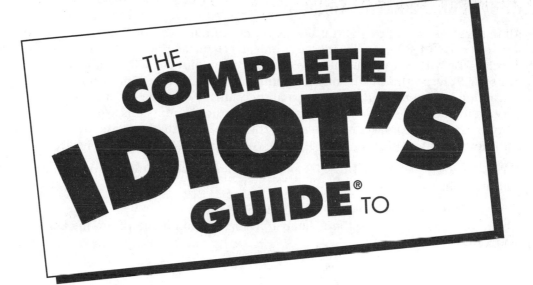

THE COMPLETE IDIOT'S GUIDE® TO

Wicca and Witchcraft

by Denise Zimmermann
and Katherine A. Gleason

ALPHA

A Pearson Education Company

Copyright © 2000 by Amaranth

International Standard Book Number: 0-02-863945-6
Library of Congress Catalog Card Number: Available upon request from the Library of Congress

03 02   8   7   6   5

Interpretation of the printing code: The rightmost number of the first series of numbers is the year of the book's printing; the rightmost number of the second series of numbers is the number of the book's printing. For example, a printing code of 00-1 shows that the first printing occurred in 2000.

Printed in the United States of America

Publisher
Marie Butler-Knight

Product Manager
Phil Kitchel

Managing Editor
Cari Luna

Senior Acquisitions Editor
Randy Ladenheim-Gil

Book Producer
Lee Ann Chearney/Amaranth

Development Editor
Lynn Northrup

Production Editor
JoAnna Kremer

Copy Editor
Susan Aufheimer

Illustrator
Kathleen Edwards

Cartoonist
Jody P. Schaeffer

Cover Designers
Mike Freeland
Kevin Spear

Book Designers
Scott Cook and Amy Adams of DesignLab

Indexer
Debbie Hittel

Layout/Proofreading
Angela Calvert
Svetlana Dominguez
Mary Hunt

Contents at a Glance

Contents

Foreword

If you are reading this foreword, it is only because I have succumbed to Witches' Local Union 719 and their promise to turn me into a newt if I didn't. Now don't get me wrong, I have nothing against newts. In fact, I kind of like them. But it is quite difficult to type manuscripts when you are one.

Newts. Witches' spells. Love charms. Flying broomsticks and cauldrons. Halloween. It's amazing how many stereotypes still exist about Wicca and witchcraft. We are living in a time when a tremendous amount of knowledge is available to the average person, and yet there still exist a great deal of misconceptions about, and even intolerance of, Wicca. Now, I am not Wiccan, but even I get raised eyebrows over my own magical life. I can only imagine what Wiccans and witches still experience.

Informative and fun, *The Complete Idiot's Guide to Wicca and Witchcraft* breaks down the misconceptions and myths about one of the most ancient and empowering traditions on the planet. It is a guide for beginners and advanced alike. Never has so much information on Wicca and witchcraft been available from a single source. The authors, Denise Zimmermann and Katherine A. Gleason, cover every facet in the world of Wicca and witchcraft, and they do so with simple respect, wisdom, and humor.

This book teaches the wonders of creating and living a magical life. From simple divination to practical spell work to sacred ritual, every aspect of this reverent and magical tradition is explored. The reader is taken by the hand and guided along the path of natural wonders with living history, practical explorations, common-sense advice, and gentle encouragement.

The Complete Idiot's Guide to Wicca and Witchcraft will weave a magical spell of new understanding, knowledge, and wonder around you and your life. And that's not just the newt in me speaking!

—Ted Andrews

Ted Andrews is an internationally recognized author and teacher. He has written more than two dozen titles, which have been translated into more than 20 foreign languages. His books include the best-selling Animal-Speak: The Spiritual & Magical Powers of Creatures Great & Small *and* How to Meet and Work with Spirit Guides, *the award-winning* Animal-Wise, *and the delightful* Magic of Believing *from the new series,* The Young Person's School of Magic & Mystery.

Introduction

Often when we feel that we need to make a change in our lives or in ourselves, we look to others for the answers. Why not start with yourself? The most powerful change that a person can make is change from within. But how do we change? Change involves learning and growth. One of the most fundamental ways to create change is through the spirit. Spiritual fulfillment is one of the primary tools that helps us on our journey to wisdom. Our ancestors knew this. And they have given us a way to make this change—the power of witchcraft.

But do witches exist? They absolutely do. Through the information in this book, you'll find out what and who witches really are. You'll also enhance your own spirituality and will grow and become empowered through the wisdom of the craft.

How to Use This Book

You don't have to run out and buy all the magickal tools mentioned in this book. You might want to read a few sections before you buy anything else related to witch-craft. As you progress through the book, you may want to try doing some spells. And we do hope that you'll try the exercises we have provided. Are you ready? Hop on your broom, hold on tight, and prepare to fly!

This book is divided into six parts:

Part 1, "Wicca Wisdom," introduces you to the beliefs and moral code of Wicca. We also discuss the history of witchcraft and its growing popularity in the present day.

Part 2, "The Wiccan Way," takes an in-depth look at Wiccan beliefs. We also examine some of the responsibilities of being a witch and introduce Wiccan ritual and some basic magickal tools.

Part 3, "So, You Want to Do Magick?" is where you'll learn how to prepare yourself for ritual. You'll also learn how and where to do ritual.

Part 4, "Working Magick," takes a closer look at ritual and celebrates the Wiccan holidays. You'll also learn about magickal natural objects and entities.

Part 5, "Any Time Is the Right Time for Magick," shows you how to work with astrology and the calendar to enhance the affects of your magick.

Part 6, "Witches' Brew: Notions, Potions, and Powders," is where you will learn all about spells—how to write them and how to cast them. You'll also learn about fore-telling the future and gain some new insight into your dreams.

At the end of the book, you'll find two helpful appendixes: a list of resources to help you learn more, and a Magickal Record sheet that you can copy and use to record your own magick rituals.

Extras

In addition, we've scattered boxes throughout the book with definitions, warnings, tips, and fascinating tidbits of information to help you learn and understand even more about Wicca and witchcraft.

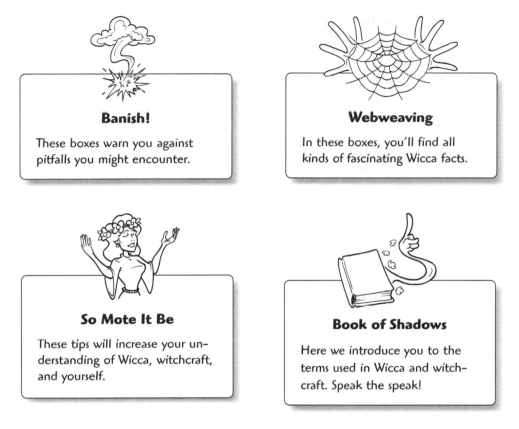

Banish!

These boxes warn you against pitfalls you might encounter.

Webweaving

In these boxes, you'll find all kinds of fascinating Wicca facts.

So Mote It Be

These tips will increase your understanding of Wicca, witchcraft, and yourself.

Book of Shadows

Here we introduce you to the terms used in Wicca and witchcraft. Speak the speak!

Acknowledgments

From Denise: I would like to thank Lee Ann Chearney and her Mom, Gloria, for giving me the opportunity to do this book. I also would like to thank Katherine and her kitty for all those late night phone sessions, lengthy conversations, and fits of laughter. To my friend and business partner Carol for her encouragement, Bunky and our Wicca students, and my boss Pat for their support and kindness, I thank you. Special thanks, all my love and appreciation to my wonderful husband Lee for his gentle kindness, support, and belief in my abilities. And foremost I would like to dedicate this book in loving memory to my father, who believed that all I had to do was open my arms and I could touch the stars.

From Katherine: Thanks to Denise and thanks to Denise again for staying up so late talking, for her good humor, generous and gracious spirit, patience, and also for all the magick. Thanks, too, go to Lee Ann Chearney at Amaranth, without whose vision this book wouldn't have happened. And thanks to Doug Rose for making the connection, Michael Thomas Ford for all the time on the phone, and Johannes Brahms (1833–1897) for the music.

Special Thanks to the Technical Reviewer

The Complete Idiot's Guide to Wicca and Witchcraft was reviewed by an expert who double-checked the accuracy of what you'll learn here to help us ensure that this book provides all you need to know about Wicca and witchcraft—special thanks to Jaylin.

Jaylin is a Wiccan Priest who has been trained in the Gardnerian/Alexandrian tradition. Currently he practices a Dragon tradition. Jaylin has been active as a witch for 10 years and now has his own coven. Jaylin also helps Denise teach Wicca to a-year-and-a-day class of solitary students at Bell Book & Candle in Baltimore.

Trademarks

All terms mentioned in this book that are known to be or are suspected of being trademarks or service marks have been appropriately capitalized. Alpha Books and Pearson Education, Inc., cannot attest to the accuracy of this information. Use of a term in this book should not be regarded as affecting the validity of any trademark or service.

Part 1

Wicca Wisdom

Witches practice magick, and they also practice Wicca—an Earth-based religion that honors a deity that is divided into male and female spirituality known as the God and the Goddess and gives reverence to the Earth. Throughout history witches have faced persecution because of misconceptions about them and their practices. But Wicca and witchcraft have survived and are going strong. In fact, Wicca is one of the fastest growing religions in the United States today.

Chapter 1

All About Wicca and Witchcraft

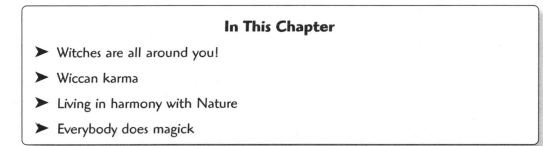

In This Chapter

➤ Witches are all around you!

➤ Wiccan karma

➤ Living in harmony with Nature

➤ Everybody does magick

Have you noticed how many witches are featured on TV shows and in movies? It used to be that you heard about witches only in children's stories or fairy tales. But these days it seems like witches are everywhere. Why? Because witches are really mysterious. Haven't you always been interested in witchcraft? Haven't you always been just a little bit envious of the witch's power and what witches know? Well, you're not alone. And that power and knowledge can belong to *you, too*.

But becoming a witch is not about power. It is about finding and developing your spirituality. It's about learning to connect with deity and with the forces of Nature. Through Wicca, you will discover what you are capable of. You will also discover a nurturing deity and will come to know who you really are.

Welcome to Wicca and Witchcraft

Denise teaches a popular class on Wicca and witchcraft. After just the first class, many of Denise's students have confided to her that they always felt something was missing from life, that a vital part of them seemed empty. But when they started learning about Wicca, students professed a sense of "coming home." And, as you'll discover, that's only *natural*.

Book of Shadows

Today the term **Wicca** refers to a religion that many (but not all) witches practice. Wicca is an Earth-based religion that honors both the God and the Goddess. The word **witch** comes from the Old English words "wicce," which means "female witch," and "wicca," meaning "wizard." A witch is someone who uses magick in his or her everyday life.

Webweaving

What series of children's books has everybody reading about witchcraft? The Harry Potter books by J.K. Rowling, of course! For the uninitiated, Harry Potter is a British schoolboy who goes to a very special school— Hogwart's School of Witchcraft and Wizardry. That Harry Potter is one popular witch—with adults and kids, too!

Wicca, the religion practiced by many witches, is one of the fastest growing religions in the United States. But what is Wicca? For now, let's just say that Wicca is an Earth-based religion founded on ancient beliefs. Wicca is a welcoming religion. Wiccans do not exclude anyone based on their race, color, sex, age, national or cultural origin, or sexual preference. Not all Wiccans are *witches,* and not all witches are Wiccan, but a lot of them are.

By the way, Wiccans don't use the word "warlock" to refer to male witches. Male witches are witches, too. A warlock is a person who has broken an oath and because of that has been ostracized from the community. If you have violated an oath you can also be warlocked or ostracized and ignored.

There are many different traditions in the Wiccan religion. We're going to talk mostly about Wiccan witches, and in this book we will use the terms "Wicca" and "witch" interchangeably. We'll explain more about Wicca, witches, and their history in the sections and chapters that follow. So, read on, have a great time learning about Wicca and witchcraft, and welcome home!

Supernatural Abilities?

Everybody has the ability to channel energy. In a sense, everything you do happens because of this ability. You decide you want a snack. So, you get up, go into the kitchen, pick up an apple, and take a bite. That's simple. You've used your physical energy to move your body. Everybody can use other more subtle kinds of energy, too. We all have an inherent power within us to 1) take control of our own lives and 2) make things happen. Because many of us have been taught by our religion, the education system, or our parents to always look to outside authorities, we have, to a large extent, repressed this ability. Using energy, or powers, to control your life and make things happen is just as much a part of the natural world as getting up from your chair.

There's nothing supernatural about a witch's abilities. Some people see these abilities as greater than ordinary and call them "supernatural," but the forces that witches use are available to all of us and are, thus, ordinary. Witches use natural energies to enhance their lives and to heal and protect themselves, their loved ones, and the Earth.

Banish!

Are you secretly hoping that a force over which you have no control will possess you? That it will make all your decisions for you and tell you how to live your life? No such luck! Witchcraft can help improve your life, but you still must make responsible choices. When you study witchcraft, you learn more about yourself, your needs, and your wants. That knowledge will help strengthen the inborn power you already have. And that, not some unseen force, just might help you decide what to order for lunch.

Or, Super Abilities in the Natural?

A witch's powers may be super or, well, powerful, but they are natural. We're not talking about powers like the ones Samantha Stevens from *Bewitched* had. What she did on that TV show often was unnatural! Just one twinkle of her nose cleaned her house in a flash. (Wouldn't that be nice?)

When you start to learn about your abilities, the natural energies you were born with, you'll start to understand what that force is—and that the energy is in all of us.

When you learn to focus on your natural energy, you'll learn to increase it, channel it, and send it out into the world. You probably won't be able to turn someone into a toad, but is that something you'd really want to do? Our natural energies make up our power, and we can use that power in the natural world to do natural things. Using your energy is not a substitute for action, though. You still have to write up your resume, mail it out, and go to interviews for that job you want. If you use your magickal energies, too, they may just help land you a great offer. Powers are a special blessing that we all have. Some witches believe that their powers come from the Goddess (we'll discuss this a bit more later in the chapter). Either way, just know that you have them. If you open your heart and mind, you can use your powers. And the more you work with them the better, the more powerful, you become.

Embracing Our Energy

The abilities you have are natural and inborn, so there is no reason to be frightened of them. Some of us are more in tune with these innate energies and thus find them welcome tools to enhance our lives. Don't worry. You won't suddenly find that green sparks shoot out of your fingers every time you are annoyed. Your powers are *yours*. You control them. You'll learn to respect your abilities and send them out to work for your own or someone else's benefit. Don't feel embarrassed by the fact that you have magickal abilities. Just because other people around you don't use or understand their abilities, doesn't mean you shouldn't use yours. That would be like ignoring the electric light on your desk and using a candle because your office mate doesn't understand how electricity works! Have fun learning about your magical abilities as you read this book. Enjoy them. Soon you will come to rely on them.

So Mote It Be

Learning about your magickal abilities is a process of self-discovery. One useful tool in such a process is a journal. If you don't already keep a journal, you might want to start one. As you learn more about Wicca and witchcraft, record your changing thoughts and feelings about yourself and the world around you. Some people like to write in their journals first thing in the morning so they can record their dreams before they forget them. Others write in the evening. Some carry their journals with them all the time so they can catch every impression. How you use your journal is up to you. Let it be fun! Include drawings or pictures from magazines, if you like.

What Do Witches Look Like?

For some of you, the first image that comes to mind when you hear the word "witch" is the Wicked Witch of the West from *The Wizard of Oz,* with her green skin and pointy, wart-encrusted nose. Or the ugly old witch from a book of fairy tales who wants to fatten up Hansel so she can eat him.

But witches, just like Christians, Muslims, Jews, Hindus, or Buddhists, come in many different packages. Denise likes to ask her students, "What do Christians look like?" Her students can rarely answer that question, but it does make them realize the global dimensions of our human diversity. And that diversity is true of witches, too. Witches are big and small, short and tall. Some witches are fat and some are thin.

Some are brunets, some blond, some have purple hair, and some have no hair at all. The very young can be witches and so can the very old. Witches are not ugly, old hags. They can be beautiful and sexy no matter what their age, just like any other person. (We think strong men and women are sexy, don't you?) And actually, witches aren't always women. As we've said, witches can be either male or female.

Webweaving

Why does the Wicked Witch of the West stick in our minds? Is it because she's so ugly? Or because we all want to command a troop of flying monkeys? Maybe. But we think it's because she represents an archetype, a universal symbol that speaks to us all. She is the shadow or "dark" side of each of us and as such she scares many of us. Others of us are more comfortable with our own shadows and don't find her that frightening. We all have a balance of shadow and light within us. The more comfortable we are with our own shadows, the less someone else's "darkness" will bother us.

The superefficient person who sits next to you at work, your best friend, or that woman at the PTA—the one who's a morph of June Cleaver and Martha Stewart—could be a witch because, in short, witches look just like everyone else.

Are You a Good Witch or a Bad Witch?

When Glinda, *The Wizard of Oz*'s Good Witch of the North, asked Dorothy, "Are you a good witch or a bad witch?" most of us, like Dorothy, just couldn't take our eyes off of her glowing white dress and jeweled red hair. Glinda and her nasty neighbor, the Wicked Witch of the West, represent the polar extremes of behavior, archetypes of good and bad. But Dorothy was the real witch. Dorothy, like most of us, must choose how she will behave; that is, what kind of witch she will be. The ruby slippers that represent her newfound powers may

Webweaving

Billie Burke, the actress who played Glinda in the original *The Wizard of Oz* movie, sure had some good ideas. She is often quoted as having said, "Age is something that doesn't matter, unless you are a cheese." We couldn't agree more! Burke was already 52 when she signed on to play Glinda. She worked in more than 30 films after *Oz*, finally retiring from the screen in her 70s.

be a gift from Glinda, but the Wicked Witch of the East had worn those same red shoes. Dorothy must *learn* how to use her powers for the benefit of herself and others. In our very real lives, we are all learning how to understand and use our potential in the best way. And, just like Dorothy, eventually we all learn that the power has been within us all the time.

Dorothy's magickal ruby slippers.

Many types of people are witches—the hot-tempered and the meek, the wild and the patient, the forgiving and the demanding, and the stubborn—just as many types of people are Christians, Muslims, Hindus, Buddhists, or Jews. Each and every one of us has the inherent ability to be nasty. It's a human failing. Witches do have the ability to behave in a negative way. But so do people of other faiths. Through spiritual understanding, Wiccan witches learn to curb the inherent human tendencies to get back at people or do negative things.

Wiccan witches do not work with the negative or with evil. Wiccans believe they must act for the good of all, including themselves. They don't believe they should benefit from another person's suffering. Sure, sometimes it's hard to deal with negative feelings that come up. But we know we don't have the good without the bad, and so we learn to deal with the negative energies, but not act on them. You may feel as if you want to rear-end the person in the SUV who cut you off as you were pulling up to the tollbooth, and that's okay. Feelings are just feelings. What's *really* important is your behavior, how you act. Actually hitting the guy in his big vehicle in a spectacular display of road rage would not be okay. And, however tempting the idea might seem, it also is never okay to try to turn him into road kill.

Banish!

Do you want to torture your ex by making him or her fall in love with you again so you can perform an extravagant revenge dump? Don't do it! Avoid using witchcraft to get back at another person or to manipulate that person. To do so would be unethical, and there's that little thing—the law of three—that says whatever you do will come back to you threefold. Ouch!

As witches, we know we have to take full responsibility for our actions. No one and nothing else is responsible for them. So, the devil did not "make" you do it! Wiccan witches are responsible for their own actions and are willing to pay the penalty for them without placing blame on others. Witches who use negative energy are always well paid back in kind for their actions. (And using positive energy also is paid back in kind.) You can always accomplish the things you need to get done without using negativity. You can reframe the question as a positive, simply turning the situation around. Or maybe there is a lesson to be learned from your inability to complete your task.

So Mote It Be

If you want to meet witches, check out your local Wiccan or New Age bookstore. Many have classes and workshops and some hold holiday gatherings that are open to the public—all good events at which to meet like-minded folk. Look in your local paper for Nature festivals or whole-life expos. If you live in a college town, find out if there's a Wiccan group on campus. Many schools have them and their membership might not be restricted to students. You might also check the Internet for Wiccan Web pages, chat rooms, message boards, even online classes. Do be careful when you meet new people, though, especially online; use good common sense.

If you are stuck in a negative situation or if something bad happens to you, try to make the best of it. One way to do that is to ask yourself, "What am I supposed to learn from this?" Katherine recently hurt herself while in her yoga class. At first she complained. (Okay, she complained a lot.) But then she asked herself what she could learn from this literal pain in her butt. After some thought, she realized that her injury was telling her she needed to slow down and take better care of her body. A piece of advice we could all benefit from! What it all boils down to is the old question: Is the glass half full or half empty? Think of the glass as half full. Count your blessings. And remember that anyone of any faith who uses other people for their own gain is acting out of negativity. Wiccan witches act for the good of all. So, be a good witch. It's for your own good.

Ever Met a Witch?

You've probably met at least one witch in your life. Maybe more! There are a lot of witches out there. And the numbers keep increasing. Of all the many religions practiced in the United States, Wicca is among the fastest growing. Witches have all different kinds of jobs. Witches are schoolteachers, bus drivers, chefs, construction workers, computer programmers, actors, nurses, bankers, doctors, lawyers, you name it. Witches are parents and even grandparents. Witches go bowling, play tennis, and attend baseball games.

When you first meet someone, do you ask that person what his or her religion is? You probably don't. In fact, in most cases, the subject rarely comes up. Remember Denise's question: What does a Christian look like? Usually you get few clues about a person's belief system from his or her outward appearance. So, because witches look just like everyone else (just like Christians!) you probably have already met a witch without even realizing it. Witches not only look like everyone else, they are a lot *like* everyone else. Witches go shopping, drive cars, eat ice cream, pay taxes, and ultimately die, just like everyone else.

What Do Witches Believe?

In the 1970s, the Council of American Witches, an organization that no longer exists, drew up a list of basic principles. We'll just paraphrase them here to give you an idea of what they sound like (for details, see Chapter 5, "So You Want to Be a Witch?"):

Book of Shadows

Is "magick" with a "k" different from magic? You bet. Both words come from the same root, meaning "to be able, to have power," but magic is what an entertainer does on stage—card tricks, making quarters disappear, sawing a hapless volunteer in half. **Magick** is the realm of witches and may include spells, healing, the harnessing of psychic forces, and even divination.

➤ We practice rites to attune ourselves with the natural rhythm of life forces.

➤ We recognize that our intelligence gives us a unique responsibility toward our environment.

➤ We acknowledge a depth of power far greater than is apparent to the average person.

➤ We conceive of the Creative Power in the Universe as both masculine and feminine. We value neither gender above the other.

➤ We recognize both outer worlds and inner, psychological worlds, and we see in the interaction of these two dimensions the basis for paranormal and magickal exercises.

➤ We do not recognize any authoritarian hierarchy.

➤ We see religion, *magick,* and wisdom-in-living as being united in the way one views the world and lives in it.

➤ Calling oneself a "witch" does not make a witch, but neither does heredity itself, or the collecting of titles, degrees, and initiations. A witch seeks to control the forces within him- or herself that make life possible in order to live wisely and well, without harm to others, and in harmony with Nature.

➤ We acknowledge that it is the affirmation and fulfillment of life, in a continuation of evolution and development of consciousness, that gives meaning to the Universe we know, and to our personal role within it.

➤ Our only animosity toward Christianity, or toward any other religion or philosophy of life, is that its institutions have claimed to be "the one true, right, and only way" and have sought to deny freedom to others and to suppress other ways of religious practices and beliefs.

➤ We are not threatened by debates on the history of the craft. We are concerned with our present and our future.

➤ We do not accept the concept of absolute evil, nor do we worship any entity known as "Satan" or "the Devil" as defined by Christian traditions.

➤ We work within Nature for that which contributes to our health and well-being.

Basically, Wiccan witches try to live in harmony with Nature and take responsibility for the environment. Wiccans believe that the Goddess is in everything and is not some force standing "out there" watching us. In the faith of Wicca, we believe in one deity—the All. We divide that into a male spirituality and a female spirituality, the God and Goddess, or Lord and Lady. Neither the male nor the female is stronger or better or more important. Wiccans also work with the demigods, different, smaller aspects of the All. The All is so big that most witches find it helpful to visualize it in a more personally comprehensible form. For example, a witch might keep on his or her altar a statuette of the Venus of Willendorf. This Goddess, with her big hips and enormous, full breasts, is the epitome of fertility and motherhood, but at the same time is part of the All. (There's more about the Venus of Willendorf in the next chapter.)

You don't have to practice magick to be Wiccan, but most Wiccans do. Magick is part of the Wiccan worldview. Wiccans honor teachers and leaders, but do not recognize authoritarian hierarchies because no one is intrinsically better than anyone else is. You can become a witch through hereditary,

Webweaving

You can recognize some witches by the jewelry they wear. A teenaged witch in a Detroit suburb was told that she could not wear her pentacle necklace to school. The American Civil Liberties Union argued in court that the prohibition violated her First Amendment rights under the U.S. Constitution. The court decided the school was wrong, and the teen returned to school wearing the symbol of her Wiccan faith.

solitary study, or by joining a *coven* where you will be taught (we'll tell you more about covens in Chapter 3, "Practicing Wicca and Witchcraft Today"). Witches are not anti-Christian, nor do they harbor negative feelings about other religions.

Venus of Willendorf.

Wiccans believe in the morals that are common to most faiths. But Wiccans do not believe in the Christian concept of original sin. Wiccans live in the now. While Wiccans do believe in reincarnation, life is to be lived for what it is in the present so that we may learn from this lifetime on Earth. As Wiccans, we do not deny ourselves pleasure or put up with unnecessary pain. We are not waiting for some reward that we will get only after we are dead. We enjoy life's pleasures so that we can learn what it means to be on this Earth and to be part of life on Earth. Wiccans believe that we all have a job to do, or a lesson to learn, or maybe a debt to pay from the last lifetime. Once we have succeeded in our mission, we must move on to the summerland where we can reflect and choose our mission in the next life.

Book of Shadows

A **coven** is a group of witches who practice their religion together. "Coven" probably comes from the Middle English word "covent," which means a gathering. The English word "convent" and "convene" come from the same root.

We believe that we are put on Earth to live in harmony with Nature, never to abuse it. While Wiccans don't believe there is a hell to punish sinners, Wiccans do believe there is a universal law, called karma, that puts our behavior on display so that we can learn from it. Think of it this way: When a small child first learns to walk, you let the child stumble and sometimes fall so that he or she can learn balance. That's what the Wiccan concept of karma does. Karma doesn't punish us; it operates like a feedback system and makes us think about our past actions.

Wiccans believe that people are basically good. A person's behavior might be unacceptable, but that person is not necessarily bad. We are all made in the image of the Lord and Lady. Nobody is born evil. Some people may act that way or harbor those energies, but the evil or negativity is not inherent.

Three Times Bad and Three Times Good

Witches know that whatever energy or actions they send out, whether it be negative or positive, will come back to them threefold. If you punch someone in the eye, that does not necessarily mean that you will get punched in the eye three times, but you may fall down the stairs and break your ankle. And that fall will be three times worse than the punch you sent out. You may get temporary pleasure out of ratting on someone at work, but in the end, you could be the one who loses your job even though you had more seniority. That's how karma works. The negativity might not come back to you right away, but it will come back. Usually it gets you at the most inopportune time. And hopefully you will remember what you did to deserve the payback and not repeat the same mistake!

If you send out positive energies, you will get positive energies in return. In this way, your life will continuously grow and get better. Think about tossing a pebble into a pond. Every positive ripple you send out has the potential to affect many, many people. In *It's A Wonderful Life*, the Jimmy Stewart movie that always plays on television at Christmastime, Stewart's character, George Bailey, is about to kill himself out of despair and frustration. But before he jumps off that bridge, an angel helps George to bring all his good deeds and kindnesses back to him. He sees all the positive ways in which he touched so many peoples' lives, and he decides not to jump. George decides to embrace life. All the good that he sent out came back to him at the moment of his despair—when he needed it most! That's a great example of Wiccan karma.

Webweaving

In 1986, a federal appeals court ruled that Wicca is a legal religion. That means that the practice of Wicca is protected by the U.S. Constitution. Ever since the ruling, more and more Wiccans have "come out of the broom closet." People estimate that there are between 100,000 and one million Wiccans in the United States alone.

And If It Harms None, Do What You Will

Because there are many different types and traditions of witches, witches believe a variety of things. If you ask 200 witches a question, you will probably get 400 different answers. But there is one core belief common to all Wiccan witches that none will deviate from. This central principle is called the Wiccan *Rede,* and it is expressed, in somewhat archaic language, like this: "An it harm none, do what ye will." If you think about it, this statement covers many of the Christian Ten Commandments in one phrase.

Wiccan witches do think about the Rede and its implications. Just like Christians, Wiccans know it is wrong to kill, deliberately hurt, steal, or bear false witness. Because the Rede does not list all the things that you should avoid, you must take responsibility for living according to its rule.

Book of Shadows

Rede is an archaic word that means "advice" or "counsel." It can also refer to a narration or story. In this context, a Rede is a good rule to live by!

"How can I cause the least harm?" This is a question that Wiccans ask themselves all the time (especially when doing magick). For some people this may mean avoiding recreational drugs, alcohol, or cigarettes because these substances hurt the body and thus cause harm. Everyone agrees that inflicting pain on animals for fun is wrong; Wiccans believe strongly in the integrity and freedom of the animal kingdom. Some witches believe in vegetarianism. Wiccans who do eat meat give thanks to the animal that gave its life in order for others to eat. They don't wear furs for vanity or take an animal's life just to be able to hang a trophy on the wall. They try to cause the least harm to all living things in Nature.

In trying to cause the least harm, many Wiccans have become serious environmentalists. Wiccans recycle and pick up trash on the street. Some Wiccans compost their food scraps or put them out for animals to eat instead of adding them to large landfill projects. For others it means buying only organic produce—fruit and vegetables that have been raised in such a way as to cause the least harm to the Earth and its inhabitants.

We'll discuss the Wiccan Rede in more detail in Chapter 5.

Witches Do Believe in God

Wiccans hold the complete pure energy of the All, of the God and Goddess most high. When you get to know a witch, you will see that witches have a great reverence for life. If, for example, a witch cuts a branch from a tree, the next action is to give something back to the tree—some compost or leaf mould to help nourish the tree in its continued growth. When a witch harvests a plant, he or she tries to do it in such a way that is the least harmful to the plant. A lot of the organizations that help animals are made up of Wiccans. Because Wicca is a Nature religion, Wiccans see the Goddess in everything. Wiccans not only see the Goddess in everything, but Wiccans honor the Goddess in everything by living in harmony with Nature.

Witches Don't Believe in Satan!

The idea that witches worship Satan is one of the most common misconceptions about witches. This mistaken idea probably developed hundreds of years ago because some Christian leaders encouraged their followers to view non-Christians as anti-Christian. If you weren't a believer in Christ, the embodiment of the good, you *must* be a believer in his evil opposite—Satan or the Devil. The all-evil Satan is a Christian concept that plays no part in the Wiccan religion.

Witches do not believe that negativity or evil is an organized force. Most of the time, negative beings act simply out of self-interest to effect their own personal gain, and, therefore, they're more like independent contractors. Neither do Wiccans believe there is a place (hell) where the damned or the evil languish and suffer. And, as we said earlier, witches do not try to gain power through the suffering or misfortune of others.

Are You Ready for Magick?

Everybody has the ability within him or her to do magick. Everybody does magick every day of their lives without even realizing it.

Have you ever …

➤ Said a little chant to find a parking place and then, *voilà*, a space appeared right in front of the building you had to visit?

➤ Made soup for a sick friend or relative to help make that person feel better?

➤ Worn a lucky outfit for a job interview or a sports competition?

➤ Thrown salt over your shoulder or knocked on wood to prevent a bad thing from happening?

Every time you ask for that parking place and get it, every time you make your special chicken soup to help cure someone, you perform magick. When you make that soup you add your own special ingredients. (We know you've got your own trademarked recipe!) And you put your own loving energy into the soup's preparation, your hope that your friend or child or uncle will feel better. The sick person eats the soup and feels better. That is magick.

Your lucky outfit is magick, too. Maybe it just gives you confidence, you say. Well, perhaps the extra confidence is all it is, but maybe there is something magickal about that, too! Every time you engage in a "superstition," throwing salt over your shoulder or knocking on wood, you are invoking part of an old belief system that predates Christianity. You're using magick.

Performing magick makes you feel good. It's a healthy form of self-expression because the magick in witchcraft comes from the power that is already within you.

If you are ready to make your life better, to take control of yourself, to empower yourself, to explore who you are and who you want to be, if you are ready to look at the world in a new and different light, then you are ready for magick.

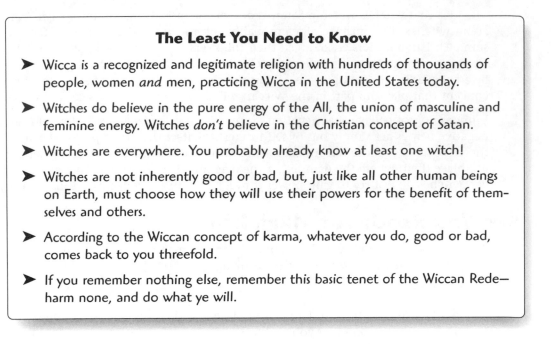

The Least You Need to Know

➤ Wicca is a recognized and legitimate religion with hundreds of thousands of people, women *and* men, practicing Wicca in the United States today.

➤ Witches do believe in the pure energy of the All, the union of masculine and feminine energy. Witches *don't* believe in the Christian concept of Satan.

➤ Witches are everywhere. You probably already know at least one witch!

➤ Witches are not inherently good or bad, but, just like all other human beings on Earth, must choose how they will use their powers for the benefit of themselves and others.

➤ According to the Wiccan concept of karma, whatever you do, good or bad, comes back to you threefold.

➤ If you remember nothing else, remember this basic tenet of the Wiccan Rede— harm none, and do what ye will.

Stonehenge
GRAND
OPENING!

Chapter 2

The History of Wicca and Witchcraft

In This Chapter

➤ Before Wicca and witchcraft

➤ The Burning Times

➤ Survival and reconstruction of the Wiccan religion

➤ Wicca now and into the future

You probably already have a sense of some of the history of Wicca and witchcraft. As a kid, you may have read novels such as *The Witch of Blackberry Pond* or the play *The Crucible*. Maybe you even *starred* in your high school's production of *The Crucible*. Or you may have visited Salem, Massachusetts, the town whose name has practically become synonymous with "witchcraft."

Some of what you have gleaned about the history of witchcraft is not pretty—accusations, trials, torture, imprisonment, and burnings at the stake. But how did witchcraft start? What really happened? Why did it happen? And where does all this history leave the modern witch today?

Searching the Spirit of Each Thing

Before Christianity, before the Roman and Greek empires and their pantheons of deities, before recorded history, people honored the spirit of each thing—trees, grass, plants, animals, rivers, and streams. The spirits of the wind, rain, sun, and moon also were important.

Paleolithic Gods and Goddesses

All over Europe, anthropologists have found small, carved female figures that date from the Paleolithic period, more than 20,000 years ago. These figures are generally referred to as Venus figures. The Venus of Willendorf is a particularly famous example. She has a super curvy figure—large breasts, a round belly, and a generous behind. Scholars believe that she represented fertility, or life-giving powers, to prehistoric societies.

Webweaving

In 1908, the limestone statuette that has come to be known as the Venus of Willendorf was found in a cave near what is now Vienna, Austria. Archaeologists believe that the 4³/₈-inch (11.1-cm) high figure comes from the period between 24,000 and 22,000 B.C.E. When found she bore traces of a red ochre pigment thought to represent menstrual blood. Similar statuettes have been found in a large area of Europe—from Western France to Western Russia. The Venus of Willendorf has become an icon of prehistoric art.

Cave paintings from around the same period depict animals, people, and a half-man, half-animal figure with horns that some anthropologists have come to call the God of the Hunt. But no one is really sure if this figure did represent a god. Many of the writers who have written on this subject had an ax to grind—they wanted to prove that men have always been dominant over women. On the other hand, more recent, feminist writers have tried to prove just the opposite. Much of the evidence left by these early societies indicates that they worshipped the life-giving potential of women and the Earth.

Nurturing a Fertile World: The Rise of Ritual

A few ancient cave paintings seem to depict religious *rituals,* with people dancing in what looks like animal costumes. Anthropologists believe these prehistoric people used rituals, such as dancing or creating paintings, to encourage animals to multiply and plants to grow.

But are rituals just confined to the distant past or strange sects? Actually, there are lots of common rituals in modern life.

For example, have you ever ...

➤ Attended a wedding, graduation, or funeral?

➤ Put candles on a cake and sung "Happy Birthday" to a friend?

➤ Rang a neighbor's doorbell while dressed in a costume and greeted your neighbor with the words "Trick or treat"?

➤ Said a prayer or blessing before a meal?

➤ Wished on a star by saying the rhyme, "Star light, star bright, first star I've seen tonight, wish I may, wish I might have the wish I wish tonight"?

So, you have participated in rituals! As you can see from this list, rituals can be quite varied. Some are solemn and serious. Others less so. And some are just downright fun. The purpose of rituals varies, as well. Anthropologists believe that the focus of rituals in early societies was on fertility—of humans, animals, and the Earth herself.

Book of Shadows

The word **ritual** describes the order or form of a religious ceremony or any detailed procedure regularly followed. A ritual is a ceremonial set of actions usually repeated in the same way over time to produce a desired effect—union with the divine or the state of consciousness necessary to perform magick.

Throughout prehistory, as rituals developed and became more complex, individuals emerged as ritual leaders. These people, the shamans, not only led rituals, but they also held knowledge of the nonphysical world.

So Mote It Be

You might want to try designing your own simple ritual. How about a ritual to give thanks for the food that you eat? Your ritual could include a brief chant or prayer that you have written. Or borrow one from a writer or poet whom you love. If you like, use music, either recorded or live, or play a recording of natural sounds, such as birds chirping, whales singing, or the roaring of the ocean. You could light candles or incense to enhance the mood. And don't forget about movement and dance. No need to worry about the choreography. Do what feels good to you. It's your ritual, after all!

Pathworking with the Shaman

Shamanism, the practice of contacting spirits through dream work and meditative trances, is probably the oldest religion, and it is still practiced in many indigenous cultures. Through fasts and meditation, shamans tread the spirit path and gather knowledge. Early shamans collected much knowledge about magick and magickal tools. Their rituals grew to encompass drumming, chanting, dancing, and often fire.

By 350 B.C.E., the Celts, an ancient people of West and Central Europe, had developed a priestly class—the Druids. Like the shamans, Druids knew about the nonphysical world. But the Druids had refined their knowledge. There were Druid healers and midwives, specialists in ritual, weather, law, and astrology. Druids were even said to be able to see into the future. Many people trace the origins of Wicca back to the Druids and their magickal knowledge. Unfortunately, as the Roman Empire grew, the number of Druids dwindled.

Of Popes and Pagans

In 371, the Roman Empire adopted Christianity as the official state religion. Roman soldiers spread the official state religion and their interpretation of it wherever they went. Often this meant killing the priests of the local religion; this slaughter included the Druids. The Christian Church gained in religious, political, and economic power.

Book of Shadows

The English word **pagan** is defined as meaning "someone who observes a polytheistic religion"— a religion that has many Gods. It is also defined as a person who has no religion. It used to mean anyone who was not Christian. This word comes from the Late Latin word that means "civilian," which in turn comes from the Latin word *paganus*, meaning "country-dweller." So, the word pagan really shouldn't carry any negative connotation at all.

From Gregory to Innocent: Papal Bull

Pope Gregory I (540–604), also known as "the Great," is credited as being one of the major forces in consolidating the power of the church and Christianizing Europe. How did he do it? He had 10,000 people baptized in England alone. He also had churches built on the sites of *pagan* temples. He reasoned that the people would continue to gather at those spots. But, instead of worshiping their old deities, they would be led in prayer by one of his priests. In many areas, people developed a hybrid religion—in outward appearance they were Christians, but deep down they still believed in the old faith. You can see this phenomenon functioning today in many parts of the world in the cult of the Virgin Mary. Many churches dedicated to her are called "Our Lady," another name for the Goddess.

After Gregory's death, despite a lot of infighting and political intrigue, the pope and the Catholic Church continued to gain power. But a series of different popes worried about the various types of Christianity that were sprouting up. To keep changes in Church doctrine in check, they employed inquisitors, men whose job it was to go out and look for Christians whose beliefs or practices varied from what the church prescribed. Christians who did not correctly follow the Church's teachings were branded heretics and imprisoned. Some were even put to death. Despite the inquisitions, more and more people became Christians or said that they were Christians.

Webweaving

When she was 13, French heroine and martyr Joan of Arc first heard a voice from God. Her voices told her to help the French king-to-be in battle. With her assistance, the king was eventually crowned, but Joan fell into the hands of her enemies. While rumored to be a witch, she was condemned for a list of offenses, including wearing men's clothes and not bowing to the authority of the Church. The theologians who tried her insisted that the voices she heard were not of divine origin. Joan was burned at the stake for heresy in 1431. The judgment against her was annulled in 1456. In 1920, the Catholic Church canonized her as a saint.

In 1484, Pope Innocent VIII wrote a bull, or letter, about witches. Earlier popes had also written about witches and how to deal with them, but Pope Innocent's letter gained much more importance. Because of the advent of printing with German printer Johannes Gutenberg's invention of movable type only a few decades earlier, this papal bull was reproduced and spread far and wide. In this document, the pope complained that neither the people nor the clergy were taking the threat posed by witches seriously enough. He insisted that everyone help his inquisitors find witches, and threatened anyone who stood in the way with the wrath of God. Some of the people convicted under Pope Innocent's bull may have been practicing witches—wise men and women who had preserved some of the knowledge of the Druids, old pagan practices, and folk beliefs—and some of them probably were not. A few of the suspected witches were accused merely because they kept cats. Cats were thought to be demons that the devil gave to witches to act as advisors and messengers.

Monk Madness: The Malleus Malleficarum

Pope Innocent's bull paved the way for Heinrich Kramer and Jakob Sprenger to publish the *Malleus Malleficarum,* or the *Witches' Hammer,* a witch hunter's manual. In fact, Kramer and Sprenger, German monks who held the jobs of inquisitors under Pope Innocent VIII, used the papal bull as the introduction to their book. The book, which is divided into three parts, came out in 1486 and is credited with starting the mass hysteria of witch persecutions across Europe.

The first part of the *Malleus Malleficarum* explains how dangerous witches are and that not believing in witches is heresy, or against Church teachings. In the second part of the book, the monks list the types of witches and how their evil doings, which include sexual relations with the devil and the ability to fly, can be counteracted. Finally, the monks demonstrate how to legally try and convict a person of witchcraft. They even suggest how best to "test," or torture, a witch to make him or her confess.

Banish!

Avoid using this information about the persecution of witches to fuel hatred of other religions such as the Catholic Church. Yes, bad things happened in the past, but harboring animosity won't help you or anyone else. Remember in the last chapter the list of basic principles drawn up by the Council of American Witches? One of the points on that list reads, "Our only animosity toward Christianity, or toward any other religion or philosophy of life, is that its institutions have claimed to be 'the one true right and only way' and have sought to deny freedom to others and to suppress other ways of religious practices and belief." Another good point from that document: "We are concerned with our present and our future." So, look ahead and avoid dwelling on the past.

Pope Innocent's bull and the *Malleus Malleficarum* led to the deaths of many people across Europe. Probably three-quarters of the people put to death were women. The monks thought that women were more likely to become witches because they are more susceptible to the influence of demons. Witches today refer to that horrible period of history as the Burning Times. Some scholars estimate that 50,000 people were killed in Europe during the Burning Times. Other people place the number as high as nine million. No one knows for sure how many people were hung, burned at the stake, or died as a result of the tests that they endured.

Enduring and Surviving the Crucible

Despite persecution, witches and their beliefs survived the *crucible* or severe trail of the inquisition and the Middle Ages, although the trouble was far from over. Repression continued into the seventeenth century, but it was less widespread.

King James I's Witchcraft Act, 1604

In 1604, King James I of England, the same guy whose name is on English translations of the Bible, passed his Witchcraft Act. Under this act, the punishment for using witchcraft became hanging. Previously in England, this crime entailed one year in jail. This act also associated witches with the devil and made any act of consorting with the devil a crime punishable by death. But James went one step further. He was so terrified of witches that he actually is said to have changed the Bible. Where the text once read, "Thou shalt not suffer a poisoner to live," in his translation it says, "Thou shalt not suffer a witch to live."

By the end of his reign, King James I had changed his mind about witches. After talking to a number of witnesses who admitted they had given false testimony and faked the physical ailments the accused witches had caused them, James I decided that witchcraft didn't exist. Despite the change in his views, the law he had enacted remained in effect.

The English witch trials of 1612, 1616, 1633, 1645, and 1649 were all prosecuted under this act, which was finally repealed in 1736. The Witchcraft Act of 1604 was also used as law in Salem, Massachusetts.

Book of Shadows

A **crucible** is a container made to heat metal at high temperatures. As such, it is extremely tough and durable. A crucible is also defined as a severe test or trial. The Burning Times certainly were a crucible for witches and for anyone suspected of witchcraft.

Salem, 1692

In 1692, America was still a British colony, and so lived under British laws. King James I's Witchcraft Act of 1604 was used to prosecute the individuals accused of witchcraft in Salem.

You may be familiar with the story of the Salem trials from Arthur Miller's play *The Crucible*. Keep in mind that the play is a work of art, not history, and that Miller took many liberties with the actual facts. (For more on this subject, see Margo Burns's Web site: www.ogram.org/17thc/.) For those of you who don't know the story of the Salem trials, several girls and young women, ranging in age from 9 to 20, started accusing the citizens of Salem and the nearby Salem Village of bewitching them. The accusers had fits, during which they cried out in pain, as if being pinched or strangled. Sometimes they were violent and disrespectful. The first four people they accused of tormenting them were a female slave, a poor woman, a widowed disabled woman, and

Webweaving

As the witch hysteria swept out of Salem and consumed other New England communities, the accusations got wilder and wilder. In Andover, Massachusetts, the son of a former governor of the state was accused of causing a dog to afflict the witch-hunting young women. The dog was tried for witchcraft and hanged.

the mother of an illegitimate, mixed-race child. In other words, they picked on the community scapegoats. But soon the accusations flew.

Devout Christians and pillars of the Puritan community stood accused. Two of the accusers admitted that they had made up their accusations, that in fact no one had tormented them. The group of accusers turned on these two young women and accused them. Soon the group of accusers traveled to neighboring towns to ferret out the "witches" in those communities. The accused soon began to accuse others in turn; those who named names were considered cooperative and were treated leniently by the court.

By the time the Salem witch scare was over, almost 150 people had been arrested and 31 people tried. Eventually, 19 people, 13 of them women, were hanged, and one old man was crushed to death with rocks. The five women who confessed to witchcraft at their trials were spared hanging and given reprieves. An additional two people died in jail. Fourteen years after the trials, Ann Putnam, the youngest accuser, admitted that the people she had accused were innocent.

A title page from Cotton Mather's famous pamphlet account of the New England witch-hunt trials, reprinted from the Boston edition for John Dunton, London, 1693.

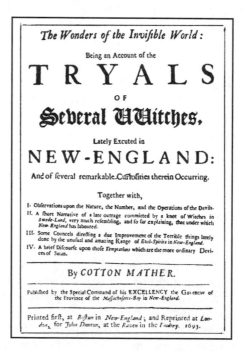

Meeting in the Shadows and Emerging into the Light

The terror that had engulfed Europe and New England simmered down, and the last execution for witchcraft took place in Poland in 1793. But neither the faith nor the magick died out completely. Practitioners of witchcraft stayed hidden in the shadows and kept their knowledge and powers secret.

Solitary Pursuits

Although witches continued to hand down their wisdom to succeeding generations, most people believed witchcraft was dead. The practice of paganism or the Old Religion survived in pockets, particularly in the countryside. Covens, groups of witches, still worshipped together, but they did so cut off from interaction with other witches. During this time, a number of covens and individual witches started to keep written records of their practices. Because witches were so isolated from one another, information that used to be passed down orally was recorded in a "Book of Shadows"—a book that contains a witch's spells and lists of magickal information.

The Crucible as a Metaphor for Persecution

In 1951, the English Parliament repealed its surviving laws against witchcraft. Two years later, Arthur Miller's play *The Crucible* was a hit on Broadway. Historically and culturally, this was a turning point for witches. Not only did witchcraft reemerge into public discussion, but the *witch hunts* were seen for what they were—persecution for no good reason. Arthur Miller's play, as everyone at the time was aware, is not about witchcraft, but about the McCarthy hearings during which time communists were the hunted. The fact that Miller was able to use the Salem trials as a metaphor surely indicates that the tide of irrational hatred against witches was beginning to turn.

In 1954, Gerald Gardner published his *Witchcraft Today*. In this book, Gardner, an English witch, comes out of the broom closet and describes the existence of the craft in the twentieth century. Gardner, a long-time student of religion and magick, believed that information handed down in his coven's Book of Shadows was inaccurate and incomplete. To remedy this situation, he did a lot of research and rewrote rituals and chants. Through these actions, he became the figurehead of the Gardnerian tradition of witchcraft. Some people see him as the founder of modern day Wicca.

Book of Shadows

The phrase **witch hunt** has come to describe a political campaign with the professed purpose of investigating activities that are "subversive" to the state when the individuals involved are not actually engaged in any such behavior. And in fact, many witches were hunted for political reasons, too.

Other witches began to come forward into the light of public scrutiny. Among them was Raymond Buckland, a student of Gardner's, who went on to found the Seax-Wica tradition in 1973 and has written numerous books about the craft.

A Return to the Natural

In 1979, National Public Radio reporter Margot Adler published her *Drawing Down the Moon: Witches, Druids, Goddess-Worshippers, and Other Pagans in America Today.* That same year, *The Spiral Dance,* author Starhawk's best-selling book, came out. Both books have introduced many people to Wicca, Goddess worship, and modern paganism. The numbers of books about Wicca and witchcraft continue to grow as the number of people interested in these topics increase. For more books on these subjects, see Appendix A, "Resources."

So Mote It Be

To increase tolerance in yourself and people around you try saying this:

> We should learn from the Earth's
> Most patient teachers
> That religious tolerance
> Be one of our features.
> In all human hearts,
> Have this light shine.
> Let us all welcome it
> Through spirit, body, and mind.
> Water it and nurture it.
> Let it continue to grow.
> So suffering and loneliness
> No longer will know.
> For what you send out
> Returns to thee times three.
> This is my will.
> So mote it be.

Add more power to this rhyme by buying a seedling plant. Nurture it, water it, and read it these words. As the plant grows, so will the tolerance around and within you.

Wiccans and witches can now practice their faith in the open. A 1986 4th Circuit Court of Appeals ruling reaffirmed that Wicca is a religion deserving First Amendment protection. Since that time, Wicca has received recognition from the Internal Revenue Service and has tax-exempt status as a legal religion. And just in case witches do encounter discrimination, there are organizations to help. In 1986, Laurie Cabot founded the Witches' League for Public Awareness. The Witches' Anti-Discrimination Lobby, the Earth Religions Assistance List, and several other organizations are active on the behalf of witches. The American Civil Liberties Union also has come to the legal aid of witches, successfully arguing in court in 1999 that a Wiccan high school student should be allowed to wear the symbol of her faith, a pentacle necklace, to school, as we mentioned in the previous chapter.

On the cultural front, people of all faiths and opinions seem to be embracing the natural knowledge that is at the heart of the Wiccan religion. Concern about the environment and the future of our planet is widespread. And people are acting on these issues by recycling and buying recycled goods, by living more simply and focusing less on the material, consumer aspects of modern day life. The increased interest in spiritual and New Age topics have led many people to explore Wicca and witchcraft, and even if these people don't become witches, they are incorporating many aspects of the faith into their lives.

Witchcraft for the New Millennium

Many people have made predictions about what life will be like as we move into the new millennium. Humans appear to be undergoing a kind of evolution of the psyche, searching for ways to live spiritually and in tune with Nature. Perhaps by the end of this millennium all the major religions will have broken down and merged together into one gentle and magickal, Earth-centered faith.

The Least You Need to Know

➤ Human kind has worshipped goddesses since before recorded history.

➤ Many, many people were killed during the Burning Times, most of them women. Some of them were witches, and some of them probably were not.

➤ Witchcraft reemerged in the 1950s and has been gaining in popularity ever since.

➤ In the United States today, witches have rights. Since 1986, Wicca has been recognized as a legal religion, and the constitutional rights of all Wiccans are protected.

➤ Wicca is one of the fastest growing religions in the United States today.

Chapter 3

Practicing Wicca and Witchcraft Today

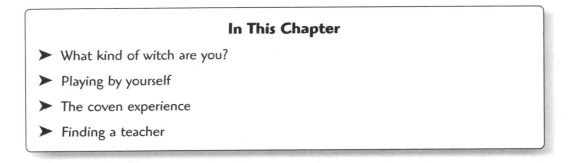

In This Chapter

➤ What kind of witch are you?

➤ Playing by yourself

➤ The coven experience

➤ Finding a teacher

Many, many people practice Wicca and witchcraft, and you can be among them. Witches practice in a variety of traditions and follow the teachings of various teachers. We'll tell you about the different traditions in this chapter. We'll also talk about solitary witches—witches who practice alone—and those who choose to join covens.

As you read this chapter you may start to get ideas about what kind of witch you want to be. We'll give you some tips about learning more and finding a coven or a teacher. Whatever you decide to do, you'll want to do some additional reading and research before you make any type of commitment.

Starting Your Practice of Wicca and Witchcraft

Beginning anything new can be scary. But isn't some of that jittery feeling excitement? We think so! If you do feel nervous, take it slow. Read through this book and read some others. You don't have to rush right out and find a teacher or a coven. Remember, this is *your* practice of Wicca and witchcraft. So, do it your way. Explore. Have fun. Do what feels right for you.

All Kinds of Witches

Just as there are many different denominations of Christians, there are various kinds of witches. Some witches practice rituals in covens. Some follow a prescribed set of traditions, while others work alone and make up their own rituals. Some witches draw elements of their practice from a number of different traditions. And some witches find their traditions within their own families.

The Witches' Coven

Simply put, a coven is a working group of witches. Covens usually have one or two leaders who are known as High Priestess or High Priest. The number of witches in a coven runs between 3 and 20. Some covens keep their membership to 13 or fewer because 13 people is the largest number you can comfortably accommodate in a nine-foot circle—a size that is considered traditional by some witches. Covens perform magick together and engage in religious rituals, according to the tradition that they follow. Every coven is autonomous. So, each coven gets to make its own decisions.

Webweaving

Some people believe that the coven was an invention of the Inquisition. Because the Inquisitors saw witchcraft as a parody of Christianity, they decided that witches must be organized in the same way that Christian monks were. At the time, monks were grouped into "convents" of 13 in honor of Christ and the 12 apostles. Other people believe that witches have worked in covens since time immemorial. Either way, modern covens do exist, and they work!

The Tradition of the Craft

Witches follow a variety of traditions, or practices. Here are descriptions of some of the different kinds:

➤ **Gardnerian Wicca.** In the 1950s, after England repealed its witchcraft laws, Gerald Gardner went public about his practice of witchcraft. He rewrote the rituals of the coven he belonged to so that they would be more accurate. Gardnerian covens have a degree system in which one learns about the craft. Individuals must be initiated by the coven and cannot initiate themselves through self-study. Gardnerian covens *work skyclad*. In addition, some try to have equal numbers of men and women in the group.

➤ **Alexandrian.** Alex Sanders founded this tradition in the 1960s. Originally based in England, practitioners work skyclad and much of their ritual is similar to Gardnerian practices, although the Alexandrians place more emphasis on ceremonial magick. Sanders called himself the "King" of his witches.

➤ **Georgian Wicca.** George Patterson founded the Georgian tradition in Bakersfield, California, in 1970. They also are known as The Georgian Church. Their rituals are drawn from Gardnerian and Alexandrian traditions with other elements added as the coven members see fit. In fact, in some covens members write their own rituals. Some Georgian covens work skyclad, and some do not.

➤ **Algard Wicca.** In 1972, Mary Nesnick combined the Gardnerian tradition with the Alexandrian to form the Algard tradition. Some people think that in practice this combination ends up being very close to the Gardnerian tradition because much of Alexandrian ritual is similar to Gardnerian to begin with.

➤ **Seax-Wica.** In 1962, Raymond Buckland, a protégé of Gerald Gardner, moved to the United States where he founded this tradition. Buckland taught the Gardnerian tradition for a number of years. Because of problems that he saw in the practice of the craft, he started his own tradition in 1973. Seax-Wica is based on Saxon traditions, but as Buckland admits, he made it up alone. Covens decide for themselves if they will work skyclad or robed. Witches of this tradition can be initiated by the coven or through self-study.

➤ **Feri Tradition.** There are a number of ways to spell the name of this tradition. You'll also see Fairy, Faery, and Faerie. Victor Anderson is credited with bringing the Feri tradition to the United States, where he has taught in the San Francisco area since the late 1960s.

Book of Shadows

Skyclad literally means "clothed by the sky." Yup, you got it—in your birthday suit. Buck naked. To **work skyclad** means to work naked.

Webweaving

Starhawk, the popular author of *The Spiral Dance,* received her training in the Feri Tradition from Victor Anderson. In 1981, she and some of the women in her coven went on to co-found the Reclaiming Collective. The Reclaiming tradition focuses on political and environmental change.

Feri teachers tend to add something of their own when they teach, so there is a strain of eclecticism in this tradition. Feris are usually solitary, or they work in small groups.

➤ **Dianic Tradition.** The Dianic Tradition focuses on the Goddess with little talk about a God. The Goddess is worshipped in her three aspects—Maiden, Mother, and Crone. There are different varieties of Dianic witch. Since the 1970s, the Dianic Tradition has been seen as the feminist movement of the craft. Some, but not all, Dianic covens are women, only.

➤ **British Traditional.** There are a number of different British Traditions, all of which are based on what people believe to be the pre-Christian practices of England. Many British Traditional groups follow Janet and Stewart Farrar, who have written a number of influential books about witchcraft. The groups tend to be structured, with training for neophytes (beginners) following a degree program. Their practices are said to be a mix of Celtic and Gardnerian traditions.

➤ **Celtic Wicca.** This tradition looks to ancient Celtic and Druidic deities and beliefs with an emphasis on the magickal and healing powers of plants, minerals, gnomes, fairies, and elemental spirits. Some of the rituals are derived from Gardnerian practice.

➤ **Northern Way or Asatru.** This tradition is based on the Old Norse gods. Practitioners generally work in re-creations of Old Norse dress. They celebrate four Solar Fire festivals and Old Norse holidays.

➤ **Pictish Witches.** This is a solitary Scottish tradition that is very much based in Nature. Some people see this tradition as being more magickal than religious.

Book of Shadows

Strega means "witch" in Italian, and the word for witchcraft is *stregoneria*. Remember Tomie dePaola's popular series of children's books about Strega Nona? That's Grandma Witch to you!

➤ **Strega Witches.** This group follows traditions from Italy. Some people trace *Strega* teachings back to a woman named Aradia in the fourteenth century. The Strega tradition is rapidly gaining popularity in the United States today.

This list, of course, is not complete. There are other forms of witch religions. And new ones are created frequently. As you can see, witches are a creative bunch!

As you probably noticed, some of the different types of witches are based on a particular national tradition. If you meet a Strega, there's a good chance that she'll be from an Italian background. But this does not mean that only individuals with Italian heritage can learn the Strega traditions. If you are drawn to a tradition, explore that tradition, whatever your background.

Solitaire

A solitaire, or solitary witch, can practice witchcraft in a variety of traditions or in no particular tradition. He or she can use none of the traditions or parts of many. As a solitaire, this witch can design a system of worship that works best for him or her. Some traditions—Gardnerian and Alexandrian, for example—say that a witch must be part of a coven to really be a witch. Some people believe that most witches throughout history have been solitaires. Others see this as a more recent development in the craft.

The proliferation of books about witchcraft has aided the rise in the numbers of solitary witches. In the past, before so much information about witchcraft was available to the general public, people seeking knowledge about one of the many traditions had to find a coven or an individual witch willing to teach them. Now, all the neophyte needs to do is head to the local metaphysical bookstore! Solitaires act and learn on their own. To some this might seem lonely. To others it means great freedom and personal empowerment.

The Eclectic Witch

An eclectic witch is just what it sounds like—someone who pulls from many different traditions, sometimes including non-European traditions such as Native American, Hawaiian, or even Buddhist. There are eclectic covens and many eclectic solitaires. Some eclectic witches lean more heavily on one tradition than on another without following any single sect or denomination. Basically, eclectic witches use whatever rituals or traditions they are drawn to—and whatever works!

The Hereditary Witch

Hereditary witches inherit the craft from older relatives who teach the family traditions. Some people believe that the traditions passed down within families represent an unbroken chain of beliefs and traditions that date back to the Old Religion of prehistory. Other people are sure that, while some family traditions can be very old, the forms of their practice are relatively recent. In rare cases, a hereditary witch might adopt someone from outside the family and teach that person the family craft.

Webweaving

The witches portrayed in entertainment media often are hereditary witches. On TV, *Bewitched's* Samantha Stevens and Sabrina of *Sabrina the Teenage Witch* are hereditary witches, as are the characters played by Nicole Kidman and Sandra Bullock in the movie *Practical Magic*.

Solitaire or Coven Life?

Choosing between becoming a solitary witch or becoming a member of a coven can be a tough decision. It involves many factors. What kind of witch do you want to be? Do you live in an area where there are covens? Are there covens of the tradition that appeals to you in your area? Do you feel comfortable in a group? Do you have the time to commit to coven activities? These are important questions. But let's examine the issue more closely.

Pros and Cons of Coven Life

As with everything else, there are pros and cons to coven life. Let's start with the positive.

The pros:

In a coven, you get a lot of support. You have people available to you who have more education in the craft than you do, so you can learn from them. There is camaraderie in a coven. You also get some structure in terms of schedule and how you go about learning the craft. Within the coven structure, you can work up to higher degrees, eventually attaining the rank of High Priestess (or Priest). The teachings of a coven have been handed down through a lineage—which is important to some people.

The cons:

The fact that there is structure in a coven can be a con for some people. The coven will make decisions about meeting times and attendance that might not fit your busy schedule. Covens have certain expectations of each and every member that you may not be comfortable with. Many covens have dress (or undress!) requirements that you might not like. The other members of the coven will judge you in that they hold you accountable for the upkeep of the laws of the tradition.

If you break the laws of the tradition of your coven, your coven and its community can oust you. If you leave the tradition and go to another tradition, you may have to start your training all over again as if you had never been trained at all. There are many traditions that will not recognize the degrees granted by covens of other traditions. Finally, the membership of the coven is a group of people you will be spending time with. If you decide you don't like another member or if the group chooses to admit a new member whom everyone likes but you, you will probably be uncomfortable. Basically, the cons to coven life are pretty similar to the cons that come with any group activity.

Pros and Cons of Going Solo

So, what about going solo?

The pros:

The solitary witch can learn at his or her own pace. A solitaire does not have to worry about earning degrees. A solitaire can follow his or her own schedule and is not bound by a coven's timetable. Solitary witches can wear whatever they want during rituals—street clothes, robes, or nothing at all. Solitary witches keep company with whom they choose and, unlike coven witches, do not have a set group they must associate with. As a solitaire, you can take on students when you want, if you want, and when you feel you are ready. Many solitaires design their own rituals.

The cons:

The downside of going solo is that you really are on your own. Help and guidance from knowledgeable witches are not going to be readily available as they would be if you were part of a coven. As a solitaire, you must go out and seek the companionship of other witches. Some witches harbor prejudice against solitary witches, believing that you are only a true witch if you have been initiated by a coven. Because the solitary witch does not earn degrees, sometimes other witches do not recognize the solitaire's level of proficiency in the craft. If you do join a coven, no matter how many years of solitary experience you have, your learning might not be recognized and you have to start again as a neophyte. Finally, the solitary witch has no lineage that he or she can look back to for guidance.

Neophyte Witch Seeks Training!

The kind of training you look for will depend on what kind of witch you want to be. But the first step is to find out what's out there. Visit your local metaphysical bookshop. Check out the books, and find out if any classes are offered. Make sure you take a good look at the store's bulletin board too; stores often display interesting advertisements and announcements. And check out their newsstand. Some Wiccan newsletters carry personal ads for neophytes seeking training. If you have access to the Internet, use it. There's a lot of information on the Web. Go to festivals and see what they offer in terms of training, and read, read, read, and read some more!

Training in a Coven

What actually happens in a coven? Perhaps you have heard stories about scary initiation rites or mandatory sexual performances. Let us dispel the myths. Read on!

Dedicated to the Craft

Each coven is different, but the process usually follows these general lines.

After you have approached a coven and told them you are interested in joining, the coven invites you to attend their open rituals. If a coven approaches you and asks you to join, steer clear of them. A

> **Banish!**
>
> Resist the temptation to become dedicated to the very first coven that you visit. Be sure that you make an educated decision. Be aware of all the resources available to you in your community before you commit. Are a few of your friends really gung-ho about a certain tradition or group? Don't let them pressure you. Make sure your decision really feels right to you!

good coven should not ask you because witches do not try to covert people to their religion. You need to ask them. When you visit the coven's open circle, you get to check out the coven, and they get to check you out. After a few visits, if all goes well, you tell the coven members that you still want to join. The coven meets and decides if they want to accept you as a dedicant or a witch in training. (In all likelihood, if you are under 18 years old and do not have your parent's support, the coven will not agree to take you.) If they do accept you, in many covens, someone agrees to be your sponsor or teacher. As a dedicant, you study the craft for a year and a day before earning your First Degree Initiation and acceptance into the coven as a member. Witches study for a year and a day because the Celtic Goddess Cerridwen is said to have stirred her brew in the cauldron of knowledge for that same amount of time.

The coven will probably give you a list of what is expected of you as a dedicant. The list may include—attendance requirements, promises that you will work hard to learn the craft, get to know the other coven members, uphold the Wiccan Rede, and keep the identity of other coven members secret. (Some witches are not "out of the broom closet" and their families and/or coworkers do not know that they are witches.) The list should *not* include sexual favors for the High Priestess, the High Priest, or any of the coven members. If it does, this is not a true Wiccan coven, and you do not want to be part of it.

The coven will hold a dedication ritual for you. At this time, you can choose your craft name. After the dedication ritual, you will be called by that name in the coven and in the pagan community. When you have dedicated, you may (or may not) be required to sign a dedicant agreement. This document is usually quite similar to the list of expectations. It may also state that you understand that being a dedicant does not guarantee initiation into the coven in the future.

During your time as a dedicant, the High Priestess, High Priest, and coven members will watch you closely. They want to see that you are serious, and they need to see if your energies mesh with the energy of the group. As a dedicant, you could do everything right and still not be asked to join the coven. Your energies may not mix with the other coven members. For the coven to survive there must always be love and harmony within the group. Each member of the coven has to enter the circle in perfect love and perfect trust. If personality conflicts rear up between members, that trust will be destroyed. A coven is not just a club. It is more like a very tight-knit spiritual (and magickal!) family.

Initiation: Earning Your Degree

Here are the steps that many covens follow in the granting of degrees of initiation. Of course, there is some variation from tradition to tradition and from coven to coven, because, as Denise likes to say, if you ask 200 witches a question you will get 400 answers!

➤ **First Degree Initiation.** A year and a day after your dedication, after study and some hard work, and provided the High Priest and Priestess feel you are ready, you can earn your First Degree Initiation. Now you are a member of the coven and a First Degree witch!

➤ **Second Degree Initiation.** A year and a day after earning your First Degree, and after more study and work, you can earn your Second Degree Initiation, if the High Priest and Priestess feel you are ready. At this point, you usually can start teaching.

➤ **Third Degree Initiation.** A year and a day from the day you earned your Second Degree, you can get your Third Degree Initiation, provided the Priest and Priestess feel you are ready. Sometimes this degree takes a little more time to earn because there's a lot to learn. Once you have your Third Degree, you attain the status of High Priest or Priestess and can break away from the mother coven or "hive off" and form your own coven. If you do that, you will be High Priestess (or Priest) and the leader of the new coven. If you don't want to start your own coven, you can stay in your mother coven with the rank of High Priest or Priestess. Depending on the coven, you may share the responsibilities of leadership. Some covens go to four degrees with the Fourth Degree representing training to be a High Priest or Priestess.

So Mote It Be

If you do visit a coven, remember that you want to check them out as much as they are checking you out. Do the coven members seem healthy and happy? Are they friendly? Do they treat each other with respect? Do the High Priestess and High Priest treat the other members with respect? Does the group emphasize Wiccan teachings, such as the Wiccan Rede, respect for the Earth and all living things? Are the members having fun? If the answers to these questions are no, if the members disrespect one another, seem miserable or grim, then this is not the coven for you.

Life as a Coven Member

Being a member of a coven is a real commitment. As a member, you are expected to attend coven functions. The High Priestess and the High Priest, in consultation with the members, decide when the coven will meet. Covens generally meet to celebrate the 8 Sabbats—holidays of the God—and 13 Esbats—holidays of the Goddess—a year.

So, right there you have almost two meetings a month! Often each coven member is assigned a part to play in coven rituals. Not attending a ritual at which you are expected is a big no-no. If you don't make it, you could ruin the ritual. As a neophyte, you will also probably meet with your teachers on a regular basis. You might also be asked to do things for the coven or your teacher—buy candles for the altar, run errands, or clean the *covenstead,* for example. Covens also take on community service projects such as cleaning up a local stream, picking up litter in a park, helping out at a soup kitchen, or cleaning cages at the animal shelter. You will be expected to participate. If you miss too many coven activities, the coven will probably ask you to leave.

But coven members do have fun together. Sometimes, schedules permitting, they go to the movies together or get together for potluck suppers. Coven members enjoy each other's company, and they learn by working closely with one another.

Book of Shadows

A **covenstead** is where a coven meets. Indoors or out, it's a place where all the witches feel safe to meet and practice their craft.

Priests, Priestesses, and Elders

Most covens have a *High Priestess* and a *High Priest.* A coven must have a High Priestess. The High Priestess is seen as the Goddess incarnate. She is the spiritual center of the coven. She leads the coven in rituals, usually teaches, and guides coven members on their spiritual path. The High Priest assists the High Priestess and is seen as the God incarnate. Elders are people who have all their degrees but chose not to be High Priestesses or High Priests. Elders don't necessarily have to be old. They just have to be experienced in the ways of Wicca and magick. Some covens elect their Elders. Sometimes Elders are called on to help the coven make decisions, especially when a controversial issue crops up. Elders can lend themselves out to young covens to aid in decision making. If there is political upheaval in the community, the local Elders might get together to form a council to deal with the problem.

Book of Shadows

A **High Priest** and **High Priestess** are individuals who have advanced knowledge of witchcraft and lead a coven. Scholars think that the English words "priest" and "priestess" come from the ancient Greek word meaning "elder."

Training as a Solitaire

The solitary witch either has to train herself or find a teacher outside of the coven structure. This can seem a daunting task at first, but it is also an enjoyable process. Remember, learning is fun! But where do you start? Read on!

A Trip to Your Local Metaphysical Store

Most cities and many towns have metaphysical stores. There you should be able to find books about witchcraft. If your town doesn't have one, check out the New Age section of one of the major chain bookstores. Many of them carry Wiccan books. If there is a women's bookshop in your area, chances are it stocks a supply of books on the craft as well. And you can always order books online. Go to a store if you can, though, even if it means a field trip. Metaphysical or Wiccan stores usually carry a lot more than just books. The sales staff at such stores can often be a valuable resource for information. In addition, many stores also sponsor classes about Wicca and witch-craft.

Wicca Workshops and Courses

If you hear about a class while visiting a store, ask questions! Ask if a witch teaches the class and if you can speak to her (or him). Find out what the witch's training is. Is the witch part of a coven or a solitaire? Is the teacher a High Priestess (or Priest)? Does the witch practice a specific tradition? Find out how long the class lasts and how much it costs. Is it just a few weeks or does it last for a year and a day? An up-and-up store that offers classes will provide a meeting place for those classes. Does it have a space for the class to perform rituals? The store should also have a newsletter that lists its events.

If you find a solitary witch as a teacher, one who is not affiliated with a store, make sure this solitaire is a reputable person. Find out if the solitaire will charge you, and if so, how much. Find out if the solitaire will ask you to do favors, and if he or she asks you to do anything immoral, illegal, or that makes you uncomfortable, don't do it! Sex should never, ever enter into it. If it does, what you are learning is not Wicca. If you go over to a teacher's house for a class, let your friends and family know where you are going and when to expect you back. A true Wiccan would never hurt you, but some people may say that they are Wiccan when they're really not.

Another great place to find workshops and courses about Wicca and witchcraft is at Nature festivals. At festivals, you know for sure that the classes will be safe because the organizers of the festival would not hire someone disreputable to teach classes at their event. There are also likely to be a lot of classes! Festivals are great places to meet people and to network. You might find a teacher at a festival, or you might find someone who knows a good one in your area.

Wicca Books, Videos, and the Internet

Again, it all depends on what you are looking for. If you are interested in the Gardnerian tradition, look for books by Gerald Gardner. If eclectic witchcraft or the Pow Wow tradition appeal to you, check out the books by Silver Ravenwolf. Raven Grimassi has written about the Strega tradition, and Scott Cunningham has written several books for solitaires. Raymond Buckland has written about Seax-Wica and has published a useful nondenominational workbook that is arranged into lessons. Check your local library or bookstore for titles.

Videos are an excellent way to learn. There's just one drawback—you can't ask questions! Raymond Buckland has a good video called *Witchcraft Yesterday and Today*. And Janet and Stewart Farrar have two—*Discovering Witchcraft: A Journey Through The Elements* and *Discovering Witchcraft: The Mysteries*. See Appendix A, "Resources," for more details about these videos.

There is a lot of information on the Internet. But be careful about giving out your information on the Net. As you know, people can pretend to be many different things when you can't see them. Be cautious in your interactions. People do teach online Wicca and witchcraft classes. If you find a class you're interested in, you'd do well to ask all the questions you would of a teacher based at a store. Be aware, however, if you do take an online class, even if you have completed training for your First Degree, a coven will probably not recognize what you have learned.

When the Student Is Ready, the Teacher Will Appear

Don't worry too much about how and where you will find your teacher. Witches always say, "When the student is ready, the teacher will appear." If you aren't ready, you can search and search and nothing will happen. But when the time is right, when you are ready for transformation, you will step on the path and somehow it will lead you to the teacher you are meant to have.

The Least You Need to Know

➤ There are probably hundreds (maybe thousands!) of different kinds of witches. Some practice traditions based on their ethnic heritage. Others do not. If you are drawn to a certain tradition, check it out, even if you do not come from that background.

➤ You do not have to join a coven to be a witch. Many, many witches practice on their own as solitaires and have fulfilling magickal and spiritual experiences.

➤ If any witch asks you to do something that is immoral, illegal, or makes you uncomfortable, don't do it! Sexual favors should never enter into your training as a witch.

➤ You will find your teacher when you are ready.

Part 2
The Wiccan Way

It's time to take a closer look at Wiccan beliefs. In Wicca, you can honor the God and Goddess in many different forms. Once you become acquainted with the responsibilities involved, you'll want to think about why it is that you want to be a witch. After that you may want to go shopping for some magickal tools and objects that you can use in ritual.

Chapter 4

Wiccan Deities: Homage to the Lord and Lady

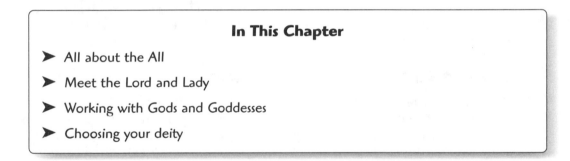

In This Chapter

➤ All about the All

➤ Meet the Lord and Lady

➤ Working with Gods and Goddesses

➤ Choosing your deity

In most faiths, you worship the God or Gods of that faith. There is no choice. In Wicca, you choose which deities you are going to work with. And sometimes deity chooses you!

You can choose which aspect of deity you are going to work with because all deities from all cultures are seen as facets of the All. So, you can work with Hera and Zeus from Ancient Greece, or you can pay homage to the Hindu deities Kali and Shiva. If you want, you can even work with aspects of Jesus, with the understanding that he, too, represents an aspect of the All. Wiccans have very personal relationships with deity. But let's slow down a little and start at the beginning.

In the Beginning, the All

Before people, before the creation of the Earth, there was the All. The All existed in knowing, stillness, and silence. The All, a female spirit, was alone. She created her other half, the male spirit. They intertwined. Even though there were now two spirits, they were still one. They became the two halves of the whole. And together they gave birth to the Universe. Then they made the solar systems, stars, moons, and planets. On Earth, they made water and land, the plants, and the animals, and humans.

The All is both male and female. No one part is better than the other part. The two parts are twin and of equal form. From their union came the seeds of life. The God and Goddess chose physical symbols to remind us of their presence. The Goddess chose the Moon, radiant and calm, yet changeable. The God chose the Sun, fiery and bright. These celestial bodies remind us of the God and the Goddess.

Homage to the Lord and Lady

In witchcraft traditions, you pay homage to both the Lord and the Lady, the God and the Goddess, as manifestations of the All. For a variety of reasons, many Wiccans choose to focus primarily on the Goddess. As Denise explains it, Wiccans are more into the Goddess because she represents that aspect of the All that is nurturing and compassionate, enabling growth, fertility, and gentleness. She can display her wrath, just as any female can, but for the most part we call up in her these gentler aspects. Many Wiccans believe that the Goddess and the feminine need to be focused stem from the domination for many hundreds of years of male-centered religions. Wiccans also work with her because of the nurturing fulfillment of her spirituality.

Who Is the Lady, and Where Is She?

The Lady is the female essence of the All. She is the nurturing part, the essence of motherhood. She is there to love us, shield us, help us to learn, and to grow. She is the one you'd call on for female spirituality because she understands the pain of childbirth, nurtures our spirits and our bodies, and encourages growth and connection within the family.

The Goddess is *immanent*. In other words, the Goddess is in everything and is everywhere. She is not some force that looks down on us from above. The Goddess dwells in every single thing—in every rock, in every cat, in every drop of rain, and inside you.

Book of Shadows

Immanent refers to something that exists or remains within. It can be something inherent. This English term comes from a Latin word that means "to remain in."

Who Is the Lord, and Where Is He?

The Lord is the male essence of the All. He is the wild, playful, and lusty aspect of deity. He is there to protect us. He is the one you may want to call for if you suddenly needed physical strength and agility. For instance, if a mugger pursued you, the Lord would help you to utilize your animal instincts in order to escape the danger. He can help you bear what life has thrust upon you by lending his speed, motion, and ability to adapt to change. Just as the Lady is, the Lord is immanent. He exists in everything.

How Do You Relate to the Lady?

You work with, respect, and honor the Lady. You don't beg for favors from her. You can see her as a Goddess from an ancient culture, or you can work with her as an abstraction. Many people feel more comfortable giving her a face and a personality. The Lady nurtures your growth. She is the abundance that the Earth has to give. She has that hidden, inner knowledge, or sixth sense, that all women have. You can pull upon that part of her to guide you and help you grow. She will teach you, nurture you, and provide for you. In return, you give her your love. Out of that love, you do your best to take care of the Earth that she has provided for you.

Luna: Maiden, Mother, Crone, and Enchantress

Luna is the Roman Goddess of the Moon. The Goddess's three phases—Maiden, Mother, and Crone—represent the three stages of a woman's life. The Maiden is an innocent, young girl. To her everything is new. She is health, sweetness, and tenderness. As the Mother, she has matured. She is all loving, protective, and nurturing. When human kind takes actions that hurt the Earth, she can get angry. And yet she still loves us, however badly we behave. She sends us signs so we, her children, can learn from our mistakes. The Crone, an old woman, holds all the things that we have learned throughout our life times. She can be stern, but she is a great teacher. She takes us back into her, into the Goddess, in death. These three aspects of the Goddess correlate to the phases of the Moon—new, full, and waning.

The Enchantress is that part of the Goddess, and of all women, that seduces. She is that sexy playful spirit that we get from the All. She is both Maiden and Mother, and as such relates to the Moon when it is new, waxing (growing bigger in the sky), and full.

So Mote It Be

Try writing about your conception of the Goddess. Jot down a few words. You don't have to write in sentences or worry about spelling. Just put down whatever comes into your head. What does she look like? How does she dress? What's the first thing that you notice about her when you see her? Does she have a scent? What does her voice sound like? And what about the God? Do they look alike, or are they different? Give yourself at least 10 minutes, then read your words over. Highlight any passages or ideas that you particularly like. Keep this piece in your notebook so you can refer to it in the future.

As a Woman: The Female Mysteries

If you are a woman, the female *mysteries* may not seem too mysterious to you. The fact that we have our periods, that we bleed every month and don't grow weak and die, is part of the female mysteries. That women can grow life inside themselves, give birth, and feed that new life from their bodies is a mystery. The hidden knowledge women possess, or women's intuition, forms a part of the female mysteries. This hidden knowledge grows within us as we mature, and transforms us from the maiden to the mother and to finally the wisdom of the crone.

Book of Shadows

By **mysteries** we don't mean stories in which a detective figures out "who done it." Mysteries, in a religious context, are special rites or knowledge that only initiates are supposed to be familiar with. The word comes from an Ancient Greek root that literally means "to close the eyes or mouth"; in other words, to keep a secret.

As a Man: The Male Mysteries

Working with the Goddess, men discover that they have a female side. They learn that crying does not mean they are weak. They learn that they can be tender and nurturing. A man who has gotten in touch with his feminine side is truly comfortable with himself and who he is. He learns that to show his emotions does not demonstrate weakness, but indicates a strength of feeling and compassion, and he will not be embarrassed by such a display.

The Charge of the Goddess

The Charge of the Goddess is an invocation that is frequently used in Wiccan ritual. There are many different versions of the charge. Here is the most widely known one:

Charge of the Goddess

When I have departed from this world,
Whenever ye have need of anything,
Once in a month, and when the Moon is full,
Ye shall assemble in some desert place,
Or in a forest all together join
To adore the potent spirit of your queen,
My Mother, great Diana. She who fain
Would learn all sorcery yet has not won
Its deepest secrets them my mother
Teach her, in truth all things as yet unknown
And ye shall all be free from slavery,
And so ye shall be free in everything:
And as the sign that ye are truly free,

Ye shall be naked in your rites, both men
And women also: this shall last until
The last of your oppressors shall be dead:
And ye shall make a game of Benevento,
Extinguishing the lights, and after that
Shall hold your supper thus.

If you like, you can adapt the Charge of the
Goddess so that it suits you. Or try this one that
Denise wrote:

Charge of the Goddess

Webweaving

The Charge of the Goddess was first published in *Aradia: The Gospel of the Witches*, by Charles Leland. In 1897, a witch named Maddalena is said to have given him the text. The Charge of the Goddess has been adapted several times by a variety of authors.

High Priest: Listen to the words of the Great Mother, the ancient one of ageless time. She was known by many among those who worshiped her. Artemis, Diana, Morrigan, Aphrodite, Venus, Cerridwen, Isis, Mary, and by many other names.

High Priestess: Whenever you have need, come to me. Assemble in a place of secret, better it be when the Moon is full and give praise to the spirit of me.

I am Queen of the Witches and those who seek the knowledge of the Craft of the Wise. From me flow all its mysteries and its darkest secrets. I will teach those who gather in my honor and seek to know all it's sorcery. There is my place of worship you shall sing, dance, feast, make music and love in my praise. For to do this in the presence of me, shall truly set you free from bondage. In my spirit you shall feel ecstasy and joy on Earth.

In striving for your highest ideals keep your heart and spirit pure. Let no one stop you or turn you aside from me.

Enter the Land of Youth through my secret door and drink from the Chalice of Life Eternal. It is there that you will find the Holy Grail of Immortality and the Cauldron of Cerridwen. Drink in the gifts of joy, knowledge, and eternal spirit that I have bestowed upon humanity.

Upon death you will receive my gifts of peace and freedom. You shall be reunited in the spirit of love with those who have passed over before you. I demand no sacrifice in my name, for to do so would dishonor the spirit of me. I am the Mother of all living things. Give reverence unto me by honoring all that I have bestowed upon the Earth.

High Priest: Hear the words of the Great Moon Goddess, She whose light illuminates the heavens and whose spirit weaves the tapestry of the Universe.

High Priestess: Cherish and protect the Earth's beauty which holds the gateway to the entrance of my temple. Call my name when you gaze upon the white Moon that stands alone in the night sky amidst the stars of heaven. Learn the mysteries of the waters and hold tightly to the desire in your hearts.

I who gave life to the universe give my soul to Nature, therefore rise up and give your soul to me. Always know that from me all things proceed and unto me all things must return. Through me, let my beauty, compassion, strength, power, humility, and the honors of my spirit reside within you. Let my rituals of love and pleasures remain in the heart that rejoices in my worship.

To those who seek to know me understand that all of your yearning will be in vain unless you know the mystery. If what you seek is not found within you, then you shall never find it without. For behold I am alpha and omega, the beginning and the end. I have always been and always will be with you.

If you use the Charge of the Goddess with a group, you want to have the person in the role of High Priest read the sections marked for him. The High Priestess reads the rest of the charge. During the Charge of the Goddess, the High Priestess is seen to become the Goddess.

How Do You Relate to the Lord?

You work with the Lord in the form of a God or as an abstraction. He is the essence of fatherhood. He is kind, gentle, and protective, but he can also show his wrath. You look to him with honor and respect and gain from him his guidance, wisdom, protection, and strength. You pull on this aspect of the All to protect and strengthen your life, in order to do what you need to do, so you in turn can protect your family. The Lord is also representative of the playfulness and heavy sexuality that we all have within us.

Nature's Royal Prince, King, and Elder

Just as the Goddess can be seen in three phases (Maiden, Mother, and Crone), the God has three phases as well. As Nature's Royal Prince he is a youth, full of wonder, curiosity, and playfulness. As the King, he has matured into a man—noble, protective, and just. And as the Elder he is an old man, wise, weathered, and strong.

As a Woman: The Female Mysteries

Working with the Lord, women get in touch with the male part of themselves. This is a strength you would call on if you were in trouble or needed protection.

As a Man: The Male Mysteries

Through aspects of the Lord, men learn to behave nobly. They learn to control through kindness and by earning another's respect, not by browbeating other people. The Lord can punish us, but as any good father does, he prefers to work by teaching us. He wants us to learn from our mistakes and live in harmony. Just as the Lord works as one with us and rules over us with a gentle hand, so men learn to accept and be among his fellows—both male and female.

Charge of the God

Like the Charge of the Goddess, the Charge of the God is an invocation. Here's a version that Denise wrote:

Charge of the God

> *High Priestess:* Listen to the words of the God who is son, lover, and consort of the Lady. He is the ancient one of time eternal, the great father who of old we know as Ra, Osiris, Zeus, Thor, Pan, Herne, Luke, and by a thousand other names.

> *High Priest:* I am the radiant Sun, king of the heaven. Come to me whenever you seek haven in my spirit. Assemble in some secret place, most notably at the eight sacred days of the wheel and give praise. Set aside the restrictions of cultural laws and, like the beasts of the forest that are of hoof and horn, run naked and free in my presence. Sing and dance, make love, and celebrate. Delight in the moment.

> My law is harmony. My love is the seed that fertilizes the Earth. My rapture is of the mind. In the grain that bursts forth and grows, I am life abundant. In the fall harvest when the grain is cut down, I am death, the gentle reaper, king of the underworld, where the living may not venture. And in spring, I am rebirth, the hidden seed of creation that bursts forth into being.

> *High Priestess:* Hear now the words of the great horned one whose song stirs the astral winds and whose music changes the season from one to the next, flowing in a smooth rhythm.

> *High Priest:* I, who am the Sun, the keeper of the lamp that sends out the light to warm the Earth, the lord of the hunt, the master of the winds that spread the seed of life. I call upon you now to arise and come unto me. Show respect for the wonder of me. Give love to others as I have given love to you. Let there dwell within you the magnificence of life, tenderness of heart, the glory of the spirit, mastery of emotions and merriment and pleasure. Keep me always in your heart for I am the giver of peace, the source of life, the father of all things and my protection blankets the temple of life, the body of the Lady and the Earth.

Who Are All the Other Gods and Goddesses?

All Gods and Goddesses are aspects of the All. Before you start to work with one of these aspects, you need to read about them. You need to know your Gods and Goddesses before you call them. Learn about their likes and dislikes. Who are their allies among the other deities? Who are their consorts? What makes them angry? How do they relate to the other Gods and Goddesses in their pantheon? We'll give you an introduction to some of the major Gods and Goddesses later in this chapter. But you'll probably also want to go to the library and look for myths about the Gods and Goddesses from the cultures that interest you.

Book of Shadows

A **pantheon** is the collection of all of the deities from one culture. It can also be a temple that has been dedicated to all of the Gods.

Banish!

Resist the temptation to pick a very dark God or Goddess just because you can. Remember your work with a deity should benefit you, not scare you. And what you do is for the good of all. Remember "An it harm none, do what ye will."

The Pantheon: Getting the Big Picture

While you are learning the craft, work with deities from one *pantheon*. Don't mix and match Gods and Goddesses from different cultures. First discover all you can about one pantheon. Later on, you can branch out and start to learn how deities from one system relate to deities from another.

Working with Deities: Sometimes Light, Sometimes Dark

The deity you want to work with on a given day will depend on what you want to do. If you are working with the Greek pantheon and you need to attract some loving energy, you may want to call on Aphrodite. Within the Hindu system, you would invoke Sarasvati, Goddess of language and wisdom, for assistance in studying for a test. You can work with any God or Goddess that you want. Some deities encompass a light energy, and others are darker. Be aware of the qualities of the deity you are working with. Know that Hecate is wise *and* that she is associated with the underworld. Athena is also wise, and she is a warrior. She does not have as dark energy as Hecate does.

Choosing Your Pantheon: Some Famous Deities

You may have read about the Greek Gods and Goddesses in school. Deities from some of the other traditions may be less familiar to you. Read up on the pantheon that appeals to you. Stories of the Gods and Goddesses are always fascinating and full of lots of drama! And the stories will give you more insight by providing some of the nuances of each deity's personality. Here are some of the major Gods and Goddesses from a number of different pantheons.

Greek Gods and Goddesses:

➤ **Aphrodite.** The Goddess of sexuality, love, and beauty. She is a beautiful and often naked young woman. Sometimes she is covered, or partially covered, in a cloth. She can be seen carrying a dove or stepping out of the sea.

➤ **Apollo.** The God of healing and the arts. He is young and handsome. He carries a lyre, a bow, and arrows. He drives a golden chariot.

➤ **Artemis.** The Goddess of the Moon, the hunt, and women. A beautiful maiden, she carries a bow and quiver of arrows. Often birds, deer, or lions accompany her.

➤ **Athena.** The Goddess of wisdom. She is a beautiful and serious young woman. A warrior, she wears a breastplate and helmet and carries a lance and a shield. Sometimes she has an owl with her. She is associated with the city of Athens and with the olive tree.

➤ **Demeter.** The Goddess of the harvest. She is an old woman and the mother of Persephone. She often weeps because she and Persephone have been separated.

➤ **Dionysus.** The God of wine, the life force, and the wildness of instinct. A young man dressed in an animal skin, he carries a staff and sometimes is seen as a bull or a goat.

➤ **Eros.** The Greek God of sexual attraction. He is a small and beautifully formed young man with wings. He often carries a lyre or a bow and a quiver of arrows.

➤ **Gaia.** The Mother Earth. She sits on a throne and holds many fruits, grains, and vegetables often in a cornucopia. She is a mature woman and usually wears a robe. Gaia is often used in craft rituals.

➤ **Hades.** The God of the underworld and of wealth. He is also king of the dead. A mature man, he wears a beard and a helmet and often is seen on a throne next to his young wife Persephone.

➤ **Hecate.** The Goddess of magic and the Moon. She can take a few different forms and is also associated with the underworld. She often carries a torch and has snakes in her hair. She can have three heads—those of the maiden, mother, and crone. She can be found at the spot where three roads meet.

➤ **Hera.** The Goddess of women. Married to Zeus, she is the queen of the Gods. She wears a crown and carries a scepter. She is mature and beautiful.

➤ **Hermes.** The God of communication, thought, and travel. A beautiful, athletic young man, he wears sandals with wings, a helmet with wings, and carries a *caduceus*.

➤ **Pan.** The God of wild places and things and of shepherds. Pan plays a set of connected pipes called panpipes. He takes a form that is half man and half goat. His legs and feet are of the goat, while his chest and upper body are that of a hairy man. He usually has horns. He is frequently invoked in pagan rituals.

Book of Shadows

A **caduceus** is a wand or staff with two snakes twined around it. At the top of the wand sit a pair of wings. Today the caduceus is used as the symbol of the medical profession.

➤ **Persephone.** The Goddess of the harvest, fertility, and spring. She often is seen sitting with Hades on a throne in the underworld, where she spends a number of months every year. Sometimes she carries a pomegranate. She is also called "Kore," the maiden.

➤ **Poseidon.** The God of water and the seas. He always carries a trident and is associated with dolphins and horses.

➤ **Zeus.** The God of the sky and the king of the Gods. He is associated with rain and clouds and often carries a thunderbolt. He is married to Hera, but often falls in love with other women. He is a bearded man of great wisdom and authority.

Roman Gods and Goddesses:

➤ **Ceres.** The Goddess of the harvest. She is described in the same way as the Greek Goddess Demeter.

➤ **Diana.** The Goddess of fertility. A beautiful maiden huntress, she is associated with the Moon and the woods. She often has dogs or a stag with her. Diana is often used in craft rituals.

➤ **Fortuna.** The Goddess of fortune and fate. She is mature and carries a cornucopia, a rudder from a ship, a sphere, and a wheel.

➤ **Janus.** The God of beginnings and doorways. He is a bearded man with two faces, one looks into the past, the other into the future. He can see the inside and the outside of all things at the same time.

➤ **Juno.** The Goddess of women and the Moon. She is married to Jupiter and is queen of the Gods. In one of her aspects, she is the Goddess of childbirth. A beautiful woman, she has dark hair and wears a robe. The cow, the peacock, and the goose are sacred to her.

➤ **Jupiter.** The God of the sky and the king of the Gods. He is described in the same way as the Greek God Zeus.

➤ **Luna.** Goddess of the Moon. She appears as the Maiden, the Mother, and the Crone.

➤ **Mars.** The God of war and agriculture. Dressed in armor and carrying a shield, Mars is a large man. His companion animals include a wolf, a woodpecker, and a vulture.

➤ **Mercury.** The God of communication, thought, and travel. He is described in the same way as the Greek God Hermes.

➤ **Neptune.** The God of water and the seas. He is described in the same way as the Greek God Poseidon.

➤ **Pluto.** The God of the underworld and of wealth. He is also king of the dead. He is described in the same way as the Greek God Hades.

➤ **Venus.** The Goddess of sexuality, love, and beauty. She is described in the same way as the Greek Goddess Aphrodite.

Hindu Gods and Goddesses:

➤ **Agni.** The God of Fire. He has razor-like golden teeth, three arms and seven legs. He carries flames, a pot full of water, and a trident.

➤ **Brahma.** The God of creation. He usually has four arms and four heads. He dresses in white and rides on a swan or a peacock. Sometimes he sits on a lotus blossom.

➤ **Durga.** The great mother Goddess. She often rides a lion and has four arms in which she carries a drum, a sword, a trident, and a bowl filled with blood.

➤ **Ganesha.** The elephant-headed God. He is the overcomer of obstacles. Besides his elephant-head, he has a potbelly. In his four arms, he carries roses, a piece of his broken tusk, a thorn, and a bowl. He often rides upon a very small rat.

➤ **Hanuman.** The monkey God. His job is to tour the world singing the name of God. He has great strength and learning and is mischievous. Often he has wings. He can be a fierce warrior.

➤ **Indra.** The God of war. Usually riding a horse, Indra takes the form of a golden or red man and carries a thunderbolt. Sometimes he rides a white elephant. His name means "strong."

➤ **Kali.** The Goddess of Earth, Nature, and destruction. With wild dark hair, a blood-smeared body, and a protruding tongue, she wears a necklace of human skulls and often stands on her husband Shiva.

➤ **Krishna.** The God of love. He takes the form of a man with blue skin. He often plays the flute.

➤ **Lakshmi.** The Goddess of fortune and beauty. Always beautifully dressed, she is golden and sits on a lotus blossom.

➤ **Sarasvati.** The Goddess of language and wisdom. She has six arms and three faces. She often rides a swan or sits on a lotus.

➤ **Siva** or **Shiva.** The God of change, transformation, and destruction. He is the creator of yoga and a dancer. A man with a third eye between his eyebrows, he carries a trident and an axe.

➤ **Vishnu.** The God of preservation. He is also seen as the liberator and the highest God. In his four arms he holds a club, a shell, a disk, and a lotus.

Egyptian Gods and Goddesses:

➤ **Amun, Amon,** or **Amen.** The God of creation. He carries a whip and sometimes is seated in a throne. He can be depicted as a ram with a coiled cobra on his head.

➤ **Anubis.** The God of the dead. He has the body of a man and the head of a jackal. Sometimes he is shown as entirely jackal.

➤ **Bastet** or **Bast.** The Goddess of the Sun and pleasure. She has a human body and the head of a cat. She carries a rattle and wears a breastplate decorated with the head of a lion.

➤ **Geb.** The God of the Earth. He often lies beneath Nut, the Goddess of the sky. He has dark skin and sometimes wears a goose on his head.

So Mote It Be

You will develop a personal relationship with the deity that you choose to work with. To help that relationship develop and to welcome that deity into your life, get a picture of your chosen God or Goddess. Many stores sell images of ancient deities. Or find a picture in a book in the library and make a color copy.

➤ **Hathor.** The Goddess of beauty, love, and pleasure. She is a woman with the horns of a cow. Sometimes all of her takes the form of a cow. She often carries a rattle.

➤ **Horus.** A Solar God and the avenger of evil. Horus is seen in the form of a man with the head of a falcon or as a falcon with the Moon as one eye and the Sun as the other. Sometimes he appears as a child standing in the back of a crocodile.

➤ **Isis.** The mother Goddess. She is associated with fertility, the Moon, magick, and resurrection. She is usually seated and sometimes holds the infant Horus.

➤ **Nephthys.** The Goddess of Earth and fertility. She takes the form of a woman with a hieroglyph on her head.

➤ **Nut** or **Nuit.** The Goddess of the sky. She is young and slim. Stars shine from within her body. She usually appears naked, arched over Geb, the Earth God.

➤ **Osiris.** The God of fertility and resurrection. He takes the form of a mummy with the head of a live man. His face often has a slight green cast.

➤ **Ptah.** The God of creation and chief of the underworld. He takes the form of a mummified man with a shaved head or appears as a dwarf.

➤ **Ra.** The Sun God. He takes the form of a man with the head of a falcon. As the Sun appears to move across the sky, so he travels through the sky. At night, he journeys through the underworld and his head takes the form of that of a ram.

Buddhist/Asian Gods and Goddess:

➤ **Buddha.** The Awakened One. The Buddha takes many different forms. He often sits cross-legged and appears to be fat and happy. Sometimes he is golden in color.

➤ **Maitreya.** The future Buddha. He takes the form of a man wearing a headdress and holding a white flower.

➤ **Quan yin.** The Goddess of mercy in the Japanese tradition. She also has cults all over China. She will protect you from danger. Newlyweds often pray to her for fertility. She is sometimes referred to as the Queen of Heaven. She is pictured sitting on a lotus, holding a vase full of the dew of compassion. In addition, she is associated with the willow tree.

Celtic Gods and Goddesses:

➤ **Brigid.** The Goddess of healing, inspiration, and craftspeople. She has great strength and can be called upon to help you endure hardship.

➤ **Cernunnos** or **Kernunnos.** The Horned God. He takes the form of a man with the horns of a stag. He is the universal father. Sometimes he has three heads. He is the consort of the Lady. He is often called in pagan rituals.

➤ **Cerridwen.** The Goddess of the Moon, the harvest, and inspiration. She can be dark, like the Crone or the darkening Moon. She is often seen as a hag, stirring the cauldron of knowledge. It takes her a year and a day to prepare her brew—the same amount of time a witch studies between dedication and First Degree Initiation and between First Degree and Second Degree Initiation.

➤ **Herne.** The God of the Underworld. He is the leader of the phantom hunt. He is usually depicted with the antlers of a stag.

➤ **Morrigan.** The Goddess of war, fertility, and vegetation. She is Queen of the demons and has three faces. In her warlike aspect, she takes the form of a bat with red eyebrows. She can also appear as a raven, crow, or horse. She will take care of the wrongdoing that someone has done.

➤ **Ogma.** The God of language and inspiration. He takes the form of a wise old man. He wears animal skins, and golden chains pour out of his mouth. He invented the Druidic alphabet.

Other Gods and Goddesses frequently used in Wiccan rituals:

➤ **Aradia.** The Queen of the witches in the Italian tradition. She is very powerful and can be called on to protect any witch.

➤ **Astarte.** The Goddess of love and war in the Middle Eastern tradition. Usually naked, she wears a necklace and carries a spear. Sometimes she stands on a lion and has horns that take the shape of a crescent Moon.

Webweaving

You may meet a man named Thor in the future. Many male witches take the name Thor as their magickal name. Hey, you never know!

➤ **Freyja.** The Goddess of love and fertility in the Norse tradition. She is a beautiful woman who drives a chariot drawn by cats. Sometime she rides on a golden boar.

➤ **Thor.** The God of thunderstorms and the life force in the Norse tradition. He is a really big guy with a red beard. In his hands, which are sheathed in iron gloves, he carries a hammer. Two goats draw his chariot.

➤ **The Venus of Willendorf.** The Goddess of fertility from prehistoric Europe. She has large breasts and a big bottom and practically no arms or feet (she's pictured in Chapter 1, "All About Wicca and Witchcraft").

The Least You Need to Know

➤ The All—the Lord and the Lady—are present in all things and in all beings.

➤ The Lord and the Lady are two major aspects of the All. They are different from one another, but equal. Gods and Goddesses from all the different pantheons represent various aspect of the All.

➤ In Wicca, you choose the form of deity that you work with, based on your personal preferences and what you want to work on. You can choose from many different traditions and many different Gods and Goddesses.

➤ You work with deities. You do not beg from them.

Chapter 5

So You Want to Be a Witch?

In This Chapter

➤ Check your motivations

➤ Taking care of your temple

➤ Remember, harm none!

➤ Magickal energy and responsibility

Wiccan witches live their lives according to the principles and moral code of their belief. These principles are not rigid, and yet, they are not always easy to follow. Abiding by the Wiccan faith can require a good deal of thought and your good actions.

In this chapter, we'll help you look at the reasons that you want to become a witch. Committing yourself to the craft is a serious step that you don't want to enter into lightly. You may want to take some time to mull over some of the issues raised in this chapter.

Why Do You Want to Be a Witch?

Do you want to gain in personal power? Do you want to live in tune with yourself and Nature? Witchcraft could be the path for you. Keep in mind that being a witch is more than saying chants, doing spells, and knowing cool stuff. Wicca is a spiritual path. It's important to look at your motivations before you set off on your journey.

A Self-Exploration

Take this little quiz and find out if your reasons are the right reasons.

1. You want to be a witch because …

    a. you want to learn more about yourself.

    b. you want to become more in tune with yourself and Nature.

    c. you want to turn your boss into a frog.

    d. your best friend is doing it.

2. You believe witches to be …

    a. keepers of magickal forces.

    b. people who can change the future.

    c. people who are content with themselves and the world around them.

    d. people who dance naked and have orgies.

3. Witches are people who associate themselves with …

    a. the Devil.

    b. a loving God and Goddess.

    c. people of like ways and minds.

    d. mystical, magickal creatures.

4. To be a witch you have to …

    a. be willing to have sex with other people.

    b. be willing to do blood sacrifices.

    c. be willing to face your true inner self and not be afraid.

    d. learn to trust yourself.

5. A witch always …

    a. tries to abide by a positive code of morality.

    b. owns a black cat.

    c. flies on a broom during a full Moon.

    d. knows the intent of her magick.

Were you honest with your answers? We hope so. After all, no one is looking—besides you!

Question 1. Answer a) is an okay answer, but b) is a better answer. Remember Wicca is an Earth-based religion, so it's not just about you. It's about you *and* Nature. You picked c)? Have you forgotten all about the Wiccan Rede? Please read the rest of this chapter carefully and go back and reread Chapters 1, 3, and 4! Answer d)—it's nice to do things with your friends; but if this is the only reason that you're interested, if you are going to be a witch, Wicca has got to be *your* practice. That means commitment of your energies, time, effort, and yourself.

Question 2. Answers a) and b)—there might be some truth in both of these answers, but c) is the best answer. Witches are happy people because they live right and use their energy wisely. Did you choose answer d)? Really? Only some covens practice ritual skyclad. And orgies? We don't think so.

Question 3. Answer a)—witches do not believe in the Devil. The Devil is a Christian concept that plays no part in Wicca; b)—yes, witches honor the loving God and Goddess; c)—you could say that a coven is made up of people of like ways and minds, but remember, many witches are solitary. And the point of the coven is to honor the God and Goddess; d)—what kind of mystical, magickal creatures? We haven't mentioned any of those, have we?

Question 4. Answer a)—as we said in Chapter 3, "Practicing Wicca and Witchcraft Today," sex should never come into your training as a witch. While some covens may practice skyclad, that does not mean that the coven members are engaged in an orgy; b)—witches do not make sacrifices. Remember the Wiccan Rede? In case you don't, we're going to talk more about it soon; c) is actually the best answer here. Sure, d) is close, but think about it this way: You need to face your true inner self and not shy away from what you find there in order to trust yourself.

Webweaving

Why are witches associated with brooms and flying? As early as 1458, an inquisitor for the church declared that believing that witches could fly was part of the true and Catholic faith. During that period in history, witches were thought to fly out of their chimneys, mounted astride sticks. By 1580, brooms became one of the vehicles of choice.

Question 5. a)—correct! This is a most important feature of witchcraft; b) is not the best answer, but ... well, yes, lots of witches do own black cats, although they also live with white cats and dogs and parakeets and gerbils, c) is also not the best answer, but Katherine admits that she really wants to try this! d) is almost right, but answer a) is better. How come? You could know the intent of your magick, and that intent could be to harm. That would not be okay. "An it harm none, do what ye will" is the witch's most important rule.

So, how did you do? Great, we're sure! Witchcraft, as you can see, involves Nature, the God and Goddess, self-knowledge, and ethics, and morality. Do you feel confident that being a witch is the right path for you? Many, many people do feel that way because witches don't just have beliefs, they have principles.

More on the Witches' Council and the 13 Goals of a Witch

In 1974, the Council of American Witches, an organization that no longer exists, drew up a list—the "Principle of Wiccan Belief." We gave you a summary of those 13 principles in Chapter 1, "All About Wicca and Witchcraft." You might want to look them over again. The Council, which was made up of 73 witches from a variety of different traditions, met in Minneapolis and prepared this document to try to dispel misleading misinformation about witches. The principles have been important in giving Wicca legal status as a religion under U.S. law. In fact, the handbooks issued to U.S. Army chaplains contain these 13 principles.

Scott Cunningham, the respected author of more than 30 books and a practicing witch for 20 years, came up with another list of important principles for witches. Cunningham details the 13 goals of a witch. Here they are:

1. Know yourself.
2. Know your craft.
3. Learn.
4. Apply knowledge with wisdom.
5. Achieve balance.
6. Keep your words in good order.
7. Keep your thoughts in good order.
8. Celebrate life.
9. Attune with the cycles of the Earth.
10. Breathe and eat correctly.
11. Exercise the body.
12. Meditate.
13. Honor the Goddess and God.

We think these are great goals for everyone, witch or not. The point of many of them is that you have to respect yourself *and* your body. Your body *is* a temple. You've probably heard that before, and maybe it sounds clichéd, but listen—your body is sacred because it carries your soul. And, because your body carries your soul, it carries the essence of the God and the Goddess. Yes, you have the God and the Goddess inside you. Even if you do feel crabby and irritable, or hungry and sleepy, or sad. So, your body is the sacred vessel of your soul, a temple, and the goal of all witches is to take care of the temple.

Following the Wiccan Way

You're probably understanding that being a witch is not just about casting spells and wearing cool outfits. Neither is it a hobby or a pastime. Being a witch means that you are walking on the Wiccan path. It's a lifestyle, and it is more than that. Being a witch is about commitment and responsibility—to yourself, to your coven (if you have one), to your community, and to the Earth.

The Wiccan Rede

Remember the Wiccan Rede from Chapter 1: "An it harm none, do what ye will"? Well, here is the full text of the poem from which the Rede is drawn.

The poem "The Rede of the Wiccae," sometimes referred to as the Wiccan Rede, was first published in *Green Egg Magazine* in 1975. Lady Gwen Thompson, a witch from the Celtic Tradition, submitted the poem. Her grandmother, Adriana Porter, had given it to her. No one is really sure how old the poem is. Some people believe it was written in the mid 1930s. Others believe that is unlikely, because the word "Wicca" was not used until the 1960s. No matter how old it is, the Rede remains a central pillar of the Wiccan faith.

"The Rede of the Wiccae" (Being Known as the Counsel of the Wise Ones)

1. Bide the Wiccan laws ye must
   in perfect love and perfect trust.

2. Live and let live—
   fairly take and fairly give.

3. Cast the Circle thrice about
   to keep all evil spirits out.

4. To bind the spell every time,
   let the spell be spake in rhyme.

5. Soft of eye and light of touch—
   speak little, listen much.

6. *Deosil* go by the waxing Moon—
   sing and dance the Wiccan rune.

7. *Widdershins* go when the Moon doth wane,
   and the Werewolf howls by the dread Wolfsbane.

8. When the Lady's Moon is new,
   kiss the hand to her times two.

9. When the Moon rides at her peak,
   then your heart's desire seek.

Book of Shadows

Deosil means "clockwise." Deosil movement in a circle is used to draw the positive. **Widdershins** means "counterclockwise." Widdershins movement is usually used in dispelling negative things, such as bad energy or disease.

10. Heed the Northwind's mighty gale—
    lock the door and drop the sail.

11. When the wind comes from the South,
    love will kiss thee on the mouth.

12. When the wind blows from the East,
    expect the new and set the feast.

13. When the West wind blows o'er thee,
    departed spirits restless be.

14. Nine woods in the Cauldron go—
    burn them quick and burn them slow.

15. Elder be ye Lady's tree—
    burn it not or cursed ye'll be.

16. When the Wheel begins to turn—
    let the Beltane fires burn.

17. When the Wheel has turned a Yule,
    light the Log and let Pan rule.

18. Heed ye flower, bush and tree—
    by the Lady blessed be.

19. Where the rippling waters go,
    cast a stone an truth ye'll know.

20. When ye have need,
    hearken not to other's greed.

21. With the fool no season spend
    or be counted as his friend.

22. Merry meet an merry part—
    bright the cheeks an warm the heart.

23. Mind the Threefold Law ye should—
    three times bad and three times good.

24. When misfortune is enow,
    wear the blue star on thy brow.

25. True in love ever be
    unless thy lover's false to thee.

26. Eight words the Wiccan Rede fulfill—
    an it harm none, do what ye will.

So Mote It Be

Why not learn "The Rede of the Wiccae" by heart? If you memorize it, then you really will have it in your heart! You haven't had to commit a poem to memory in a million years? Work on one couplet at a time. The rhyme will help make the words easier to remember. Write the couplet out a few times on scrap paper. Post the couplet in places where you'll see it—on your computer monitor, the dashboard of your car, the door to the refrigerator, the bathroom mirror. Before you know it, you will know it! Then you can add another one.

Honoring the Wiccan Rede

So, that's the Wiccan Rede. We think it's quite beautiful. But, what, you ask, does it mean? Let's take a look, line by line:

1. You must keep the Wiccan laws with an attitude of perfect love and perfect trust. If you don't completely agree with what Wicca is about, you might want to rethink your choice to follow the Wiccan path.

2. Respect people and Nature. Treat them both as you want to be treated.

3. Witches generally cast a circle around them when preparing to do magick. The circle is cast three times because three is a very magickal number. It stands for the three phases of the Goddess and God, and it's the number of creativity. In addition, there is the threefold law that says events usually happen in threes.

4. Witches speak their spells in rhyme because it gives the conscious mind something to do. While your conscious mind is busy listening to the words, your unconscious can tap into your energy and the energy of the God and the Goddess—and magick is done.

5. Be gentle. Sit back and listen. Wise people don't blab; they listen.

6. When the Moon is waxing, or getting bigger, move around the ritual circle clockwise to bring good things toward you.

7. When the Moon is waning, or getting smaller, move around the circle counterclockwise to take away negativity. Wolfsbane is dreaded because it is a poisonous plant.

8. When the Moon is new and has just become visible in the sky again after being dark, salute the Lady and welcome her by kissing your two fingers.

9. When the Moon is full, go after your heart's desire. At that time of the month, you can ask anything of her.

10–13. These couplets describe various elements associated with the four directions.

14–15. There are nine different kinds of magickal wood that are often burned in the cauldron during rituals—apple, birch, fir, hawthorn, hazel, oak, rowan, vine, and willow. But never burn the elder (that's a kind of tree, too). Elder trees are the Lady's tree, and in honor of her they are always spared.

16–17. The turning of the wheel refers to the cycle of the year. Beltane is one of the year's major Sabbats, or holidays. It occurs in the spring. Yule, another Sabbat, sits on the opposite side of the wheel of the year, at the time of the winter solstice.

18. Take care of Nature, and respect it for the Lady's sake.

19. Watch what happens when you throw a stone into water. The ripples spread out from where the stone landed. In much the same way, your actions, like the stone, send out ripples that affect everyone and everything around you.

20. Don't allow the idea of profit to sway you. Don't take money for your magickal work.

21. People will associate you with the company you keep. If you hang around with fools, you may just be seen as one, too.

22. Basically, this means it's good to be with friends.

23. Pay attention to the threefold law. Whatever you do, good or bad, comes back to you three times.

24. When you are in trouble, visualize a blue *pentagram* on your forehead. The pentagram will protect you.

25. Be loyal in love, but if the sucker isn't loyal to you, forget about him (or her)!

26. Eight words sum it up—if it harms none, do what you want.

There are other versions of Rede poems. There's a nine-line version by Amber K, a popular author of books about the craft. In fact, there is a whole Web site devoted to the Wiccan Rede. Check it out at http://pagan.drak.net/sheathomas/. Whichever version of the Rede you prefer, you must agree that it contains a strong moral code. These principles are central to the Wiccan faith.

To Know, to Dare ...

The witches' pyramid describes the necessary conditions you must meet to perform magick. You must be ready to ...

1. Know who you are and what you are. You have to *know* the rules. You must *know* what magickal rites you are going to be doing. And you must *know* your intention.

2. Dare to do what you are planning. Do you *dare* to follow through?

3. Will the magick to happen. Do you have the ability and the *will* to follow through? Can you *will* your energy to make it happen?

4. Keep silent and not brag or boast about what you have done. You don't take your magick for granted, but you sit back quietly, watch, and know that you are growing.

All You Need to Put Yourself in Tune with Magickal Energy

You really don't need much to put yourself in touch with magickal energy. Remember magick is in you. Magickal energy is something that we all possess. Then how come you haven't been performing magick since you could walk? Well, there are some prerequisites. First off, you must try to solve your problem using mundane means. In other words, if you want to get your security deposit back from your former landlord, and he isn't coughing it up, you need to write him a letter. Send it registered. Tell him you will take him to court. After you have exhausted all the non-magickal means at your disposal, only then should you do magick.

Magickal Purpose

Before you perform an act of magick, you must be 100 percent clear on why you are doing it. What do you hope to achieve? Why are you using magick in this case? Have you really tried to attain what you want through nonmagickal means? Are you sure that your actions are for the good of all and not just for your own self-interest. Are you sure that your magickal action will not harm anyone? If you come up with clear and positive answers then you can proceed.

Book of Shadows

A **pentagram** is a five-pointed star. It is made of five straight lines and contains a pentagon inside it. When surrounded by a circle or a pentagon, a pentagram becomes a pentacle. A pentacle is a symbol of the Wiccan faith.

Webweaving

Remember the scene from Shakespeare's *Macbeth*, when the three witches are gathered around their cauldron? This is what they say: "Double, double, toil and trouble, Fire burn and cauldron bubble." He may not have described witches in a favorable light, but that Will sure had a way with a rhyme!

Magickal Concentration

In order to use your magickal energy, you must be able to concentrate. You have to focus intently and visualize the magick—actually see what you want to have happening happen in your mind. When performing an act of magick, you will build up a huge amount of energy with your powers of concentration. Then, when the energy is really intense, you send that energy out to work for you. Don't worry. You can do this. And we'll be telling you more about it, and giving more detailed directions, later.

A Good Finger

Once you have built up your magickal energy, direct the energy toward the place you want it to go. In ritual, Wiccans usually use an athame, a special ritual knife (more about these in Chapter 6, "What You Need to Do Magick"). If you don't have an athame, you can use your finger. Remember, the magick is in you, not in the tools that you use. Using an athame is helpful, though. The ritual objects help you focus your mind. The tools give the conscious mind something to settle on so that the subconscious can work. The symbolism of the athame speaks to your subconscious, as well. Because the subconscious works with images and symbols and not words, just seeing the athame can get your subconscious primed.

Banish!

Didn't your mother always tell you it was rude to point? Well, especially so if you are a witch! But seriously, if a person knows that you are a witch, and you point your finger at that person and say something in rhyme, you could really do some damage. Even if you are just kidding, you could hurt that person psychologically. So, don't joke around about your powers. You also want to avoid intimidating others. Even if you are mad. Even if the person deserves it. Remember the Wiccan Rede, and don't point!

Your Place in the Universe

As a witch, you need to know your place in the Universe. You are only a minute part of the whole Universe. But you are connected to every other part of the Universe. Everything affects you, and what you do affects everything. No matter how small an action you take, someone, or something, will feel it. If you sneeze in Cleveland, some one in South America will feel it. Each and every thing that you do has an effect, no matter how small.

If you do magick, it can truly change things. None of us can fully comprehend how much change we can create. As a witch, you need to respect this. Remember the image of the stone thrown into a pool of water? Think of the ripples moving away from the center as your energy moving away from you. As the ripples of energy spread out, they affect and change everything they touch. You can change things. You can have major impact on people and their lives. With this power, comes responsibility—to other people, to animals, to the Earth, and to yourself.

The Least You Need to Know

➤ Witches have ethics. If you are going to be a witch, you must understand the witches' moral code, the Wiccan Rede, and you must try to live by it.

➤ Living by the Wiccan Rede includes taking care of yourself. Take good care of your body; it is truly your temple.

➤ Magickal energy lives inside of you. In order to use that energy, you have to learn to concentrate. You also must be totally clear on the reasons why you are using magick. And they better be good reasons!

➤ All of your actions have effects. Especially magickal ones! You might not see the effects immediately or you might not see them at all, but know that everything that you do causes a reaction somewhere in the universe. For this reason, we all must use our powers wisely.

Chapter 6

What You Need to Do Magick

We've looked within at your reasons and motivations for becoming a witch. Now, it's time to look without at the material things that witches use. Some of the objects we discuss will be familiar to you and some of them will be less so.

If you love "stuff," especially magickal stuff, you'll have a great time reading this chapter. You'll also want to plan to do some shopping. But we'd like to suggest that you read through the chapter before you start making purchases and be prudent in your buying. You don't need to go broke to be a witch!

Secrets of the Witch's Magickal Cabinet

Do you want to see all the secret stuff that's in a witch's magickal cabinet? Of course you do! Well, we can't show you everything, but we will give you a good idea. You can practice your visualization skills (they're important!) to see what it all looks like. We're not going to find any eye of newt, toe of frog, or fillet of snake, but you will see cauldrons and candles and powders and herbs and ....

Choosing Your Magickal Toy Chest

When choosing the things that will be part of your magickal toy chest, remember that the journey, or in this case the looking and shopping and looking some more, is half the fun. You don't need to buy every item that we discuss in this chapter. Let things come to you slowly. Keep some adventure and mystery in the process. Trust your intuition. If you are absolutely and totally drawn to an object and you must have it, well then, that's the one you're supposed to have, so go ahead and get it. On the other hand, if you think you need to buy a cauldron, for instance, and you see a few, but you don't really like any of them, don't settle and buy one just because you feel you should own one. Look around you as you go about your daily activities. You never know what you might find on the street, and those things that you find by "accident" are there just for you.

What Are Magickal Tools?

Magickal tools are any objects used during ritual or while doing magick. They are used only for magick and ritual and for no other purpose. Magickal tools can be fancy items—objects that are inscribed with magickal symbols or have stones or crystals set in them to pull in and enhance magickal energy—but they don't have to be ornate. In ritual, each tool has symbolic significance. For instance, the athame, a ritual knife, symbolizes the male, and the chalice symbolizes the female. Any object that has been charged with energy to do magickal work becomes a magickal tool. Because tools are charged to help you make the magick happen, they are not to be used for any other purpose.

Book of Shadows

A **poppet** is a magickal doll. A witch concentrates on the magick that she wants to do while she makes a poppet. The word comes for the Middle English word "popet," which meant "child" or "doll." Today, in the United Kingdom, poppet means "a darling." And, yes, it is related to our word "puppet."

How Do You Use Magickal Tools?

Just as the case with mundane tools, each magickal tool has its own use. The way in which you utilize a given tool depends on the tool and on what kind of magick you want to do. Magickal tools aid you in doing magick in a variety of ways. They help you to focus your attention and energy. And, because the subconscious works with images and symbols, they tell your subconscious mind it's time to get to work, too. When using tools such as herbs, powders, *poppets*, oils, candles, and cords, you focus your energy and put it into the tool. You can then use the tool to hold the energy, or you can use the tool to send the energy out.

For example, if you made a poppet for a child who is ill, you'd put all kinds of healing energy into it. Then you'd give the poppet full of healing energy to the child to hold and look at, but not to play with. The poppet holds your healing energy and helps the child to get better. If you put your energy for trying to find a new job into a candle, when you light the candle your energy is sent out to the universe to work for you.

There are also ritual tools—such as the athame and the chalice—which are used in celebrating the Wiccan religion. Ritual tools are used during ritual to cast a circle, to represent the Lord and Lady, to welcome deity, to cleanse, to make sacred space, and to cut energy. Ritual tools are not used in the act of magick. They adorn altars, and are used in celebrating Sabbats and Esbats. Because they represent the Lord and the Lady, ritual tools take on great symbolic significance during ritual.

Storing Magickal Tools

The place where you keep your magickal tools is important. You can store them in a closet, a wardrobe, a desk with big drawers, or a cardboard box. You don't need to spend a lot of money on something fancy. But you do need to keep your tools in a safe space—a place where other people won't handle them or discover them by accident. You want to be absolutely sure that small children and animals won't get into your stuff. Some of the herbs you acquire may be toxic. This is also true of magickal oils. Some dogs (and children!) have even been known to eat candles! And you wouldn't want your Aunt Martha to accidentally stumble upon your supplies and have a heart attack at the sight of your figure candles.

Besides protecting people from your tools, you need to protect the tools from other people. Once you have cleansed and put away the objects you use in magick and ritual, only you and people who have your permission should touch them. You don't want just anyone handling your tools. The tools will absorb energy from whoever touches them. And you want to know what kind of energy your tools have. You also want to make sure that your magickal tools are not used for mundane purposes.

So Mote It Be

Here's one way to make sure that your husband, girlfriend, or roommate doesn't use your magickal broom to sweep out the garage. Instead of keeping the broom under lock and key, disguise it. If you buy a cinnamon broom, you can decorate it with dried flowers, herbs, ribbons, or stones. Tie a bow around it, and then hang it on the wall. People will think you have discovered a great piece of folk art! And who would take your wonderfully handcrafted object down from the wall and get it dirty? Only you need to know that this fancy broom is one of your magickal tools.

Before you put your tools away, make sure they have been cleaned. Cleaning will get rid of any dust, dirt, or fingerprints. Before using them again, make sure they have been cleansed. Cleansing will clear the energy from your tools. There are lots of ways to cleanse. You can use a smudge stick, set your tools out under a full Moon, or anoint them with holy water that has been blessed in the name of the Goddess. (See Chapter 9, "Preparing to Do Ritual.") Consecrate them, and let the Lord and Lady know that you will use them only for the good. Don't let anyone else touch them after they have been cleansed. If anyone else does touch your tools, you'll need to re-cleanse them to clean that person's energy from them.

Witches Love Toys!

We all like stuff, right? Especially cool stuff, and witches are no exception. If you have visited a metaphysical store, you've probably seen the wide variety of paraphernalia, magickal tools, and all-around great stuff you can buy. If you have not been by your local metaphysical store, you're in for a treat!

A Basic Magickal Inventory for Beginners

The most common mistake a new witch makes is to run out and buy a huge amount of stuff. You'll want to get some things, but be reasonable. Some tools you may not need for years, and others you may not need at all. And some products—such as essential oils—don't keep. You don't want to be stuck with a closet full of rancid oil! As you meet people and learn magick, your collection of supplies will grow and grow. You'll buy what you need as you need it. Don't worry about having the "right" stuff right away.

Banish!

Resist the temptation to whip out your credit card and buy one of every item that you see at the metaphysical store. The same goes for online shopping. We know, it looked like such a good deal. But if you don't really need it, it's not a good deal, no matter how low the price!

You can start out with simple things. If you don't have an athame to use in your ritual, you can use your two fingers held together, or use a wand. You can draw a pentagram on a piece of paper for your altar instead of buying one. You will need candles and bowls for salt and water. You should have a broom to sweep out the energy in your ritual space. If you don't have a censer for burning your incense, you can use a small cauldron. Or use a ceramic dish with some sand in the bottom. You don't have to go broke and buy a carload of things. Start small and build up slowly.

Here is a list of basic items. Remember, don't let this list trigger uncontrolled buying. Some of the things here just may come to you! And some of the items may be things that you already own. Remember, too, once you have cleaned, consecrated, and used a tool for magick, you can never use it for mundane purposes again.

➤ **Altar cloths** come in all shapes and sizes to fit your altar. You can make them as magickal as you like. They are both bought and made in different colors to represent the Sabbats or to decorate the altar. If you have a very special one and don't want to worry about wax or oils dripping on it, you can either put a small topper over it or set your candle or work on a place mat.

➤ **Amulets** are nature made-objects used in protection or with magickal intent.

➤ An **athame** is a double-edged knife, approximately 6 inches in length, which is used in ritual to represent the male phallus. Athames are usually dull because they are never used to cut anything but energy. Traditionally, athames had black handles. Many witches own athames made from a variety of materials, including crystal, pewter, steel, bone, and copper. Some are plain, and some are very fancy. Because an athame is a ritual tool that you will use frequently, be sure to pick one that is special to you.

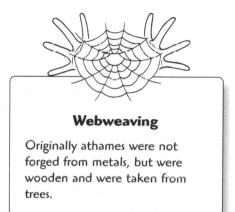

Webweaving

Originally athames were not forged from metals, but were wooden and were taken from trees.

➤ **Baskets** are used for many things. Plain baskets are good to keep your magickal notions, potions, and powders organized. That way you can find everything you need, when you need it.

➤ **Bath salts**, both plain and magickal, are used in the ritual bath taken before doing ritual or magick. They help calm and relax you and make your bath a special treat. **Bath oils** are used alone or in conjunction with bath salts and have the same purpose as bath salts.

➤ **Beads** are used in decorating talismans, medicine bags, feathers, and many other objects.

➤ A **bell** is used in ritual when calling in the quarters and deity (asking the four directions and the God and Goddess to join you). At the end of ritual, the bell is rung to let the elements return to their realms.

➤ A **bolline** traditionally is a white-handled knife with a curved blade. This is your working knife. It is used to cut a variety of things—string, clay, herbs, candles, or what have you—while doing magick or ritual.

➤ A **Book of Shadows** is your personal magickal book. In it you record your spells, magickal information, dreams, chants, or any other material that has to do with your workings in the craft.

➤ **Bowls** are important for your altar. You will need at least two small ones. In one keep salt, in the other water.

➤ A **broom**—a magick one—is used to sweep out negativity from an area where you are going to do ritual or magick.

Book of Shadows

Scrying is a kind of divination. To **scry** means to look at an object in such a way that the conscious mind becomes quiet. In that quiet, it becomes possible to see things that haven't happened yet. Water held in a cauldron is often used for scrying. So are crystal balls and candle flames.

➤ **Candles** of various shapes, sizes, and colors are used in magick and on the altar. **Candleholders** of various shapes and sizes are needed to hold the type of candle you are working with.

➤ The **cauldron** represents the womb of the Goddess and is used to cook, burn, *scry,* or hold things that are used in ritual or magick.

➤ **Chalices** represent the female. They are used to drink wine from during ritual. A chalice is also used in doing the great rite—a symbolic unification of the male and female in which an athame is lowered into a chalice. Many witches own more that one. You always seem to find a great one that you just must have. Keep an extra inexpensive one on hand in case someone in ritual doesn't have one.

➤ **Charcoal** is used to burn powdered incense or herbs.

➤ **Clay** can be used in poppet magick. It comes in all colors and can be formed into many shapes.

➤ A **censer** is a special container used to burn incense. Censers often have feet so that the heat they contain will not scorch the surface upon which they rest. Some censers have chains attached on top so that you can lift them easily and spread the smoke from the incense around the room.

➤ A **compass** is used to determine where your directions are. It's a hard call in the north wind when you are facing south!

➤ **Cords** of different thicknesses and colors are used to do binding magick.

➤ **Crystals** and **gems** are used in magick, healing, ritual, and talismans among other things. Your collection of these pretty objects will continue to grow and grow.

➤ **Crystal balls** come in various sizes and colors. They are used for pulling in energy and scrying.

➤ A **decanter** is used to hold wine during ritual.

➤ **Divination tools** such as tarot cards, runes, pendulums, and the I-Ching are used in looking into the future, to aid you in decision making, and in doing magick. It's best to learn more than one type of divination.

➤ **Feathers** are used in magick to represent the element of Air.

➤ **Felt** is used in poppet magick, in making pouches and dream pillows, or to wrap items to cover or protect them.

➤ **Fiber stuffing** is used for filling pillows or poppets.

➤ **Herbs** are used in healing and in magick, and can include dried plants or spices, dried corn, and even tobacco.

➤ **Holy water** is used to cleanse and consecrate ritual tools and magickal items. **Holy oil** is used to consecrate ritual tools and magickal items.

➤ **Incense** comes in stick, cone, and powder form. In ritual, it is used to represent the element of Air. It is also used in Air magick—magick in which you call upon the element of Air—and to cleanse ritual or magickal tool.

➤ **Lighters** are great to have on hand to light your candles.

➤ **Magickal inks**: homemade, dragon's blood, or dove's blood. No, these inks are not really made from the blood of a dove or dragon. They are specially made from herbs and resins to enhance your magickal spells. These inks come in a variety of colors, and some have essential oils added.

➤ A **magick mirror** is a mirror that has been cleansed, treated with herbs and magickally charged to help you see things as they really are or as they should be.

➤ **Magick pens** can be quills, hand-blown glass, or antique. These are very special pens that are used only for writing your magick spells or in your Book of Shadows.

➤ A **mortar and pestle** are used to grind your herbs to a fine powder.

➤ Tapes of special **music** are used in ritual and magick. The music helps you ground, center, and relax, or it helps you build a cone of power or celebrate in dance.

➤ **Needle and thread** are used to sew magickal bags and poppets and to attach talismans or amulets.

➤ **Oils** of various types—essential, fragrance, and herbal—are used to consecrate, anoint, or charge people and tools both in ritual and magick.

➤ **Parchment paper** is paper that is usually enhanced with cloth fiber. It is used when writing magickal spells or rituals.

➤ A **pentagram** can be used as jewelry. It is also placed on the altar for protection.

➤ A **pocketknife** is great for cutting or carving.

Webweaving

Four of the five points of the pentagram represent the four elements—Earth, Air, Water, and Fire. The fifth point stands for Spirit.

➤ **Pouches** are used for keeping crystals, tarot cards, herbs, jewelry, or anything else special.

➤ **Powders** come in various colors. Mixed with herbs, they are used in magick or to mark boundaries.

➤ **Scissors** are used for cutting cords for binding spells or cloth for poppets.

➤ A **scrying mirror** is usually made of black glass and is used in divination or magick.

➤ **Sea salt** is used on the altar to represent Earth. It is also used in making holy water and in magick.

➤ **Seeds** are used in magickal ritual. Various kinds are used to represent different intents in your magickal working.

➤ **Smudge sticks** are bound herbs and grasses used in cleansing an area or item.

➤ **Statues**, which represent the God or Goddess you are working with, are usually placed on the altar.

➤ **String** is used in beading, tying, or binding objects.

➤ **Talismans** are man-made objects or symbols that have magickal intent placed in them.

➤ A **wand**, which can be made from a variety of materials, is used to direct energy.

➤ **Wooden spoons** are used to stir notions—magickal mixtures, potions, and powders.

For More Advanced Magick

When you get more advanced, you'll want to start collecting all types of herbs, stones, and oils. Eventually, as your magickal work gets more in-depth, you'll start writing your own spells and making your own talismans and amulets. Some of the advanced equipment can get expensive. But as you become more adept, you grow stronger psychologically and more able to focus, and the tools become less important. Some witches can even do all their magick with just their fingers! As you gain experience, you'll also learn how to find the stuff that you need quickly when you need it. And you'll learn to make substitutions for the things that you don't have just the way an experienced chef can figure out how to make a dish without all the ingredients listed in the cookbook.

Where to Find Magickal Stuff

There are lots of places to find magickal tools—stores, catalogs, and online. You can also find great magickal stuff at flea markets and even in your own backyard! Or you can get creative, make like Martha Stewart, and build your own.

Metaphysical Stores, Catalogs, and the Internet

When shopping at a metaphysical store, compare prices. Remember, in a lot of respects, shopping for magickal tools is just like the kind of shopping you do almost every day. Make sure the store you choose to buy from is a place where you feel welcome. Does the sales staff say "Hello" and offer to help you? Or do all the store employees sit in a corner, smoke cigarettes, and ignore you?

Make sure the store you go to has a knowledgeable sales staff, too. You should be able to ask questions and get answers. If they can't answer your questions, they should offer to find out for you or refer you to someone who can help you. Ideally, you want to shop at a store that has a witch working in it.

Banish!

If you go into a store with a list of things that you plan to buy and the staff tries to convince you that the magick you plan to do can't possibly be done without several additional expensive items, stay clear of that store. They could be trying to sell you things that you don't need. Also beware of a store that tries to sell you everything once they find out that you are a new witch. The best kind of metaphysical store is one where they tell you to slow down. You don't need to buy everything. And you certainly don't need to buy it all at once.

Catalogs can be great. You can read them in bed, and they can be very educational. For new witches catalog shopping can have drawbacks, though. You have to know what it is you're buying because there usually isn't someone to answer your questions. Prices in catalogs can be good, but remember, you have to add the shipping and handling costs.

There are thousands of Internet sites that sell magickal stuff. Again, make sure you shop around. Most sites carry a lot of the same merchandise. One of the great things about shopping on the Net is that the stores are always open. The problems? Just like with catalogs, there isn't always someone to answer your questions, and you need to know what it is you want. Another disadvantage to shopping online versus in a store: Stores often carry one-of-a-kind items made by local artists and craftspeople. Frequently the artists who make magickal tools are Wiccan themselves so a lot of their positive energy goes into the product. These kind of goods generally aren't sold online because they can't be mass-produced.

Flea Markets and Found Objects

Flea markets are excellent places to find magickal stuff. That weird metal pot with three legs that the antique dealer didn't know what to do with? It's a cauldron. Take it home and, before you do anything else, cleanse it. (We'll tell you how to do that in Chapter 9.) Because you have no idea who owned it before you did, what they did with it, and what kind of energy that person had, you have to clean away any energy that is residing in your new treasure. If you don't, it could mess up your magick.

Found objects are things that you literally find. Sometimes these finds are gifts from Nature. You could be walking down the street and come upon a raven feather or a duck feather just lying there waiting for you. Or you could find a rock with a perfect hole through it. Or a branch fallen from a tree that would make the perfect wand. Found objects can also be someone else's trash. It's really true that one person's trash is another person's treasure! You could find a pair of deer antlers, a symbol that represents the Lord, that someone else is throwing out. Take them home, cleanse them, and put them to good use!

Magick Craft: Making Your Own

Usually, when people make their own magickal tools, they gather their materials from Nature. If you take something from Nature, you need to give something back. For instance, if you take a branch from a living tree to make a wand, you should then give the tree some compost, fertilizer, or a good long drink of water. Or you could leave out some breadcrumbs for the birds. If you do cut something from a living plant, make sure that you do it in the right season so as not to hurt the plant.

Banish!

Resist the temptation to cut a branch from a tree when the tree is in bloom. Yes, it looks pretty all covered with blossoms, but taking a branch at that time could hurt the tree. It's better to wait until fall or winter when the tree has gone dormant.

The beach and the banks of rivers are great places to look for materials for crafting your own magickal instruments. Rocks that have been smoothed in the water can make great runes—stones with letters of a magickal Germanic or Nordic alphabet drawn on them—and divination tools. Just add a little paint, and they are ready. Small shells and pebbles can be used in making rattles. There are all kinds of things that the Earth will give you. Scallop shells can make great bowls for your altar. If you find a piece of wood with a flat surface, you can inscribe it with a pentagram. If you keep your eyes open, you will find things. Just make sure that you don't pick every wildflower in the meadow. If you do, make sure that you sprinkle some of the seeds outside so a new generation of plants can grow up. And give something back to those plants-to-be as a way of saying thanks.

Oh, What to Wear? What to Wear?

Do clothes make the witch? Well, we wouldn't say that. But clothes certainly do have a function in witchcraft. And they do more than just keep you warm. Just like magickal tools, magickal clothing can help you to focus your mind. Clothes can also help create a mood, enhance energy, and they can be fun.

From High Priests and Priestesses to Covenmaids

The High Priest and Priestess of a coven often wear crowns. Sometimes the other members of the coven wear jeweled headbands and sometimes not. In some covens, the High Priest and Priestess change the color of their robes to symbolize the change in the seasons, while the rest of the coven wears the same color robes throughout the year. They also may have special robes for performing special ceremonies, such as initiations, Wiccannings (child blessing), or handfastings (Wiccan weddings).

A coven that wears robes usually decides what kind of robes all of the members are going to wear. The robes all may be identical, or they may just all be the same color. In some covens, the color of the cord around the robe denotes the magickal degree an individual has attained. As a solitary witch, you can decide what to wear and when to wear it.

Can Witches Do Magick in Street Clothes?

If you have to, you can do magick in street clothes. You can also do ritual in street clothes. As a beginner, however, it is really difficult to keep the mind sufficiently focused when surrounded by mundane things. When you gain more experience and become more adept, you will be able to maintain your concentration better and will have greater success performing magick in street clothes.

Secrets of the Witch's Wardrobe Closet

Remember how we said that you don't want to use your magickal broom for a mundane purpose like sweeping out the garage? Well, the same is true of your wardrobe. Okay, we know you probably wouldn't go clean the garage in a silk dress. The point is when you put on an article of clothing from your magickal closet, it tells your subconscious mind it has magick to do. So, keep your magickal clothes special. That way you'll be sure that your subconscious gets the right message at the right time.

A Cloak of Stars: Skyclad

As we first mentioned in Chapter 3, "Practicing Wicca and Witchcraft Today," some covens and solitaires prefer to practice magick and ritual skyclad, or naked. Many witches feel that clothing restricts their energy, so they feel better working without clothes. Working skyclad can also help you to accept your body as natural. Once you get used to it, just seeing your body and feeling the air on your skin can be very liberating. Some covens go skyclad for the same reason that Catholic school kids wear uniforms—it emphasizes that everyone in the circle is equal.

A Renaissance depiction of four skyclad witches by the German master Albrecht Dürer, 1497.

So Mote It Be

Before you attend a coven meeting, find out if they practice skyclad or robed. You wouldn't want to show up in your magickal birthday suit only to find the whole group robed and hooded. If they do practice skyclad, bring along a robe just in case. You may want something that you can slip into and out of quickly. And you may have to walk some distance from where you leave your street clothes to the spot where the ritual will be held. If the coven practices robed, ask what you should wear. Chances are you can pull out that little black robe that you've been saving for just such an occasion.

Robes, Dresses, Hoods, and Shoes

Many solitary witches like to wear purple because it is a magickal color. During the summer, you might wear green to symbolize the Goddess and Earth all in leaf. You can pick a color to correspond with the type of magick or ritual you are going to do. Or you can pick a color just because it looks good on you. As a solitaire, you can wear whatever you want—a dress or slacks, robes and a hood, or nothing at all. Whatever you wear, remember to keep that outfit (or outfits) for magick and ritual only. You don't want to use any of your magickal wardrobe for regular day-to-day wear. Keep your magickal clothes magickal by keeping them special.

When choosing an outfit, keep in mind that you will be working around candles and possibly other open flames. Your clothing should be made of something with cotton in it. Cotton and cotton blends are not nearly as flammable as synthetics. What's worse, many synthetics melt as they burn and …. Well, ouch! Also, be careful of wide sleeves that will dangle down into the flames.

If you decide to wear robes, you can dress them up any way you want. Sew on magickal symbols or embroider them if you know how. You can even make your own robes. Some witches like to wear robes with hoods. The hood is really useful when you are working in a group because, if you're having trouble concentrating, you just have to pull your hood up. Like a horse with blinders on, you'll be able to see only the thing you need to focus on and won't be distracted by the people on either side of you. The cord that you wear as a belt around your robe can be the same color as your robe or a contrasting one. The cord at your waist can also hold your athame, pouches, charms, or medicine bags.

Some people love capes. They're so stylish and dramatic. Capes are usually worn outdoors over robes in cool weather. If you do wear a cape, you may start out with it on, but as ritual or magick work proceeds, you may need to take it off. Witches raise a lot of energy when they are working, and all that energy means heat.

Many witches do not wear underwear under their robes. (Say that three times fast!) Witches also typically do not wear shoes when doing magick or ritual. Being barefoot gives you greater access to the Earth's energy and can help you feel more grounded.

The Ultimate Accessory: Jewelry

Witches love magickal jewelry and, like your magickal clothes, you want to keep your magickal jewelry for magickal occasions. You should not wear magickal jewelry for your regular day-to-day activities. That jewelry should be worn only during ritual or when doing magick.

Many solitaires wear crowns. In a coven, usually only the High Priest and Priestess wear crowns. As a solitaire, you are a Priestess or Priest so there is nothing wrong with wearing a crown. Witches often wear magickal rings and pendants or other special jewelry to hold back the hair so it doesn't get near flames. Medicine bags or pouches worn around the neck or hanging from a belt are also popular.

The metals you choose can be important. Gold jewelry represents the Lord, while silver stands for the Lady. Some witches wear both kinds for a balance between the Lord and Lady. Others choose to wear only gold or only silver. The designs you choose in jewelry also have significance. Images of the Moon are images of the Goddess. The Sun represents the God.

Banish!

Resist the temptation to touch someone else's magickal jewelry. Just like you don't want people to touch your magickal tools, another witch doesn't want you to touch her beautiful necklace. Because magickal items, including jewelry, are charged with energy, they are very compelling. They look like something you want to touch! But touch someone else's things only if that person has given you permission to do so. By the same token, don't let anyone touch your jewelry. If they do, cleanse your things so that you don't have that person's energy hanging around you.

Adorning with Body Art

Many witches who work skyclad will paint magickal symbols on their bodies with washable body paint. Sometimes the designs, which can be quite elaborate, have to do with the special magick that the witch is doing. Other witches get tattoos that tell the world what type of magick they are into or just that they practice magick to begin with. Tattoos can also represent totem animals, fantasy creatures, or Nature itself.

The Least You Need to Know

➤ The most common mistake a new witch makes is to buy too much stuff. Acquire your tools slowly. Enjoy the process and see how many of your magickal things come to you.

➤ Don't let anyone sell you things that you don't need. Also, don't convince yourself to buy something that you don't really like just because you think you need it.

➤ Make sure to keep your magickal tools in a safe place away from children and people who might try to use them for mundane purposes or handle them and leave their energy behind.

➤ Keep your magickal clothes and jewelry special. Don't wear them for everyday.

Chapter 7

Observing Ritual the Wiccan Way

Most religions use ritual in some way. Wicca is no exception. In Wicca, like in many other faiths, you do ritual to honor deity. But in Wicca you can do magick as part of your ritual, and you can even write your own ritual.

As you practice ritual and become more familiar with the steps involved, your sense of spirituality will grow and expand, and you will come to feel more and more connected to the All. You will discover that as you become more spiritual, your life will start to change. You will learn to appreciate the world around you and all the wonderful gifts that the Lord and Lady have given us.

What Is a Wiccan Ritual?

A Wiccan ritual is a means of creating consecrated ground or sacred space in order to pay homage to deity. Ritual is also used to do magick and to work with the energy of the God and Goddess. Ritual consists of a set of actions that are performed in a particular order. While there is a basic structure to rituals, they can be changed and varied to some extent.

Ritual is also a time when Wiccans get together with other people whom they trust. Within the ritual circle, individuals in the group can share their thoughts and feelings. Anything said within the circle must be kept confidential.

Why Perform a Magick Ritual?

People perform ritual for the same reasons that they go to church. Ritual is special, and it gives you a taste of the sacred. Ritual puts you in a state of mind in which you can relate on a personal level to deity. It creates the necessary conditions for you to perform magick. It also allows you to connect with others in a spiritual way. Performing ritual creates order and harmony in your life. It is a way to nurture and heal yourself. It also helps you to live by a moral standard. Doing ritual will enable your energy and allow you to pull upon the energy of the God and the Goddess. Ritual will help you focus and keep things in perspective. While doing ritual, you might realize just how small you and your problems really are.

Inside the ritual space, you'll feel safe. It's a great place to meditate. If you do ritual alone, it also gives you a great opportunity to sit back, look at your life, and get some clarity. In such a situation, there's no hiding between you and deity. At times like that, the God and Goddess can really get in there and help you figure out what you need to do.

Webweaving

Anthropologists believe that all societies throughout history have performed ritual. In addition, they believe that rituals have been and are still being performed all over the world. Rituals are and have been used for religious purposes, to do magick, or both.

So Mote It Be

It's a good idea to do a tiny ritual every day to honor the Lord and Lady. After your morning shower, light a candle and sit in front of it. Just a 10-minute meditation every day will remind you that deity is in your life. And you can remind deity that you are here, too! Then you can go about your business. This little dose of daily ritual will help put order and purpose back into your life, and you'll be amazed at how much it will help you deal with all the stresses of your day.

When to Do Ritual

Wiccans perform ritual in circle in honor of the holidays—the Esbats, which are celebrated once a month, and the Sabbats, which occur about every six weeks (read more about Esbats and Sabbats later in this chapter, and more extensively in Chapters 13, "Esbats: Moon Magick," and 14, "Observing the Sabbats"). Witches also get together in circle for ritual any time they want to formally honor the Lord and the Lady, or when the group wants to do magick. But ritual does not have to be confined to special occasions. You can do ritual when you have a problem you need to work out, when you're feeling empty, or when you need to heal. You can do ritual when you feel you need the energy of Lord and Lady to help you or if you are planning to do some major magickal working. You can use ritual when you need to think about your life in a safe space. This can help you deal with any issues that may come up and help to make your life complete.

When Not to Do Ritual

Avoid participating in ritual when you are sick. If you are working with other people, you will be in close quarters and will just give them the bug that you are harboring. Doing ritual when you aren't feeling well, even when alone, isn't a good idea. We all tend to be cranky and distracted when we are sick. You want to be able to keep the full force of your attention on ritual you are involved with. In addition, ritual demands a lot of your energy. You want to be able to give 100 percent. If you can't, then it's better to wait until you're feeling better.

It's also not a good idea to do ritual when you are very tired or in a hurry. Ritual needs your undivided attention. It's hard to stay focused when you are nodding off or worrying about running out to pick up the kids after soccer practice.

Another time to avoid doing ritual is when you are angry. Anger can send your energies off in undesirable directions or just take your focus away from the work at hand. It also puts a strain on the other members of the circle. They won't be able to relax when there are negative energies floating about. You also want to make sure that you are comfortable with all the people in the ritual circle. If you are in the middle of a feud with one of them, don't do ritual with that person. Or if you feel that you don't share the same beliefs with other people in the circle, don't participate. Remember, you want to be in the ritual circle "in perfect love and perfect trust."

Before you start ritual, make sure that you feel okay, that you're well rested, and that you don't have issues with any of the people with whom you are going to be doing ritual. This will help to keep your focus where it should be and help to ensure that everyone has a good ritual experience.

All Kinds of Wiccan Ceremonies, Rites, and Rituals

Because Wicca is a religion, there are many different Wiccan rituals and ceremonies to mark the many sacred passages in our lives. There are rituals for death, for entering the faith, for joining people together in love, for child blessing, for initiation, for magick, for healing, and for celebrating Esbats and Sabbats. You can do ritual alone or with a group. The choice is yours.

Performing Ritual as a Group

In a coven, the High Priest and Priestess lead ritual. Often coven members are assigned jobs—calling in *the quarters,* lighting the candles, or ringing the bell. If you get together with a group of solitaires to perform ritual, usually someone will take on the role of the High Priest and some will act as High Priestess. You might be assigned to call in the quarters or to bring cake, wine, candles, or incense. Or your job might be to help set up or clean up.

Covens meet to perform ritual together regularly—for the 13 Esbats and the 8 Sabbats. Some may work together at other times as well. Groups of solitaires can work together if they have something that they all want to plan to do together. Some solitaires meet for the holiday rituals as well. Or they can do ritual together for a common purpose—a healing, some magick that needs to be done, or to celebrate a special occasion such as a Wiccaning or handfasting. But most of the time they work alone, hence the name solitaire.

Book of Shadows

The quarters is another way of saying the four directions—North, East, South, and West—and the elemental powers— Earth, Air, Fire, and Water—with which they are associated.

Banish!

Avoid becoming overly casual in your ritual. Yes, as a solitaire, you can do what you want and you can wear what you want, but ritual is still ritual. A little formality and organization show your respect for the God and Goddess. It'll also help you maintain respect for yourself.

Ritual Solitaire Style

As a solitaire, you design your own ritual for specific purposes and can emphasize elements of the ceremony that appeal to you. And you can wear whatever you want—robes, a fancy outfit, or you can go skyclad. Working on your own, your ritual will not be as elaborate as one performed in a group. Because you are on your own and must do everything yourself, you need to be organized. When you are planning your ritual, make a checklist so you can be sure that you have everything you will need. Go over the list before you start your ritual and gather all your tools together. You don't want to keep cutting a hole in your magick circle to go find things. (Read more about entering and leaving a magick circle in Chapter 11, "Cast a Magick Circle.")

Moon Magick: Esbats

There are 13 Esbats, or Wiccan Moon rituals, every year. At this time, witches honor the Goddess in ritual. You can celebrate an Esbat at almost any time of the month. You can honor the Goddess when the Moon is full, and her energies are at their peak. If you want to do magick and draw on her strength, the full Moon is a great time to get her help in achieving your heart's desire. Or you can celebrate an Esbat on the waxing Moon, a good time to bring positive things toward you; or on the waning Moon, a time to get rid of the negative. The astrological sign the Moon is in also affects the character of an Esbat, but we'll talk more about that in Chapter 13.

Sacred Times: The Witches' Sabbats

There are eight Sabbats a year. On the Sabbats, witches work with the God in ritual. Sabbats mark certain natural events—the solstices and equinoxes, and the midpoints between these occurrences. Some Sabbats are celebrated in the daytime and others are observed at night.

Making Magick Takes Preparation, Body, Mind, and Spirit

Before you do magick in ritual you have to be prepared. You have to know the intent of your magick, and you have to be sure that you will be working at a good time. Then you have to get all your tools together. Go over your checklist to be sure that nothing is missing and check to make sure your robe or outfit is clean. Prepare the room that you are going to use by moving the furniture, if necessary. Unplug the phone so that no one will interrupt you, and take off your watch so it and thoughts of your busy day don't distract you.

Here are some additional steps you may want to take to prepare yourself for ritual:

➤ Fast during the day. Many people don't eat all day before ritual, but drink juice to keep their blood sugar up. If, however, you are on a special diet because of a health condition, please stay on that prescribed program.

➤ Take a ritual bath. Use special soaps and oils. Allow the water to help you feel grounded.

➤ Meditate and visualize the magick you are going to be doing.

After you have bathed, dress yourself in your ritual outfit and magick jewelry. Ground yourself by feeling your connection with the Earth and cleanse the area you'll be working in. Now you're ready to start your ritual.

All the Parts of a Wiccan Ritual

There are many elements that are common to all Wiccan rituals. We'll list them in order here and tell you about each in greater detail in coming chapters.

To perform ritual, you ...

➤ Decide to do it.

➤ Cast a magick circle.

➤ Focus your mind.

Book of Shadows

Cakes in the context of ritual doesn't necessarily mean big gooey chocolate confections. You, or the coven you visit, could use cookies or bread. The cakes are a ceremonial snack that the group shares and for which they give thanks to the Goddess.

➤ Call in the quarters.

➤ Call in deity.

➤ State your reason for doing ritual.

➤ Work magick, if that is what you need to do.

➤ Perform the great rite. In a solitary ritual, you don't need to do this. The High Priest and High Priestess of a coven perform this aspect of ritual, which represents the union of the male and the female aspects of the All.

➤ Partake of *cakes* and wine.

➤ Relax and communicate with others in the circle.

➤ Refocus.

➤ Say farewell to the quarters and deity.

➤ Take down the circle.

How to Design a Wiccan Ritual

As you learn more about Wicca, you'll want to start to design your own rituals. You'll become familiar with the structure of ritual and soon all the elements will fall into place naturally. Before you start writing, you may want to consider a few other topics that could have a bearing on what you do and how you act during ritual.

A Guide to Wiccan Ritual Etiquette

If you keep in mind that a Wiccan ritual is a serious religious rite, you shouldn't have too much trouble observing proper etiquette. When you are doing ritual with other people, make sure that you aren't late. If you've been told they plan to start at 7:30, arrive at 7:00 so you have time to change into your ritual outfit and to chat. Make sure that you have brought all the things that you said you'd bring. If you were sup-posed to bring the candles and you leave them on your kitchen table, you will have ruined ritual for everyone. If you have allergies or can't drink wine, bring your own beverage and snack so you can partake at the proper moment. As a guest, always ask if there is something that you can bring—just the way you would if you were going to someone's home.

Before ritual starts, make sure that you have removed your watch and pager. Double-check your bag to make sure that your watch, pager, and cell phone won't make any noise. Nothing can ruin concentration during ritual like a ringing phone.

Be polite and respectful to other people in the circle. If someone makes a mistake, try not to giggle. Stay focused on ritual and don't joke or goof around. If you know that someone you absolutely can't get along with will be in the circle, don't go. Wait until the two of you have patched things up instead of spoiling ritual for everyone with your negative energies. If you suddenly need to leave the circle because you are feeling ill or are very uncomfortable, ask the High Priest and Priestess to cut a door in the circle for you so you can leave. If they won't, thank the God and Goddess, cut the door yourself, and leave.

Dressing Up: Choosing the Right Clothes and Jewelry

As a solitaire, you can do whatever your little heart desires. You can wear robes or a fancy outfit. You can swathe yourself in silk or wear nothing at all. Make sure that whatever you do wear is special. If you're going to be doing ritual with a coven, find out what the members are going to be wearing before you leave the house. They may practice skyclad, or they may wear a special color of robe. Even if they do wear a special color, as a guest you can usually wear black. Bare feet are typical during ritual so that you can feel your connection with the Earth. If ritual is going to be outside, you can wear shoes if you want.

Your jewelry should also be special. Wear it only for ritual. And make sure that your magick jewelry does not include a watch, which can be distracting.

Inviting Friends and Family to Share

Covens usually work in a closed circle. In other words, only members of the coven can attend their rituals. Some covens occasionally hold open rituals in which others can participate. A ceremony such as a handfasting or Wiccaning might be conducted in an open circle so that the friends and family of the people involved can be there.

As a solitaire, you can invite a special friend or family member to join you in your ritual circle. You might want to do that if you are going to be doing healing work. Before you do invite your special person, make sure that he or she is of like mind and really understands what Wicca is all

Banish!

Resist the temptation to invite one of your friends to join you in ritual just to show off your new knowledge. There's nothing wrong with being proud of your accomplishments, but showing off won't do you or your friendship any good. And, in a ritual context, such an action would be disrespectful to the God and Goddess.

about. If you are going to do magick within your ritual, chances are your friends and family will not understand. In such a case, it is probably better not to invite anyone to join you.

Animals Join In

When you do ritual, animals can move in and out of the circle as they please. Because animals have pure energy and they enter the circle in perfect love and perfect trust, they can join you at any time in any ritual. If you have a familiar—animals or even plants with which you can psychically communicate—it will want to participate. One cat familiar we know won't leave the circle till someone cuts a door for him! (For more about familiars, see Chapter 15, "Summon, Stir, or Call.")

If, however, your animal is rowdy and badly behaved, you probably would do better to exclude him or her. You need to be sure that the animal in question will not knock over candles, jump on the altar, or bother other people in the circle. You don't want the dog licking everyone or barking while you are trying to meditate. Before you start ritual with a group, do make sure that all the people in the circle are comfortable with having the animal join in—you wouldn't want to set off someone's allergies or dog phobia.

Recording Your Wiccan Ritual

You want to keep records of your rituals. Writing down what you have done and when you did it will allow you to keep track of how often you're really doing ritual. You'll also have an accurate look at what you have been doing ritual for. If you're not working magick in a given ritual, it is not so important, but if you are, you need a record. Your magickal records will allow you to keep track of the outcome of your work. You'll also be able to see your progress as a witch. Most witches use a simple form (see Appendix B, "Magickal Record") and fill it out before they have taken down their circle.

Crafting Your Witch's Book of Shadows

Witches keep their magickal records in Books of Shadows, and you will need your own Book of Shadows, too. As you learn, you'll add to it frequently, and your book will grow and grow. If you join a coven, you may be given a copy of the coven's Book of Shadows. But even so, you will want to keep records of your own.

Grimoires and Books of Shadows

Some witches use their *Book of Shadows* (BOS) for everything. They keep their spells and personal information all in one book. Others have two separate books—a Book of Shadows and a *grimoire*. A grimoire is like a recipe book. It contains your spells and the magickal information that you need to do your working. A separate Book of Shadows can be much more personal. In it you can record your dreams and their meanings, your magical workings, and records of your rituals. You might make note of a premonition that you had or write about your feelings after ritual.

Denise likes to keep two books. That way she can take her grimoire with her when she goes out to teach a class or do ritual with others. Her Book of Shadows remains at home and stays private so no one sees it but her.

Why Start Your Own BOS?

It's a good idea to keep records. This way you can see your progress as a witch and watch how you get stronger and stronger in your magickal workings. You also need a place to record your spells and rituals. If you write them down, you can start to see what works best for you in terms of timing and the type of spell you do. And there are so many different spells and uses for those spells that you could never keep them all in your head.

Book of Shadows

A **Book of Shadows** (BOS) is a witch's personal book of magick. Think of your Book of Shadows as your magickal diary. A **grimoire** is like a Book of Shadows, but not as personal. It holds information about ritual, spells, potions, and how to prepare magickal tools. It can also contain lists of angels, spirits, and the magickal properties of objects found in Nature.

Witches' Knowledge: What to Put in Your BOS

If you are keeping a Book of Shadows and a grimoire, put all your spells and rituals in the grimoire. This way if you want to share a spell with a witch friend, you don't have to worry about her reading your scribblings about the erotic dream you had the other night and the meaning of that dream. Keep your personal information—your thoughts, plans, ideas, feelings, and dreams—in your Book of Shadows. You will also include information such as the kind detailed on the Magickal Record sheet in Appendix B of this book. If you have just one book, then everything goes into it. You'll need a lot of space, so buy a big book!

How to Choose Your BOS and Organize It

You'll need to have lots of room in your Book of Shadows. If you are keeping two books (and we suggest it), you'll want a loose-leaf notebook for your grimoire so you can remove and add pages, and a nice hardbound book for your Book of Shadows. Or you can write your Book of Shadows on your computer as long as you know that it's secure there.

The old thought was that if you didn't hand-write your Book of Shadows and grimoire yourself you weren't really putting your energy into it. Now witches see the issue somewhat differently. What does a computer do but translate the actual energy you use in typing into words on the screen? There are many advantages to using a computer to write your book. You can choose a font that looks old-fashioned, fancy, or gothic. You don't have to worry about making mistakes or ruining sheets of the expensive paper you bought. You can add clip art, drawings, or photographs. If you like borders around your text, you can have those too. You can do whatever you want to make your book magickal and special to you.

Some witches like to download information from the Internet. They print it out and add it to their books. Some people don't ever print out their books but keep them in electronic format. Some covens have such large Books of Shadows that they keep them on CD-ROMs and print out each page as they need it. Of course, you can write by hand if you want to. Maybe you know calligraphy and your Book of Shadows will be a true work of art.

Whatever you decide—to keep one book or two, to write by hand or by machine— you want to keep your information organized. Put dividers in your book and arrange everything alphabetically. It's no use having the information if you can't find it. Keep all your ritual notes in one section and facts about the Gods and Goddesses from the various pantheons you have been researching in another section.

Where to Keep Your BOS and Who Should See It

Because your Book of Shadows contains information about your magickal workings, it is a special and sacred object. Give it a place of honor, the way you would for a family Bible. Most people keep their Book of Shadows hidden in the cabinet with their magickal tools. You want to be sure that your book is safe, that no one will make fun of it, play with it, deface it, or destroy it. Your book is private, and only you or another witch whom you have authorized should see it. You want to be sure that whoever does see your book won't disclose its contents to anyone or do anything to harm the book or you.

So Mote It Be

When you do ritual don't bring your whole Book of Shadows into your circle. Your book is going to get heavy and cumbersome. Just remove the sheets that you need for ritual and put them in plastic sleeves. This way your nice paper and special magickal graphics won't get creased or damaged while you're working. If you accidentally spill something, the sleeves will keep your spells dry, and if you drip hot candle wax on your pages, you can just peel it off the plastic.

What Happens to Your BOS When You Die?

If you are a member of a coven and you die, usually your High Priest and High Priestess get to decide what will happen to your Book of Shadows. It may become part of the coven's Book of Shadows, or they may decide to give it to another coven member. In some covens, each member has a copy of the coven's Book of Shadows and that, because it is coven property, goes back to the High Priest and Priestess.

Often a witch will leave her Book of Shadows to another witch with whom she is close. Some people have their books burned. Others have their books buried with them. Sometimes witches who teach leave their books to their first student or to a student of whom they were particularly fond.

The Least You Need to Know

➤ Ritual is a time to get in touch with the God and Goddess. You can use ritual to heal, to do magick, or to celebrate a Sabbat or Esbat.

➤ To do ritual, you must prepare and organize yourself and your equipment.

➤ It's important to record your rituals so that you know what you have done and so you can keep track of the efficacy of your magick.

➤ Use a Book of Shadows or a grimoire, or both, to record your magickal business. Put your spells, chants, and rituals in your grimoire. Write down your personal musings, the results of your magickal acts, and whatever else you want to include in your Book of Shadows, which is for your eyes only.

Part 3

So, You Want to Do Magick?

Magick is not all hocus-pocus. We're talking about creating real change. And that takes dedication, preparation, concentration, and focus. In this part, we'll show you how you can dedicate yourself to the craft and prepare to do ritual. We'll also discuss places to do magick, magick circles, pentacles, and pentagrams.

Chapter 8

Dedicate Yourself to the Craft

If you're serious about your interest in Wicca and witchcraft, dedication is your next step. Dedication is an exciting and serious commitment. It means that you have chosen to walk the Wiccan path. Your dedication is a personal issue. It is not something that you do because your friends are doing it. When you dedicate, you make a personal commitment to the Lord and Lady.

You can dedicate as a solitaire or as part of a coven. If you dedicate within a coven, that action does not necessarily make you a member of the coven. In many covens, you do not become a member until you have passed your First Degree Initiation. Whether you dedicate on your own or in a coven, dedication is a serious step. You'll want to meditate on this commitment and spend some real time thinking about it before you set off on the Wiccan path.

First, Take Your Magickal Name

As you've probably noticed, a name says a lot about a person. In the past, names such as Miller, Cooper, or Smith indicated the professions of the people attached to them. These days, a name doesn't tell you that, but it can still divulge a lot about someone.

From just a name you can probably discern a person's gender, ethnic background, and sometimes even their religion. A name can give you a good impression or a bad one. It can remind you of someone you like or admire who shares that name—an old friend, an uncle, or a movie star—or someone you loathe.

Webweaving

A magickal name can be one word or two or more words or names that you put together. Examples of this kind of name include those of two popular authors—Starhawk and Silver RavenWolf. Creating a name in this way actually has an ancient tradition. The modern English name "Roger" comes from the Anglo-Saxon Hrothgar, which literally are the words "fame" and "spear" combined.

When you become dedicated to the craft, you get to choose your magickal name, the name other witches and members of the Pagan community will call you. Your magickal name is also the name by which the Goddess will know you.

The Significance of a Magickal Name

First of all, your magickal name is important because that is what all the people you meet in the Pagan community will call you. So, you want it to be a name that you like now and that you will continue to like in the future. You will also use your magickal name when you talk to the God and Goddess.

In addition, your name should have some real significance to you. You want it to reflect your goals, dreams, ideals, and aspirations. Your magickal name should give others an idea of who you are and what you stand for. It can also serve to remind you of these things and serve as an inspiration to you on your path.

Why Take a Magickal Name, and When?

Have you ever felt limited by your name? Some people do. Janes can really feel plain or ordinary. And Michaels can feel like a dime-a-dozen because there are so very many of them. When you become a witch you open up a whole new universe of possibilities. You don't want your preconceived notions of who you are to hold you back from your limitless potential.

In addition, having a magickal name that you use only in the pagan community can help that community be special to you. It can also protect your privacy. For some people, keeping their status as a witch secret is important. Others are more public and don't care who knows about their beliefs and practices. But it is nice to know that you have the choice.

Usually you take your magickal name upon dedication. This is a signal that you are committing to the Wiccan path.

Choosing Your Magickal Name

You can choose a name because you like it or because it gives you a special feeling. You might pick the name of a God or Goddess whom you are particularly drawn to. Or you might like the name of a famous Druid, such as Merlin. Your name could come to you in a dream, or it can be one that you have always dreamed of using!

One witch that we know took the name Summoner because she summons things. Denise lived in the Middle East for a number of years, and because she was very moved by the life stories of the women she met there, she chose the name Shaharazad. You may remember Shaharazad (or Sheherazade) from the *Tales of the Arabian Nights*. In order to save her own life, Shaharazad told her new husband, who was in the habit of killing his brides, a story every night. Her husband was so mesmerized by her tales and her creativity that he kept putting off the hour of her death. By the time she told him a thousand and one stories, he had fallen in love with her and no longer wanted to kill her. Denise also particularly likes this heroine because her story emphasizes a woman's creativity and intelligence, her ability to take care of herself, and her ability to survive.

If you aren't drawn to a special character, you can choose a name from something in Nature for which you have a particular affinity—Tree, Forest, or Willow, are examples of such names.

Banish!

Resist the temptation to grab at the first "witchy" sounding name that pops into your head. Yes, Samantha, Sabrina, and Tituba are cool names. And one of these names might be right for you. But don't just settle for the first name you think of. Maybe there is another, more significant name just waiting for you to find it.

What Your Magickal Name Says About You

Some magickal names conjure up very strong images—Raven, Bear Heart, Grendel, Hawk. Others are softer and more gentle—Moon Feather, Ash, Gandalf, Snow Blossom. You want to consider what your name is going to say about you. You want your name to go with you—your body, your mind, and your spirit. This is not to say that if you are a small woman you can't take a strong-sounding name. And if you are a big muscle-bound guy you don't have to stick with rough, tough names like Thor.

Coming to Your Magickal Name: A Self-Exploration

You don't have any ideas for a magickal name? Answering these questions will help you in thinking about it. Get out your notebook and spend some time writing about each question. You may want to meditate on each answer. Or think about it just before you go to bed, and you might find an answer in your dreams. You can work on one question at a time. Or scribble out answers for all of them, come back, and add more thoughts as they occur to you. Remember there are no wrong answers!

1. Do you have an affinity for a particular God or Goddess whom you have read about?

2. Do you have a favorite myth or legend? What is it? Who are the characters? With which one do you identify most strongly?

3. Is there a species of animal that is special to you? What qualities does that animal have?

4. Are you particularly drawn to one of the four elements—Earth, Air, Water, or Fire? What about other natural substances such as different types of wood or metals?

5. What is your favorite plant? Favorite flower? Favorite tree?

We hope that these questions have stirred up some ideas. Your magickal name probably won't jump out and grab you, but if you're patient we believe it will come to you.

So Mote It Be

Here's a fun way to look at some potential magickal names. Write out each name that you are considering on a slip of paper. Keep your pen and notebook handy, and put the slips into a hat or a paper bag. Give the bag a good shake. Imagine that the name that you draw will be yours forever. Draw out one slip. Then, without thinking too much about it, write down whatever feelings come up for you, even if they sound silly. Put the name back into the hat and draw again. If you keep getting the same name, consider that to be significant. Does seeing the name over and over annoy you? Or do you find some comfort in the repetition?

The Name of Rebirth

In a lot of ways, when you dedicate and take your magickal name, you are reborn. A whole new you is emerging and your magickal personality is born. In many faiths, now and throughout history, people take a new name to show that they have undergone this transformation. Their new name also indicates that they have made a commitment to their beliefs and to the laws that embody those beliefs.

Numerology: Your Destiny and Life Path Numbers

Many people use *numerology* to help select their magickal names. Numerology? Isn't that about numbers? Well, it is, but numerology is not just math. It's also concerned with letters, names, addresses, and other significant personal information.

The first step in using numerology to help select your magickal name is to determine your Destiny Number. Your Destiny Number is derived from your birth name, the name that is on your birth certificate. Yup, that means you have to include that hideous middle name that no one knows about except members of your immediate family. Among other things, your Destiny Number reveals your life purpose, your spiritual mission, and the target that you are aiming for in life.

To calculate your Destiny Number, write down your full birth name and assign each letter a number based on the following chart. Add up the numbers for each name. Reduce the numbers for each name. Then add all the reduced numbers together, and reduce the final number to a single digit number. Whew!

Book of Shadows

Numerology is the metaphysical science of numbers. Numerologists study the significance of names and numbers and relate them to each other to learn about the human condition. Numerology can help you discover who you are, where you're going, and who you will become.

Numbers and Letters

1	2	3	4	5	6	7	8	9
A	B	C	D	E	F	G	H	I
J	K	L	M	N	O	P	Q	R
S	T	U	V	W	X	Y	Z	

We'll calculate Katherine Anne Gleason's Destiny Number so you can get the hang of it.

KATHERINE	ANNE	GLEASON
2 1 2 8 5 9 9 5 5	1 5 5 5	7 3 5 1 1 6 5

First, add all the digits of the first name together:

2 + 1 + 2 + 8 + 5 + 9 + 9 + 5 + 5 = 46

Reduce 46 (4 + 6) = 10 (1 + 0) = 1

Then add the numbers of the second name:

1 + 5 + 5 + 5 = 16

Reduce 16 (1 + 6) = 7

Next add the numbers of the last name:

7 + 3 + 5 + 1 + 1 + 6 + 5 = 28

Reduce 28 (2 + 8) = 10 (1 + 0) = 1

Now add up the three reduced numbers:

1 + 7 + 1 = 9

Katherine's Destiny Number is 9.

Okay, but what do you do with this number? We're getting there. Let's say Katherine was thinking of taking the name Elphaba as her magickal name. Let's look at that name numerologically.

E L P H A B A

5 3 7 8 1 2 1

5 + 3 + 7 + 8 + 1 + 2 + 1 = 27 (2 + 7) = 9!

The name Elphaba has the same Destiny Number as Katherine's birth name. This indicates that Elphaba would be a good choice for Katherine. (Although Katherine likes this name a lot, she probably would not use it because she is very close to a being who already bears that name—her cat! But we think it is cool that they have the same Destiny Number, don't you?) If the magickal name you have selected produces a number other than your Destiny Number, you can change the spelling of the name or alter the name by adding or taking away a letter. Or you can use your Life Path Number instead.

Your Life Path Number describes the path that you will take in life and the talents and abilities that will aid you on the way. You find your Life Path Number by adding together the digits that represent the month, day, and year you were born. Then you reduce that number to a single number by adding the digits together. Here's an example of how to do that.

Webweaving

Pythagoras, the sixth-century B.C.E. mathematician who came up with that formula about the hypotenuse of a right triangle, is considered to be one of the fathers of numerology. He believed that the numbers 1 through 9 were symbolic representations of the stages of human life.

Webweaving

There are many books on numerology that can explain the significance of your Destiny Number, Life Path Number, and other numbers that are important in your numerological chart. We recommend *The Complete Idiot's Guide to Numerology,* by Kay Lagerquist and Lisa Lenard (Alpha Books, 1999).

Birth date: September 11, 1968 (9/11/1968)

September = 9

11 (1 + 1) = 2

1968 (1 + 9 + 6 + 8) = 24 (2 + 4) = 6

9 + 2 + 6 = 17 (1 + 7) = 8

So, if you were born on September 11, 1968, your Life Path Number is 8. And you might want to choose a magickal name with a numerological value of 8. For more insights on numerology and Wicca, see Chapter 25, "Divination."

Your Name in a Magickal Alphabet

Some witches use *Theban Script* to write their name on talismans and amulets. It is sometimes called Honorian Script or the Honorian Alphabet. It can also be referred to as the Witches' Alphabet, but many people consider that term to be a misnomer. Using this special system of writing can help you to focus your energy and send it into the object that you are inscribing. You can even try Theban Script for spells and ritual.

Book of Shadows

Theban Script is a form of writing that can help you focus your energy and send it into the object that you are inscribing. Some believe Theban Script arose during the Middle Ages; others believe it to be a more recent development. Witches of the Gardnerian tradition and many others frequently use it. Some ceremonial magickians—individuals who practice magick in a ceremony that is devoid of religious content—use it as well.

Theban Script

A	H	O	V
B	I	P	W
C	J	Q	X
D	K	R	Y
E	L	S	Z
F	M	T	
G	N	U	

Mark for end of sentence; period.

Practice writing your magickal name (or your mundane name, if you don't have a magickal one yet) in Theban Script, or use Theban Script when you make entries in your diary. If you use the script a little every day, pretty soon you'll know it by heart.

Can You Change Your Magickal Name?

In some traditions, a witch first takes his or her magickal name upon dedication. Then, a year and a day later, at the time of First Degree Initiation, he or she takes another name. A witch may also rededicate under another name if the magickal name chosen no longer fits. When you first enter the craft, you'll learn and grow a lot. Because of all the change that you will be experiencing as a person, it is not unusual to feel that you need to take a new name after some time. As a solitaire, you can change your name when you want. But it is probably not a good idea to do it frequently. You don't want to give yourself an identity crisis!

A New Path in an Old Way of Life

In many ways your life will change when you dedicate yourself to the craft. And in many other ways it won't. You will still have the same family and friends. You will probably live in the same place and hold the same job, or you will continue to go to school. For many people, their external lives do not look much different, but inside they feel the change.

What It Means to Dedicate

Dedication means just that—dedication. When you dedicate yourself to the craft, it means that you have looked at the craft, studied, and made a decision to walk the Wiccan path. When you make your dedication, you let the Lord and Lady know that you welcome them into your life, that you have chosen the craft, that you will follow the path of the witch, and will observe the Wiccan law—"An it harm none, do what you will." You also are making a promise to respect the Lord and Lady.

So Mote It Be

As a way of celebrating your dedication, why not do something nice for the Earth and her creatures? Feed the local wildlife, visit animals at a shelter, or dig in some compost around the base of a tree. Alternatively, you could send money to an organization that fights pollution or protects endangered animals. Or join a clean-up crew at a local park or stream. Or form your own cleaning brigade. When you're done, take yourself out for coffee and a slice of cake.

When you dedicate you don't just take your magickal name, you take an oath that you will live by the Wiccan Rede. In a coven, you usually also promise not to reveal to nonmembers any of the information that you learn about from the coven.

Taking Your New Name in Dedication

At your dedication ceremony, you'll take your magickal name. In a coven ritual, the High Priest or the High Priestess will ask you by what name you will be known in the circle. From then on, that will be the name the coveners call you.

As a solitaire, you can self-dedicate. During your self-dedication ritual, you can tell the God and Goddess what name you are taking.

How to Do Your Own Self-Dedication

You can write your own self-dedication ceremony or use the one that follows. Look at a few other books for ideas, and don't forget the Internet. There's loads of information about Wicca and witchcraft out there. Whatever you do, make your dedication ritual a special time for you.

Dedication Ritual

1. First decide if this is truly what you want to do. Look deep within yourself and meditate on the question. Ask yourself, "Is this the path I want to walk?" If you decide that Wicca is truly your calling, you can proceed with your ritual.

2. Set up your altar. To do this, place the following objects on the surface you have chosen to work on:
   - ➤ A pentagram for protection
   - ➤ One silver candle for the Goddess
   - ➤ One gold candle for the God
   - ➤ One illuminator candle (you will light all the other candles from this one)
   - ➤ One bowl of holy water
   - ➤ One bowl of salt
   - ➤ Your athame
   - ➤ A censer
   - ➤ A candle snutter
   - ➤ A chalice
   - ➤ A bottle of wine or juice and some cakes
   - ➤ A libation bowl
   - ➤ The words of the dedication that follows (unless you want to improvise what you want to say to the God and Goddess)

You will also need a lighter or book of matches to light your illuminator candle and incense.

3. Lay out your ritual robe (if you plan to wear one) and your magickal jewelry.

4. Draw your bath. To the water add …

   ➤ One tablespoon of sea salt.

   ➤ A couple of drops of jasmine essential oil.

   Light your bath candles. Play meditative music. Get in the tub and relax.

   Breathe in the essence of the jasmine. Think about the ritual you will be performing and what it means to you. Meditate on the changes you will be making within yourself and your life. Are you ready to face the challenge? Think about your relationship with the Lord and Lady. Cleanse your mind as well as your body.

5. After bathing, drying, and dressing for the journey you are about to take, go to the altar and prepare your sacred space.

6. First consecrate your elements. (See Chapter 9, "Preparing to Do Ritual.")

7. Now take your water and walk the circle deosil (clockwise) and say:

   "As I walk this circle round
   I cleanse and consecrate this ground."

8. Next sprinkle your salt around the circle and say:

   "First with Water then with Earth
   With negativity banished there's joyous rebirth."

9. Take the incense censer and walk the circle saying:

   "Next with Fire, then with Air
   Leaving us only with purity fair."

10. Take your athame and mark the boundaries of the circle pulling up the circle as you go. (For details of how to do this, see Chapter 11, "Cast a Magick Circle.")

11. Stand in front of your altar and light the illuminator candle with a match or lighter. Welcome the God and Goddess and thank them for coming.

12. Begin your Dedication to the Goddess by saying the following:

   "Goddess, I stand before you in this sacred place of power.
   open my heart to your spirit.
   I open my mind to your wisdom.
   I dedicate myself to the learning of your mysteries.
   I dedicate my life to following the Wiccan path.

   O Great Mother, take me into your fold.
   Protect me, teach me, heal me, and empower me.
   Breathe your spirit in my body and make me complete.

Teach me to see through eyes that are wise.
Teach me to feel through a heart that is compassionate.
Teach me to drink through lips that speak of kindness.
Teach me to hear through ears without prejudice.
Teach me to live in oneness with the Earth.

Great Goddess, Queen of the Craft of the Wise, I come to you as Your [son or daughter] [magickal name].

From this day forward I will follow your light and strive to learn the mysteries."

13. Light the silver candle with the flame of the illuminator candle.

14. Begin your Dedication to the God by saying the following:

"God, I stand before you in the sacred place of power.
I open my heart to your spirit.
I open my mind to your wisdom.
I dedicate myself to the learning of your mysteries.
I dedicate my life to following the Wiccan path.

O Great Father, take me into your fold.
Protect me, teach me, heal me, and empower me.
Breathe your spirit in my body and make me complete.
Teach me to see through eyes that are wise.
Teach me to feel through a heart that is compassionate.
Teach to drink through lips that speak of kindness.
Teach me to hear through ears without prejudice.
Teach me to live in one with the Earth.

All powerful Lord, consort and protector of the Lady, I come to you as your [son or daughter] [magickal name].

From this moment forward I will follow your light and strive to learn the mysteries."

15. Light the gold candle from the illuminator candle.

16. Pour the wine in the chalice and get your cakes.

17. Before you eat and drink, pour some of the wine and break off some of your cake into the libation bowl for the Lord and Lady.

18. Now drink wine, eat the cakes, and reflect on this ritual and how you have taken the first big step in changing your life.

19. When you are finished eating and drinking, thank the Lord and Lady for attending your dedication and snuff out the gold candle and the silver candles.

20. Take your athame and walk widdershins (counterclockwise) around the circle and to take it down. (See Chapter 11 for directions on how to do this.)

21. Snuff out your illuminator candle and clean up. Make sure you take the contents of the libation bowl, the Lord and Lady's portion of the feast, and give it back to the Earth. Go outdoors and pour it on the ground.

Congratulations! You have dedicated yourself to the Wiccan way of life.

You may have enjoyed reading this dedication ritual, but keep in mind that ritual is primarily designed to be experienced, not read about. In other words, try it out!

The Least You Need to Know

➤ Your magickal name is a reflection of who you are, what you stand for, and what you hope to become.

➤ Your magickal name is special. Only people in the craft and the pagan community need to know your magickal name.

➤ Your dedication is a moving experience in which you take your magickal name and invite the Lord and Lady into your life.

➤ A dedication ritual is best experienced, not just read about.

Chapter 9

Preparing to Do Ritual

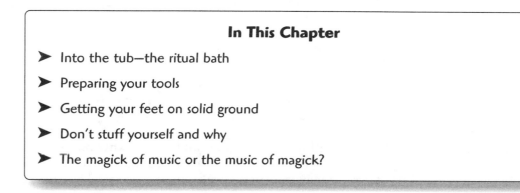

In This Chapter

➤ Into the tub—the ritual bath

➤ Preparing your tools

➤ Getting your feet on solid ground

➤ Don't stuff yourself and why

➤ The magick of music or the music of magick?

Ritual is an important part of the Wiccan faith. In ritual you honor the God and the Goddess. You can also practice magick within ritual. Because ritual is such a central aspect of the faith, you want to make sure that you are properly prepared before you start.

In this chapter, we'll tell you all about what you need to do to prepare for ritual. You'll learn how to ready your body and your mind. You'll also learn how to prepare your altar elements and tools. We'll even suggest some recorded music that you can use during ritual or before to get you in the proper mood.

A Cleansing Ritual Bath

Taking a ritual bath is one of most important pre-ritual steps. The bath helps prepare the subconscious mind for ritual. If the point is to be clean, why not just take a shower? While a shower is good for cleaning your body, it does little for your mind. A shower will leave you fresh, but it does not relax you the way a bath will. When in the bath, your heart rate slows and the body and mind find peace.

Why a Bath Is Important and When to Take It

The ritual bath is important much the way your magickal clothes and tools are important. They signal your subconscious mind to get to work. The bath helps you let go of negativity and distracting thoughts and focus your mind. It gives you the opportunity to reflect on your self and your intentions. Time in the bath is also enjoyable and refreshing! When you climb out of the tub, it's almost as if you are being reborn.

You should take a ritual bath before you do any formal ritual, especially magick, to make sure you don't have negative energy stuck on you. In preparing for ritual, after you have assembled all your tools, gone over your checklist, prepared the room, unplugged the phone, removed your watch, and checked to make sure your ritual outfit is clean, you can get into the tub. But you can take a ritual bath at other times, too, even if you are not about to do ritual. You can use a ritual bath to reflect, meditate, get grounded, and connect with deity. Just make sure that your bath is slow and relaxing. Whatever you do, don't rush! This bath is special and can be magickal in its own right.

How to Take a Ritual Bath

To prepare your ritual bath, put essential or magickal oils and/or herbs in the water. Use only a couple of drops, because you want only a subtle essence of scent. (You don't want to run everyone else out of the circle!) Choose your herbs based on your personal preference or on the kind of ritual or magick you plan to do. Turn off that glaring overhead light in the bathroom and light candles. You want your bath to be a special, magickal time for you. While you're soaking, think about ritual and any magick that you will be working. Meditating in the bath can be a powerful and yet gentle way to connect with deity.

Enjoy a luxurious ritual bath.

Let the water soothe you, and allow yourself to feel nurtured. If you like, play soft music while you're in the tub to complete the special atmosphere.

As you are stepping out of the water, let go of any negativity. Imagine that it has stayed in the water and that you are letting it flow down the drain away from you. This way when you emerge from the tub, you will be cleansed physically *and* mentally. Put on your clean robe or outfit (or stay as you are in your birthday suit!), and you are ready for ritual.

Consecration: A Means of Empowerment

After you buy or finish making your magickal tools, you need to *consecrate* them. Consecrating your tools before you use them rids the tools of any negative energy they may be harboring. It is also a way of dedicating your tools to the Lord and Lady, to the good of all, and empowering them with positive energy.

Before you consecrate your tools, you need to consecrate the elements on your altar. (We'll be telling you more about altars in the next chapter. So, if you miss something here, don't worry.) To consecrate your elements, do the following:

> **Say:**
>
> "O element of Earth, may all negative energies depart and only positive energies remain. This is my will, so mote it be."
>
> As you say these words, draw a banishing Earth pentagram in the air over the bowl of salt on your altar. (For more on banishing pentagrams, see Chapter 12, "The Witches' Symbol.")
>
> **Then say:**
>
> "O element of Water, may all negative energies depart and only positive energies remain. This is my will, so mote it be."

So Mote It Be

If you are lucky enough to live near a natural body of water, you can take your ritual bath in it. We said natural, because swimming pools, with all their smelly chlorine, don't count. You can bathe for ritual in a pond, lake, stream, river, hot spring, or ocean. As you exit the waters, imagine Venus, the Goddess of Love and Beauty, rising for the first time from the foam of the sea.

Book of Shadows

To **consecrate** something means to bless it or make it sacred. The word carries the connotation of physical change, as well. In the Catholic Church consecrate is the word used to describe the transformation of the bread and wine into the body and blood of Christ. And that's a big change. When you consecrate your tools, you also dedicate or devote them to the Goddess and the greatest good for all.

Draw a banishing Water pentagram in the air over the bowl of water on your altar.

Then say:

"O element of Fire, may all negative energies depart and only positive energies remain. This is my will, so mote it be."

Draw a banishing Fire pentagram in the air over the candles on your altar.

Then say:

"O element of Air, may all negative energies depart and only positive energies remain. This is my will, so mote it be."

And draw a banishing Air pentagram in the air over your incense.

Then say:

"O Spirit, may you charge and protect this altar from any negativity. May your blessing be upon it as I dedicate the work of this altar for positive purposes only so as it harm none. So mote it be."

Once you have consecrated your elements, take three measures of salt and put them in the water to make holy water. As you do this, say: "One to purify the body, one to purify the mind, and one to purify the heart. The spirit will bind them all as one."

Webweaving

The five elements are Earth, Air, Water, Fire, and Spirit. In Wicca, each element is associated with a direction in the ritual circle. Earth's direction is north, and Air is east. Water is west, while Fire is south. Spirit encompasses all directions because it surrounds and is part of everything.

Take your athame and sprinkle the salted water over it. As you do this, say: "With the element of Water, I wash away any negative energies from this athame so that only positive energies remain."

Sprinkle salt over the athame and say: "With the element of Earth, I wash away any negative energies from this athame so that only positive energies remain." Or you can sprinkle the salted water on the athame and say: "With the elements of Earth and Water, I wash away any negative energies from this athame so that only positive energies remain."

Then, wave the athame over a lit candle and say: "With the element of Fire, I wash away any negative energies from this athame so that only positive energies remain."

Next, pass the athame through the smoke from your incense and say: "With the element of Air, I wash away any negative energies from this athame so that only positive energies remain."

Finally, hold the athame up to the Lord and Lady and say: "O spirit, may you charge and protect this athame from any negativity. May your blessing be upon it as I dedicate the work of this athame for positive purposes only so as it harm none. So mote it be."

Go through this process with all of your altar instruments and with anything that you want to place on your altar, use in ritual, or make holy. As you probably can imagine, the first time you set up your altar it can take some time! After the first time, you don't need to reconsecrate all of your tools unless someone else has touched them without your permission. Each time you pull up the circle your tool will be consecrated by the sacred space.

After you've consecrated an object, no one should touch it but you. If someone does touch one of your consecrated things, you will have to reconsecrate it to get rid of that person's energy. Make sure you consecrate everything that you're going to use in ritual, including your magickal jewelry. You can consecrate your clothing in the same way, if you like, but you don't need to. It is enough just to know that your clothes are clean. Or you can put them out under the full Moon. (You don't need to consecrate your clothes because you don't use your robes or other clothing to do magick. They just serve to get you into the right frame of mind.)

What Does It Mean to Charge Your Magickal Tools?

Charging magickal tools is a way of waking them up and enlivening their positive energy. One of the easiest ways to charge your tools is by laying them out under the full Moon at night. If you can, spread them out in the light of the full Moon for a couple of hours or even over night. After some time in the moonlight, the energy of the Goddess will penetrate your tools and they will be ready to use. If you want to add the God energy, you can spread them out under the Sun.

If you live in an apartment, you can place items for charging on your balcony or windowsill. Just make sure they don't fall off! Or place them in a patch of moonlight that filters in through your windows. Alternatively, you can hold your tools up toward the full Moon on a night when she is shining and ask the Goddess to bless them.

A Charging Ritual for Your Magickal Tools

The first step in a charging ritual for your tools is to cleanse and consecrate them, as outlined earlier. Then take your tools out under the full Moon. If you own quartz crystals, bring them with you and place them on or beside the tools to be charged. The crystals will help to pull positive energy to your tools.

Sit on the ground near your tools. Take a few deep breaths, or spend a few minutes in meditation. Envision the moonlight filling each tool with power. Ask the Goddess to bless your tools and fill them with light. If you can leave the tools outside overnight, do so. If not, wrap them up, carry them inside, and store them in a safe place where no one else will handle them. You can do the same thing with the God, except you would place your tools under the Sun at noon when it is high and bright in the sky. (We don't recommend this for candles because they will melt.)

Learning to Ground Yourself Before Ritual

If you don't ground yourself before doing ritual, your energies will not flow the way they should. Your energy will be erratic and your magick may not do what you want it to. When you ground yourself, you align the *chakras*, or energy centers of the body. In addition, grounding allows you to receive the natural flow of energy from the Earth and enables you to become one with the Earth. It also helps to prepare your subconscious to do the work it needs to do.

Book of Shadows

Chakra means "wheel" in Sanskrit, the ancient language of India. The chakras are round, spinning discs of energy that lie along your spine from your tailbone to the top of your head. Hindus, Tibetans, Taoists, and Hopis all use chakra systems to explain the various energies in the body.

Visualization Techniques You Can Use

There are many different visualization techniques that you can use to ground yourself. Denise has her students envision that they are becoming trees. You can use this image or find another one that works for you.

Here is how you do Denise's tree visualization:

Sit up straight in a chair with your feet flat on the floor. Place your hands on your knees and relax your shoulders. Breathe slow deep breaths. Relax your abdominal muscles, and let your tummy move in and out as you breathe. Close your eyes and start to picture yourself as a tree. Your head and shoulders are the branches, your legs and body are the trunk. Take some time to really imagine yourself with branches and a trunk. See the picture in your mind grow clearer and sharper. Then, as you continue to breathe, deep slow breaths, picture roots growing from the bottom of your feet. With each exhale, push down your roots deeper and deeper and imagine them growing longer. Watch them grow farther and farther into the Earth.

As your roots grow, they mature and bring you the nutrients that all trees need. As you breathe in, pull up cool, dark nutrients and water from the ground into the tree. As you breathe in, see the nutrients fill the tree. As you breathe out, feel your roots grow longer and stronger into the Earth. The nutrients you are taking in are the blessing from the Goddess. But this is only half of what we need to thrive—we also need the blessing of the Lord, the Sun.

As you breathe out, pull down the golden rays of the Sun into your branches, down through your trunk, and into your roots. As you breathe in, pull in the cool nutrients of the Earth. Breathe out and feel the golden light of Sun entering from above.

Breathe in and feel the Earth's nutrients filling you from below. Feel the rhythm—pulling in the Sun from above as you exhale and drinking in the nutrients from the ground as you inhale. Picture the tree getting bigger and stronger and healthier. Feel the air and sway in the breeze.

After you have gone through this exercise and given it your full concentration, you will be grounded and ready to work.

So Mote It Be

Are visualization and meditation hard for you? Do you sometimes avoid doing things that you find difficult? Do uncomfortable emotions come up for you when you sit still? Well, it's really true that practice makes perfect. The more you work at focusing your mind in meditation or visualization the easier it will become. If you practice every day for just a little while, you will get better and better. And it's nice to take 5 or 10 minutes out of your day to relate to deity. As your sense of connection grows stronger and stronger, you will be less plagued by unpleasant feelings. You'll be able to sit for longer periods of time. And your visualizations will grow sharper and clearer.

Focus Is No Hocus Pocus

Focus is a really important part of doing ritual and magick. If you can't focus, you won't be able to get into ritual, and you won't enjoy it. And neither will you be able to do magick. Focusing is what channels and directs the energy you use. If you can't concentrate your mind on that task, your energy gets nowhere.

Focusing is not some esoteric art. Just like every other day-to-day activity, the more you practice focusing, the better you get. So practice, okay?

Fasting Before Ritual

Almost all religions use fasting to some extent. Fasting can be the total abstention from food and drink, or it can be more moderate. Christians, Hindus, Jews, Jains, and Muslims fast. So did the ancient Celts, Egyptians, Mexicans, Peruvians, and Greeks. (Kind of makes you want to reach for a snack, huh?)

Many people fast during the day when they are going to do ritual in the evening. Some will eat breakfast, skip lunch and dinner and drink only fruit juice and water during the day. Others might eat lunch and then have nothing but juice later, and still others will have lunch and a light dinner. Whatever you do, don't eat a big meal before ritual.

There are several reasons why people fast on ritual days. When you eat, especially a large meal, your blood pressure goes up. Your blood pressure also rises when you raise energy during ritual. So, if you eat a huge meal before ritual, you put your heart on double duty. Not only does it have to work hard to help you digest all that food, you're also asking it to pump blood to put out a lot of energy for ritual.

Banish!

Say you are getting ready to do ritual. You sit down and close your eyes to meditate, but your eyes keep popping open and your mind continues to whirl. If you can't ground yourself and get focused, then you are not ready to work. Avoid working when you aren't prepared! If you're doing magick, your magick could go in a direction other than the one you intended.

A large meal also might make you sleepy. Hasn't that happened to you before? You eat and, because all your energy is going into digestion, you have to lie down for a while. You don't want to feel like you need a nap when you're trying to build power! Rather you want to be alert and at your peak so you can build up all the energy that you need for your ritual.

Fasting is cleansing and leaves you feeling light. As a technique, fasting has been used for thousands of years to help the mind move away from the every day and focus on the magickal and spiritual. If you decide to fast, make sure that you drink juice and plenty of other fluids. If you are diabetic or have another illness, you may not be able to fast. And that's okay. Fasting is not necessary, but it can make magickal work manifest more easily. Healthy people without existing illnesses should be able to fast for some of the day or at least a short amount of time before ritual.

Magick Music

Banish!

Do not fast if you have any medical condition that might be aggravated by such an action. Consult your primary care physician before undertaking any kind of fast.

It's great to use music before ritual—when you take your ritual bath, for instance. You can also play music during ritual. Music has a direct effect on the mind on both the conscious and subconscious levels. You can order meditation tapes or pagan dance music online or buy them at New Age or metaphysical stores. If you visit a store, you should be able to listen to the music before you buy it. You need to be sure you like it and it will work for you. All stores receive demo tapes from the producers, so there is no reason that you can't listen first and buy later.

Using Music in Ritual

Music can be used in several ways during ritual. For example, you can play pagan dance music to help you build a cone of power—a large amount of energy that you will later release to carry out your magick. For this purpose, you want to select a piece that starts out slow and gets faster and faster. The faster you dance, the more energy you raise.

Or you can use music to help you celebrate sacred events. It is traditional (in many different traditions) to do a dance of celebration around the Maypole during *Beltane*. Witches dance at some of the other Sabbats, or holidays, too.

And, of course, you can use soothing music to make you feel safe and calm for your meditation during ritual. Some people like to play New Age tapes. Others like classical music. Still others prefer natural sounds—birds chirping in the rain forest, the roar of the ocean, or even the singing of whales.

Chants: Find Your Magickal Voice

Listening to a tape or CD of chants is a great way to get you in the mood for ritual. There are all kinds of chants—from Gregorian to Sanskrit to Wiccan. Try listening to a few different types and see what appeals to you. You could listen to chants while you take your ritual bath, or learn a few chants and sing them to yourself. You can chant even if you don't like the sound of your own voice.

When chanting, you don't need to sound like a grand diva. The point is to focus on the chant and its intent. The Lord and Lady want to hear from you even if you can't carry a tune. One of Katherine's yoga teachers does not sing well at all. But he leads great chants and everyone always wants to chant with him. When he chants he is totally wrapped up in what he is doing and so devoted that people around him can't help but be moved by his energy. So, try chanting—even if your singing makes the dogs howl!

Within ritual, you can use chants to build your cone of power. Just the way you would with drumming, you start out slow; then you build the pace

Book of Shadows

Beltane is a Wiccan holiday that is celebrated on April 30. The celebration of this festival has a lot in common with the May Day that you probably know. Read more about Beltane and the other Wiccan holidays in Chapters 14, "Observing the Sabbats," and 15, "Summon, Stir, or Call."

Webweaving

The group Kiva, and we mean group as in band, has a great CD of Wiccan dance music and chants. The album is called *Renewal*, and it features tracks you might want to use in your next ritual.

and raise the volume. You chant faster and louder until you feel ready to burst with the energy. But don't pop. Direct the energy you've raised into your magick tool or object. We'll tell you more about just how to do that in Chapter 16, "Why Do Magick?"

You can also use chanting in ritual to re-ground yourself or to put yourself in a certain mindset. Slow, rhythmic chanting can be very soothing and calming. It can also help to open your heart to deity just the way singing a hymn would. And sometimes witches chant or sing their spells. But we're getting ahead of ourselves. You'll find out more about spells in Part 6, "Witches' Brew: Notions, Potions, and Powders."

So Mote It Be

Here are some musical selections you might want to check out. You can use them during ritual or listen to them while you are preparing for ritual to help get you in the proper frame of mind:

➤ Loreena McKennitt, *The Visit*, WEA/Warner, 1992

➤ On the Wings of Song and Robert Gass, *From the Goddess*, Spring Hill Music, 1989

➤ Reclaiming & Friends, *Chants: Ritual Music*, Serpentine Music, 1987

➤ Mike Rowland, *The Fairy Ring*, Emd/Narada, 1982

➤ Troika, *Goddess*, Emd/Narada, 1996

Drumming

When you are building a cone of power you might want to play a drum. Drumming is an excellent way to build up energy. It's a scientific fact that when people listen to drums their heart rates speed up as the tempo of the drumming increases. With your heart beating to the beat, there's no telling the amount of energy you'll raise!

You can use a handheld drum, tambourine, rattle, your fingers against a hard surface, or anything else you can keep a beat with. You should start out soft and slow. Then increase the speed and volume. Keep drumming, getting faster and louder and faster and louder. Pretty soon you will notice that your heart is beating faster, too. You'll feel your energy rise up.

Drumming also can help to keep you focused. When you drum, the beat grabs your attention. The physical action of your arms reinforces the attention your mind is giving to the sound. Your body and your mind are intent on one thing—the beat. And that's a great way to get ready for the work you are going to do.

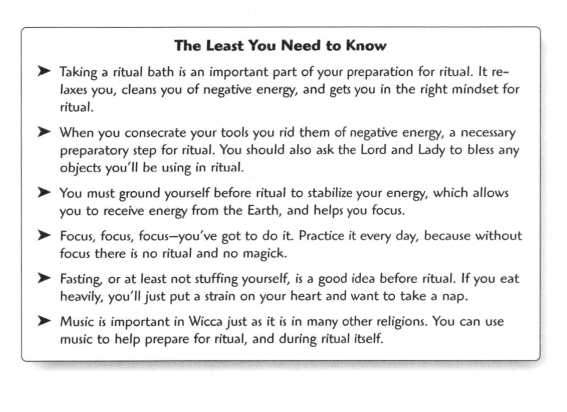

The Least You Need to Know

➤ Taking a ritual bath is an important part of your preparation for ritual. It relaxes you, cleans you of negative energy, and gets you in the right mindset for ritual.

➤ When you consecrate your tools you rid them of negative energy, a necessary preparatory step for ritual. You should also ask the Lord and Lady to bless any objects you'll be using in ritual.

➤ You must ground yourself before ritual to stabilize your energy, which allows you to receive energy from the Earth, and helps you focus.

➤ Focus, focus, focus—you've got to do it. Practice it every day, because without focus there is no ritual and no magick.

➤ Fasting, or at least not stuffing yourself, is a good idea before ritual. If you eat heavily, you'll just put a strain on your heart and want to take a nap.

➤ Music is important in Wicca just as it is in many other religions. You can use music to help prepare for ritual, and during ritual itself.

My Sacred Place
(please do not desecrate)

Chapter 10

Where to Do Magick

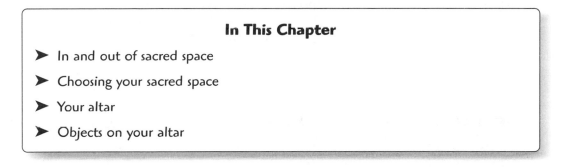

In This Chapter

➤ In and out of sacred space

➤ Choosing your sacred space

➤ Your altar

➤ Objects on your altar

There is a time and a place for everything. But what kind of place do you need to do magick? Do you have to find a castle with towers and a dungeon? Or an isolated meadow surrounded by huge cypress trees? Those sound like locations with some magickal potential, but actually, many witches do their magick and ritual at home in their living rooms.

In this chapter, you'll learn about sacred space—an area you can use for ritual. Our discussion of sacred space should help you decide on what kind of space you'll need for ritual. We'll also tell you about altars and how to set one up. We'll even tell you how to make a portable altar that you can carry with you.

Sacred Rituals Need a Sacred Place

When you were a kid, didn't your mother tell you not to play ball in the house? Then she'd always tell you to go outside. Humans have designated areas for specific functions probably since we lived in caves. Maybe even before that. We sleep in bedrooms, bathe in bathrooms, dine in dining rooms. And we worship in special rooms or buildings set aside for that purpose—temples, churches, synagogues, and mosques, to name a few. You should hold ritual in a special place to keep ritual *sacred*.

Often places of worship have been built on spots of naturally occurring power. Some sites that are currently home to a religious building or shrine have been occupied by just such a structure since before recorded history. With that many years of devotion, probably any place would start to feel pretty special. And you usually can feel it. Haven't you ever walked into a house of worship and been hit by the energy of the place?

Book of Shadows

Our word **sacred** comes from the Middle English word meaning "to consecrate." So, an object or place that is sacred is one that has been consecrated. It is also something that has been devoted to worship or set apart for a single use.

What Makes a Sacred Place Sacred?

In many respects, because the God and the Goddess live in all things, you could argue that the whole Earth is a sacred place. But most witches would agree that to really make an area sacred you need to cleanse the space of negative energies and consecrate it. A place that has been made sacred in such a way is a great space in which to spend time. You can relax there, meditate, or communicate with deity. Sacred space is safe space—somewhere you feel not just comfortable, but welcome.

How Is a Sacred Space Different from a Magick Circle?

Sacred space is space that has been cleansed and consecrated. A magick circle is also an area that has been cleansed and consecrated, but it is more than that. A magick circle is an area of protection. Before you pull up a magick circle in which to do your workings, you need to cleanse and consecrate the area. Then you make your circle inside the consecrated space. The magick circle protects you from other entities and prevents any undirected energies from escaping and causing harm. (For more about magick circles, see Chapter 11, "Cast a Magick Circle.")

Coming to Your Sacred Wicca Space: A Self-Exploration

Your choice of the space you are going to use as your sacred space will depend on what you are planning to do there. If you intend to do ritual alone, you won't need a lot of room. The same is true if you want to meditate or communicate with deity. But, if you're having a group of pagan friends over to celebrate a holiday, you'll need a large room or an area outdoors that can accommodate everyone.

How do you pick the spot for your private religious and magickal activities? That all depends on your personal preferences and on what is available to you. Here are some questions that can help you determine the qualities you'd like in your sacred space:

1. Would you rather be indoors or out?

2. Do you like to have a lot of things around you—pictures, knickknacks, and souvenirs—or do you prefer a space free of clutter?

3. Is there a space in your home or surroundings that feels particularly powerful or attractive to you?

4. Do you need to keep your ritual and magickal activities secret from those you live with?

Sit in the area that you are thinking of using for ritual, and ask yourself the following questions about the space:

1. Do you feel safe in the space?

2. Does it afford you enough privacy? Remember you will be chanting and possibly drumming in the space. So just being out of someone else's sight may not be enough.

3. Do you feel good in the space? Does it feel as if it could be an area of power for you?

Probably the most important features of a place where you choose to do ritual are your feelings of safety and privacy. If you don't feel safe in the area you have chosen, you will not be able to perform ritual there. The sense of what is adequate privacy may seem to be an entirely individual matter. However, we guarantee that you will find it hard to concentrate on your ritual if you have joggers running by staring at you every three minutes.

Webweaving

Since the time of the ancient Romans, and maybe even before that, sacred space in the form of an altar or a temple has been a safe area where slaves and those accused of crimes could find sanctuary. In Roman times, any act of violence against a person taking such sanctuary was considered to be an insult to the gods.

Setting and Respecting Sacred Boundaries

You should cleanse the whole area that you will be working in. It can be as small as the space around you—usually a 9-foot circle is big enough to work in. Or, if you are working with a group, the space you cleanse may have to be very large—say a quarter of an acre. If you have gone to the trouble of cleansing and consecrating an area for a specific purpose, create some landmarks or visible boundaries so you know where your consecrated space begins and ends, ensuring that you won't stray outside the area.

Once you have made a magick circle in which to work, you should stay inside the circle. If you need to leave, you have to cut a door in the circle to do so. Many witches believe it is best to locate a door in the circle in the north or east. To create a door, you cut the energy field of the circle with your athame.

If you are working alone, leave your broom to guard the door while you are out of the circle. (Many witches leave their brooms by the door of their house or apartment for the same purpose.) If you are working with a group, the person who cuts the door, stands by as guardian. When you return and have reentered the circle, you must remember to seal the door. With your athame, close up the space that you have cut and remember to move in the opposite direction that you did when you cut the door. In other words, if you cut the door from left to right, you will seal the door by moving from right to left. When you cut a door, you draw energy from the circle and leave a void. The energy is drawn into your athame. When you seal the door, you take the energy out of the tool and make the circle complete again. Should you forget to seal the door, you will risk being visited by entities that you probably would rather not meet.

Once, a few years ago when working with a large group, Denise pulled up a circle, but then cut a door to get something she needed from outside the circle. When she came back, she got distracted and forgot to seal the door after herself. Twenty-four hours later, she got sick, and she stayed sick for two and a half months! None of her doctors could figure out what was wrong with her. They gave her antibiotics and anti-inflammatories, but she just got sicker. She ended up having to breathe from an oxygen tank. One day, as she was growing weaker and weaker, she sat down to think, and she remembered the day that she hadn't sealed the door. She thought that incident could be the root of her troubles because she knew that a negative entity would go after the person who had pulled up the circle. She called a friend, and they did a magick healing ritual. During ritual, the friend felt nauseous, and she got a terrible headache. Denise's headache vanished. Within 12 hours Denise was back to normal, as if she had never been sick at all, and her friend felt fine, too. Denise never forgot to reseal the door again.

The moral of the story? Remember to seal the door, if you have cut one! If you are working with other people, have someone stand guard at the open door. When working alone, leave your broom to guard the door. If you keep in mind that the circle is there to protect you and that you need to honor and respect sacred space, you shouldn't have any problems.

Banish!

Stories about witchcraft mishaps can be frightening, but avoid dwelling on your fears. Remember that every worthwhile activity carries some risk. Behave responsibly in your craft activities, just the way you do when you drive a car, cross the street, or go skiing, and you'll be just fine.

Crafting an Altar

In many religious traditions all over the world people keep *altars* in their homes. Some of these altars are devoted to a single deity, others to an individual's ancestors, and still others to a group of gods and spirits. Altars are often designed along traditional lines, or they are just a corner in a room. As a Wiccan, you get to create your own altar.

What's So Special About an Altar?

Your altar is your special area for magickal workings and religious observance. It should be used
only for these purposes. You can think of it as your
Wiccan workbench. You can use your altar as a
work area when combining herbs or dressing candles, for instance. Your altar also is a central space
where you can keep many of your magickal tools—
salt, holy water, and athame to name a few. (See
the section "What Goes on Your Altar?" later in
this chapter for more.) If you are able to leave your
altar set up when you aren't working, it will represent your honoring of deity even when you are not
present. In that sense, the altar can function as a
shrine and tribute to the God and Goddess. Your
altar is also another important tool that helps you
focus your personal power.

Book of Shadows

An **altar** is a working surface,
such as a tabletop, that is to be
used only for magickal or religious
purposes. The English word comes
from a Latin word that meant
"material for burning sacrificial
offerings."

What Do Altars Look Like?

If you have privacy concerns, your altar does not have to scream, "A witch lives here."
Some people use the mantle over the fireplace as an altar, and to the naive visitor it
just looks like they have an interesting and creative sense of interior design. If you
need to, there are many ways to disguise your altar.

Altar Specs

Your altar can be a regular table. It can be round or square. It can be triangular or ob-
long or oval. Your altar can be of any shape, size, or height that you like. You can use
what you have or make something especially for your purposes. You could use a crate
with a cloth over it, an old desk, or that pink Formica table that you bought 10 years
ago and now are totally sick of. Or you could go a more natural route and use a large
flat rock out in the woods, or the cut surface of a tree stump in your back yard. All you
have to do is cleanse and consecrate the table or surface you have chosen, add an altar
cloth, and presto—there's your altar.

Altars Big and Small

At many metaphysical stores, you can buy small altars that hang on the wall. They
look like knickknack shelves with a little drawer at the bottom where you can store
things. Most of them have a mirror or a picture at the top so they look quite decorative. If you do decide to go with a small altar, try not to let it get too small. You should
have enough room for your candles, ritual objects, and magickal workings. If you're
lucky enough to have the space, spread out your tools on a large table. This way you'll

have plenty of room to work and enough surface area to add your own personal touches to the collection of objects you keep on your altar.

Location, Location: North, South, East, West

Usually a permanent altar is placed in the northern or eastern section of a room, but if your space constraints don't allow for such a placement, you can put it where you have to. Within a magick circle, whether you are indoors or out, you also should try to set up your altar in the north or east. Keep it oriented so that when you stand to work at it you are facing one of those directions. If that simply isn't possible or practical for the area in which you will be working, set up the altar in such a way that you are comfortable. During ritual, you also can keep the altar in the center of your magick circle. Some witches prefer to have the altar centrally located because the center of a circle is the spot of strongest energy. In addition, if you are working with other people, a centrally placed altar will allow everyone in the circle to see the work being done.

Sanctuary: Indoor vs. Outdoor Altars

Many witches prefer to work outdoors. What better way to honor the God and Goddess than to be among Nature? Despite this preference, many are not able to work outside, it is difficult to find a safe and private space outdoors. Even if you have a backyard, you may not have sufficient privacy to practice ritual there. As a result, most witches do ritual inside. Besides ensuring privacy, there are other advantages to working indoors. If you work indoors, you can have a permanent altar that you leave up to honor the God and Goddess after your ritual is over. In addition, when you do an indoor ritual you will have all the comforts of your home, including the bathroom.

Banish!

Don't practice an impromptu ritual in a park or other public place. Children playing or joggers running by will distract you. What's more, you may attract a good deal of attention yourself and maybe even the police (especially if you've been brandishing your athame). If you want to use a park or other public place for ritual, plan ahead. Get a permit, if you need one, and talk to the local police precinct before you begin and before a frightened bystander calls them.

Permanent vs. Moveable Altars

Some witches set up their altars in a spare room, in a corner, or even in a closet and never move it. It's nice to have a space, even if it is tiny, where your altar can live. For others, because of space constraints or a lack of privacy, the altar has to be moved or taken apart and put away after ritual is done. Ideally, because your altar serves to honor the God and Goddess even when you aren't there, you should have a permanent altar. It's also nice to come home after a long day and see your religious and magickal items all laid out and ready to use. And, of course, having a permanent altar can save you clean-up and putting-away time. If, however, a permanent altar is not an option for you in your present living situation, don't worry. A temporary or moveable altar is just as good in the eyes of deity. And witches have probably used them for hundreds and hundreds of years.

What Goes on Your Altar?

Here's a list of basic tools for your altar:

> ➤ One or two illuminator candles
> ➤ A silver candle to represent the Goddess
> ➤ A gold candle to represent the God
> ➤ A pentagram
> ➤ A censer
> ➤ Water and salt in bowls
> ➤ An athame
> ➤ A chalice
> ➤ A bell
> ➤ A wand

So Mote It Be

Avoid overcrowding your altar. Remember, your altar is both a place of worship and a working surface. You should have space to do your workings. You don't want your altar to start to look messy. That would be disrespectful to the God and Goddess, and to yourself, too. Put away the things you don't need when you're done with them.

You should also keep a lighter nearby to light your illuminator candles. Some people keep one under their altar or in a nearby drawer, so they always have one when they need it. It's a good idea to keep a large bottle of water under your altar, too. You might get thirsty during ritual or you might have to douse some flames! You might also want to consider investing in a small fire extinguisher to keep near your altar. Candles can fall over or suddenly flare up. And wouldn't it be better to be prepared for such an occurrence? As Denise says, "There's nothing in the world worse than a flaming witch."

You can keep your wand on your altar if you want. There are all kinds of other things you can put on your altar—a representation of your *totem animal*, crystals, herbs you plan to use, images or statuettes of the God and Goddess you are working with. If you don't have a censer, you can use a small cauldron, which is also great for burning other objects and for fire magick. If you can't afford to buy that beautiful pewter pentagram that you saw in your metaphysical store last week, don't worry. Draw a pentagram on a piece of paper, and while you are saving your pennies, use it on your altar instead of the fancy one. Your paper pentagram will serve the purpose just as well.

Here's another tip: The country of Morocco uses the pentagram as its symbol. A pentagram appears on the Moroccan flag and on some Moroccan currency. If you can get a Moroccan coin, you've got a pentagram for your altar or to carry with you!

Book of Shadows

In Native American tradition, a **totem animal** is an animal that represents a clan or a family. The word "totem" comes from an Ojibwa word that means "my family mark." Some witches and some covens have totem animals, or power animals, that help them in their magickal work. Such an animal does not have to be a pet. Neither does it have to be a real live physical entity. Rather, the spirit or the power of the animal is called upon.

If you choose to work with the Goddess alone, you can honor her in her three phases—Maiden, Mother, and Crone—with three separate candles—white, red, and black. If you can't find a silver candle to represent the Goddess, you can use three candles to represent the three phases on your altar instead. If you choose to work with just the God, you can honor him in his three phases (Prince, King, and Elder). His candles are black, gold, and white.

Book of Shadows

Cowry shells are shiny, tropical shells used as money in some areas of Africa and the South Pacific where certain varieties are considered valuable. The cowry shell is thought to be a yoni—a symbol of the woman's vulva.

Porta-Pagan: Carrying Your Altar with You

Some witches carry a small altar with them all the time, either in a little bag on their persons or in a box in their cars. This way they are able to do ritual anywhere, which is great if they run into friends. When driving, a witch with a porta-pagan might stop if she saw a dead animal by the side of the road and do ritual to help the animal pass over.

If you'd like a little porta-pagan, check out your local metaphysical store. You'll probably be able to find everything you need in miniature there, around your house, or in Nature. Most stores will stock tiny pewter athame charms. (If you can't find one, remember that you can always use your two fingers held together instead.) Add two birthday candles, a small pentagram like one you would wear around your neck, little scallop shells from the beach to hold your water and salt, a small bag of salt, and a *cowry shell* to represent the Goddess. Put all of these items into a little velvet bag. All you need to do is add water, and you'll be ready for ritual.

The Least You Need to Know

➤ An area that has been cleansed and consecrated is sacred space. You make your magick circle inside sacred space.

➤ If you have to leave a magick circle, you must cut a door in the energy so you can get out. While you are out, make sure that someone stands guard at the door; or, leave your broom by the door to watch it for you.

➤ *Always* seal the door after you have returned to circle. If you don't, you could be exposing yourself to negative entities that will mess with your magick or with you.

➤ You can make sacred space almost anywhere. If you plan to do ritual, you must feel safe in the space you choose, and there must be enough privacy so that others do not distract you.

➤ You can use any flat surface for your altar. Ideally, you should have enough room to accommodate your candles, ritual objects, and magickal tools.

Chapter 11

Cast a Magick Circle

In This Chapter

➤ The geometry of it all

➤ Casting the circle

➤ Sharing in the circle

➤ Taking down the circle

At this point, you probably are starting to get a feel for Wiccan ritual and for magick. Maybe you've selected a space for your altar and set it up. Maybe you've performed a dedication ceremony for yourself and taken a magickal name. If you've done that, you even have a little ritual experience under your belt. Now, we're going to get more specific about ritual and one of ritual's major components, the magick circle.

Whenever you are going to do magick, you should put up a magick circle. One of the reasons you do this is to keep any undirected energy that you stir up inside the circle. The magick circle also protects you from any outside magickal beings. Inside your circle is a place where you are safe and where only things that you invite can come in. It's a place where you should feel comfortable and relaxed so you can meditate, visualize, and build up your cone of power or energy.

What Is a Magick Circle?

A magick circle is a protective area of energy that you create to work in. Some people like to think of it as a magick bubble. They believe the idea of a bubble better represents the three-dimensional nature of this protected area. A magick circle or bubble is not just a line on the floor. It goes through the floor and surrounds you on all sides.

When you pull up a magick circle, you want to think of yourself as being inside a sphere of protective energy. In addition to protecting you, a magick circle serves to hold and concentrate your energies.

Webweaving

Ceremonial magickians—those individuals who practice magick in a ceremony that is devoid of religious content—also create a circle inside which to work. Because they often summon creatures from other realms to help them with their magick, they need the circle to protect themselves. The creatures they call are not always friendly.

Book of Shadows

The **Watchtowers** or the Guardians of the Watchtowers are powerful entities associated with the four elements and the four directions. Ceremonial magickians and some witches use them. Some witches envision them as archangels. Because the Watchtowers are very powerful, you want to use them only if you need them.

When to Cast a Circle, and When Not To

Whenever you want to do magick, you need to cast a circle. The circle will protect you from any outside influences or little creatures from a different plane who want to meddle with your magick or with you.

If you are sick or exhausted, you should not cast a magick circle. You should plan to do magick only when you are feeling well. You also should not cast a circle when you are unprepared. Remember that you need to plan your magick and be focused on your intent. Finally, never cast a circle when you are angry. The circle is supposed to be full of your positive energy, not your annoyance or wrath.

Round vs. Square

Because a circle has round edges, not corners and straight edges, it's hard to break into one. (Circles denote continuous strength; corners are weak joints.) A circle also has no beginning and no end; it just goes around and around and is both the beginning and the end. If, when you are casting a circle, you walk the perimeter of a square room, the circle will pass through the walls so that it holds the entire room. Or you can caste a smaller circle inside of the room. Either you end up with your room sealed inside a protective bubble, or you have a protective bubble inside your room. If you plan on working with the *Watchtowers* (more on them later in this chapter), you will need to create your circle inside a square because the Watchtowers need corners to sit on.

Getting Started

You've planned your ritual. You've made sure you have all your tools. You've taken your ritual bath. You're dressed in your robes and magickal jewelry. Now what?

How to Cleanse the Sacred Space

Your first step is to cleanse your sacred space, the area in which you plan to do ritual, by sweeping out all the negativity. With your magick broom, sweep out the negative energy, and don't forget to sweep the corners!

While you sweep, say this little rhyme:

> Sweep, sweep with this broom
> All bad out of this room.
> Sweep, sweep all good in
> The bad to never return again.

Once you have swept out all the negative energy, you need to consecrate the area. To do this, walk around the room in a circle three times. Each time, carry a representation of an element—first Water, then Earth, then Fire and Air—from your altar.

First take your bowl of water and walk deosil (clockwise) around the circle. As you walk, say:

> I walk the circle once around
> To cleanse and consecrate this ground.

Then pick up your bowl of salt. (Remember that salt represents the element of Earth.) As you walk deosil around the circle say:

> I walk the circle once again.
> Between the worlds all time can bend.

When you are finished with your second tour around the circle, pick up your censer, which should have smoldering incense in it. (The burning incense and the smoke from the incense represent the elements of Fire and Air.) As you walk deosil around the circle for the third and final time, say:

> I walk the circle thrice this time
> For the protection of the Lord and Lady are mine.

Now you are ready to get to work on your circle.

How to Define the Circle

Some people will make an actual mark on the ground in chalk or will use a length of rope to define the edge of their circle. Placing something that you can see at the edge of your circle is a good idea when you are working outdoors in a large circle. Otherwise, you might forget where the boundaries of your circle are. Working indoors, you probably don't need to use actual physical markers, because you will have limited space.

Once you have walked the circle three times with your elements, take your athame, wand, sword, or staff and trace the edge of the circle with it as you walk deosil around again. Walk slowly, but with purpose. In your mind, see yourself pulling up a circle.

How to Put Up the Circle

To pull up the magick circle, you need to concentrate and use your powers of creative visualization. Some people, as they walk around the edges of the circle, imagine a white light flowing through them, through their athame or wand, and out. They see it pouring out in the form of white fibers that spin out until the whole circle is co-cooned. Some people see the circle as a bubble that grows up from the floor, curving overhead until it meets on top. Some people visualize plates of armor surrounding them, and others see the circle as made up of the scales of a dragon. You can even imagine the circle as a magick web that grows so it is all around you. It doesn't mat-ter what image you pick, just be sure it works for you. You'll probably need to work with the same image for a while before you can tell if it works. Remember, practice does make perfect.

So Mote It Be

Are you having trouble visualizing your magick circle? Well, try this. Go to your local video store, rent a copy of *The Wizard of Oz,* and pop it into the VCR. Pay careful attention to the scene right after the house falls on the Wicked Witch of the East. What happens? Glinda the Good Witch arrives. How does she get there? She floats in a shimmering pink bubble—and that is one super magick bubble. Watch the scene a few times if you need to. Feel free to change the color of the bubble. You want your bubble to be custom-made just for you.

Where's the Altar?

You can place your altar in the north part of your circle, in the east, or in center of the circle. Your decision about placement will depend on what you're planning to do. If you want to sit in the center of the circle and drum, you should place the altar to one side. If you have a group, it's nice to keep the altar in the center where everyone can see.

Summon, Stir, and Call: Calling in and Working with ...

The are many different entities that you can ask to help you with your magick. We'll introduce some of them here and tell you all about them in greater detail in Chapter 15, "Summon, Stir, or Call." You can summon or tell some of these entities to come to your aid. Others you can stir, and still others you can call or ask to come. It all depends on who and what you want to work with.

The Elements

As we have mentioned before, there are four elements—Earth, Air, Fire, and Water. Each element has a color, direction, and certain other characteristics. Because the elements are all around us and in that sense never leave us, if you want to work with them, you can summon them.

➤ Earth's color is green, its direction north. Earth is associated with beauty, growth, nurturing abundance, and the bounty of the Earth. Earth also represents prosperity, wisdom, and sensation.

➤ Air's color is yellow, its direction east. Air is associated with communication, education, the realm of the intellect, wind, and sound. Air is also linked to creativity, meditation, divination, and awareness—in short, anything that flows through the air and any energy that passes quickly. The way that you communicate to deity and the way deity communicates to you is tied up with the element of Air.

➤ Fire's color is red, its direction south. Fire represents the passion and desire burning inside all of us. As sexuality, Fire is the most physical and the most spiritual of elements. Fire is also linked to courage and feelings. It is the element of change, and the spark of spirit within us all.

➤ Water's color is blue, its direction west. Water is associated with psychic energy, emotion, intuition, the subconscious, and cleansing. We all have Water within us and are subject to its ebb and flow. Contemplation of the element of Water also reminds us that we all have heights and depths of emotion. It is also the element of reason.

Webweaving

Some witches keep their altars in the center of the circle but make sure that the altar faces north. North, you will remember, is the direction associated with Earth, and many feel that because we live on Earth we should align ourselves in this way. North also is considered a direction of power. Other witches face their altars east, the direction of the rising Sun and Moon.

The Elementals

The elementals are personifications of the four elements. The elemental associated with Fire is the salamander. Undines, or water nymphs, are associated with Water, while sylphs are associated the element of Air, and gnomes are associated with the element of Earth. If you want to work with the elementals, you can summon them.

The Deities

All deities from all pantheons are manifestations of the All. To work with them, you call them respectfully and ask them to attend your ritual.

The Ancestors

Some people refer to the Ancestors as the Ancient Ones. They can actually be your ancestors. (You may be related to someone who was very powerful.) Or they can be magickal people from history such as Merlin or a famous witch from the past such as Aradia. Usually they are thought of as potent magickal people. However mighty and powerful they might be, they are not Gods. When you ask for the help or presence of the Ancestors, you stir them. They are asleep, so you want to wake them gently. You wouldn't want to have a bunch of crabby Ancestors hanging around your ritual.

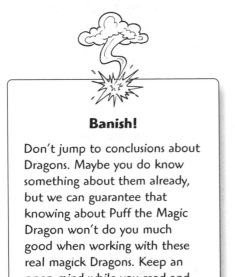

Banish!

Don't jump to conclusions about Dragons. Maybe you do know something about them already, but we can guarantee that knowing about Puff the Magic Dragon won't do you much good when working with these real magick Dragons. Keep an open mind while you read and don't cram all this new information into a framework that is already in your mind.

The Watchtowers

There is one Watchtower for each of the four directions. Sometimes the Watchtowers are referred to as the Guardians of the Watchtowers. Various authors have come up with different theories to explain who the Watchtowers are. Some people see them as the stars of heaven. Raven Grimassi, a popular Wiccan author, has described them as ancient people of Earth that the Gods put here to watch over us. In a lot of ways, you can think of the Watchtowers as the bouncers in the bar. They're big. They're tough, and you don't want them to mess with you. If you want the Watchtowers' presence, you stir them. Like the Ancient Ones, the Watchtowers are sleeping. You might want the Watchtowers to be present to watch over you if you were doing a dedication or an initiation ceremony.

Dragons

There are five Dragons—Fire, Air, Earth, Water, and Spirit. The Dragons come from a long line of truly awesome, noble creatures. If you work with them, you need to have a lot of respect for them. They can get angry, and like a force-five tornado, that is a frightening thing. Dragons, like the Ancestors and the Watchtowers, are sleeping. If you need them, you stir them gently.

Entering and Exiting a Magick Circle

We talked about leaving a magick circle in an earlier chapter, but we'll give you a little recap here. If you need to leave, you must cut a door in the energy that makes up the circle. Or have someone else cut a door for you. You can't just walk through the circle without using a door. Doing so would break the circle and allow whatever energy is in the circle to get out. It would also allow any magickal beings in the vicinity to get in. The person who cuts the door in the magick circle must stand guard at the door, and then seal the door when you return. If you are working alone, leave your broom to guard the door, and when you come back, remember to seal the door yourself.

If you are outside a circle that has been cast, you also need someone to cut a door for you so you can enter. But why would you be outside of the circle? Because you were late for ritual! Don't be late. If you are working with a group of people, plan to arrive half an hour before ritual starts. This way you will have time to get changed and settled before ritual starts. It's very rude to be late, especially for ritual. Entering late can spoil everyone's concentration, and that could ruin the whole ritual.

Working Magick Within the Magick Circle

When working magick, stay within the circle you have cast. The circle is there to protect you and your magick. The circle also helps to hold your personal power until you are ready to release it and send it out to do your work. Think of the circle as your magickal office. That's the place you receive and make magickal calls, the place where you aren't subject to a lot of interruptions from friends and family. It is the place for you to focus and do your work.

After the Magick Is Done

After you have completed the magick or celebration segment of your ritual, you start to wind down. You share cakes and wine with the other people in the circle and with deity. There's also time to talk before you say farewell to the God, Goddess, the quarters, and any other powers who

Webweaving

Aleister Crowley, the infamous magickian, is said to have stepped out of his magick circle once while working. The story goes that he had gone out into the desert and summoned a particularly nasty demon. Somehow Crowley ended up outside the circle. His assistant dragged him back in, but the demon had already affected Crowley badly. People say that when he returned from the desert he looked decades older.

have been in attendance, and before you take down the circle. If you are alone it is a time to reflect or communicate with the Goddess. Or you can use this time just to relax in protected space.

Relaxation: Good Communication

After you have completed the magick work in your ritual, you relax and have some cakes (which can be cookies, bread, or muffins) and wine (or juice). But before you partake of your cakes and wine, break off a piece of cake and put it in the libation bowl. Pour a little wine into the libation bowl, too, and set the bowl aside for deity.

While you enjoy your magickal snack, you can talk to your fellows in the circle. This is a great time to share, discuss the issues of the day, plans for the future, and any troubles that people have.

If you practice ritual on your own, you can talk with deity while you have your cakes and wine or take this opportunity to record your ritual in your Book of Shadows. This is also a great time to meditate on an issue that is bothering you. Or communicate with your familiar (an animal, plant, or created being with which you can communicate telepathically), if you have one. If you like, you can just curl up, rest, relax, and recharge after expending all that energy in magick work.

Conversation Within the Circle

When working with other people, you will probably engage in conversation inside the circle about a variety of topics. You might turn to the feelings that ritual left you with; or someone in the circle might give the leaders of ritual a bit of constructive criticism or point out a mistake that someone made during ritual. One thing that you never talk about is what you want to happen as a result of your magick. That is a subject you discuss only with deity. Conversation within the circle can get very personal, and often people will discuss difficulties they are having in their lives. Whatever comes up in circle remains in the circle. You must keep anything you hear in the strictest confidence and never gossip about it. If you gossip, that is a sure way to get thrown out of the circle and excommunicated.

How to Take Down the Circle

First you say farewell to the quarters and thank them for coming. Then say farewell and thank you to the Lord and Lady. Obviously, you speak to the God and Goddess with respect, but remember to maintain that respect for the quarters as well. You'll want to thank each quarter for coming to your circle and for protecting you during ritual. Then say to each quarter, "We bid you hail and farewell." If you think of the quarters as honorable guests who have been visiting in your home, you shouldn't have any trouble giving them the proper respect they deserve.

After you have bid the quarters and the Lord and Lady goodbye, start to take down the circle. With your athame (or whatever you used when you cast the circle) start in the east and walk widdershins (counterclockwise) around the edge of the circle. Imagine the energy of the circle getting sucked into your athame, as if it were a vacuum cleaner. See the energy moving through the athame and travelling up your arm, through your body, then down your legs, out the bottom of your feet, and into the Earth.

So Mote It Be

Visualizing the quarters might help you in talking to them. When you speak to the North, which is associated with Earth, try to see a large majestic mountain. Imagine the East, which is associated with Air, as a silent tornado whirling in place in front of you. Think of the South as Fire in the mouth a volcano, silently burning, but ready as any moment to unleash its power. For West, which is represented by Water, picture an enormous wave constantly folding over itself. If you can see these awesome forces of Nature and talk to them, you won't have any trouble coming up with the right words of respect.

The Circle Is Open, But Never Broken

At the very end of ritual, after you have taken down the circle, you join hands with the others in the circle. The High Priestess or whoever is leading says, "The circle is open, but never broken." This statement signifies that even though you are no longer in circle, you still have that connection to deity and the elements, and as you entered the circle in "perfect love and perfect trust," you sill have that bond with each of the other members in the circle. Then she says, "May all beings and elementals attracted to this ritual be on their way harming none."

The circle members respond by saying, "Merry ye meet, and merry ye part, and merry ye meet again." Then everyone exchanges hugs and kisses, and you wish everyone well until the next time you can be together.

At this point, you should record what you did using a Magickal Record form. (See Appendix B, "Magickal Record.") If you are working with friends, you might want to relax with them some more. You might find that you're very hungry after ritual, so make sure you have some good things to eat in the house. After all, you deserve something yummy after all your hard work. If your friends stick around, you'll probably want to wait till they go home before you complete your records.

After your guests have left, and you've recorded your ritual, put away your tools so nothing happens to them. Take the bowl of salted water from your altar and the libation bowl with cakes and wine in it outside and give the contents of both bowls back to the Earth by emptying them on the ground. Do not pour the water and wine down the drain. These are gifts that you need to give to deity by placing them on the ground for the animals to eat. In this way, we—people, wild things, and even insects—all share in the Earth's abundance. Rinse the bowls out and place them back on your altar.

After ritual, you will probably feel charged and full of zip and energy. You can sit and read until you feel sleepy, or just relax and reflect on what you have done. Eventually you will calm down.

Even if you are a little hyper, you will probably feel great after ritual. You will feel spiritually nourished, and you'll probably sleep wonderfully well. Often people sleep deeply and have prophetic dreams. So, keep your notebook or Book of Shadows handy in case you need to record anything first thing in the morning.

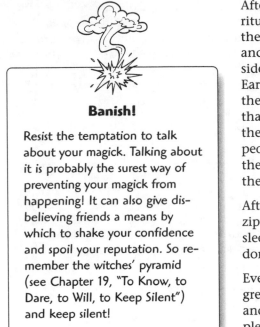

Banish!

Resist the temptation to talk about your magick. Talking about it is probably the surest way of preventing your magick from happening! It can also give disbelieving friends a means by which to shake your confidence and spoil your reputation. So remember the witches' pyramid (see Chapter 19, "To Know, to Dare, to Will, to Keep Silent") and keep silent!

So Mote It Be

You've finished your ritual and you're just too buzzing with energy to sleep. What to do? Don't turn on the TV. Try shaking out some of that energy and putting it back into the Earth. To do this, swing your arms over your head and from side to side. (Make sure you don't hit anything while you are doing this.) When your fingers feel all tingly, bend down and place your hands flat on the floor. Imagine all that energy rushing down your arms and back into the Earth.

The Least You Need to Know

➤ A magick circle is not just a flat, two-dimensional circle. It is a sphere or bubble that completely surrounds and protects you.

➤ Before you put up your circle, you need to cleanse and consecrate the area in which you will be working.

➤ Use your athame and your powers of creative visualization to pull up the circle. If you have trouble visualizing the circle, stick with one method that makes sense to you and keep practicing until it becomes clearer and clearer.

➤ Never, never gossip about something that someone has said in circle. If you do, you will ruin the trust that others have put in you, you'll probably get kicked out of the group, and you may be barred from other groups in your community.

➤ When finishing up your ritual, take the time to be courteous to all the entities that you asked to come. Make sure that you thank the Lord and Lady, the quarters, and anyone else whose help you have drawn on.

➤ During ritual you will feel the connection between you and deity, you and Nature, and between you and the others in the circle. Even after you have taken down the circle, these bonds will not be broken.

Chapter 12

The Witches' Symbol

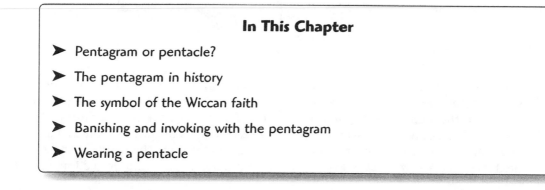

In This Chapter

➤ Pentagram or pentacle?

➤ The pentagram in history

➤ The symbol of the Wiccan faith

➤ Banishing and invoking with the pentagram

➤ Wearing a pentacle

Catholics have crosses, some Jews wear a Star of David, and the Crescent Moon has long represented the Islamic faith. Most religions have a special symbol or device, and Wicca is no exception.

Wicca's symbol is the pentagram. Pentagrams have been around for thousands of years. Despite the misconception held by many people, pentagrams have never been used as a sign of evil. They have always been used as a sign of protection against evil. Given the strong reaction that some people have to pentagrams, you'll want to think seriously about whether you want to wear a visible one as a symbol of your faith or whether you want to keep your faith and its symbol private. The information in this chapter should help you decide when and where the pentagram is right for you.

All About Pentagrams

To some people the very word pentagram conjures up thoughts of evil—satanic rituals, sacrifices, and the injury of small children and animals. The association of pentagrams with devil worship is relatively recent. The pentagram has a long history and once was even used by the Catholic Church. Today it is a symbol of the Wiccan faith.

Pentagrams vs. Pentacles

A pentagram is a five-pointed star. It's a lot like the star that you drew as a kid without picking your pencil up from the paper, but the sides are interwoven. Because the pentagram can be drawn with a single line, it has also been called the Endless Knot. Other names for the pentagram include the Devil's Star, the Witch's Foot, and the Goblin's Cross.

The pentagram: a symbol of the Wiccan faith.

A pentacle is a pentagram with a circle drawn around it. It can be made of wood, stone, metal, or clay. It is a powerful symbol of protection, and there is usually one placed on the altar. Pentacles and pentagrams can be either physical or abstract in Nature. If you draw a pentagram over an object, the object is just as protected as if you placed a tangible pentagram on or alongside that object. The pentacle and the pentagram have always been associated with mystery, magick, and protection against evil.

The pentacle.

How Old Is the Pentagram?

Archeologists have found pentagrams on Mesopotamian potsherds that date back to 3500 B.C.E. Pentagrams also appear in ancient Egyptian, Greek, and Roman art. Pentagrams were even used by Christians in the early Middle Ages.

In the twelfth century, because of the writings of Hildegard of Bingen, a Benedictine nun and abbess, the pentagram became the central symbol of the microcosms, the reflection on Earth of the divine plan and the divine image.

What Does the Pentagram Stand For?

Hildegard of Bingen saw the pentagram as representing the human form because we have five senses—sight, smell, hearing, taste, and touch and five "members"—two legs, two arms, and a head. And, because humankind was made in God's image, she also saw the pentagram as representing God.

Other Christians saw the pentagram as representing the five wounds of Christ. As such, it was considered a potent protection against evil. Earlier Hebrew tradition associated the pentagram with the Pentateuch, the first five books of the Bible. It was also seen, at that time, to represent truth.

In the late Middle Ages, the pentagram was used as a symbol of knightly virtues. In the well-known English poem *Sir Gawaine and the Green Knight,* which dates from the second half of the fourteenth century, the pentagram's points stand for chastity, chivalry, courtesy, generosity, and piety.

During the Inquisition, the pentagram first became associated with evil and the devil in the form of Baphomet. In the popular imagination of the time, the pentagram was thought to represent the head of a goat, the devil, or a witch's foot.

Today, the pentagram and the pentacle are symbols of the Wiccan faith and of neo-paganism. Many witches wear one on a daily basis for protection. Some display their pentacle jewelry to show pride in their religion. Others wear one, but keep it to themselves.

Five Points

The points of the pentagram and pentacle represent *Akasha* or Spirit and the four elements, substances that are crucial to all life. In some pentagrams, each

Webweaving

In 1964, Sybil Leek, who was once considered to be "Britain's Number One Witch," founded the Witchcraft Research Association. The association had its own magazine, which was called *Pentagram*. Unfortunately, both the magazine and the association were short lived. They both folded in 1966.

Book of Shadows

Akasha is a Sanskrit word used to describe the concept of Spirit. Spirit is seen to unify the four elements. It also transcends them. Some see Spirit as the essence or quintessence of a thing. Akasha is often described as space or ether—the background upon which reality is perceived.

point is the color associated with that element's point. Some witches also view the five points as representing the three aspects of the Goddess—Maiden, Mother, and Crone—and the two aspects of the God—dark and light.

Pentagram points repre-sent Akasha, the Spirit, and the elements: Air, Earth, Fire, and Water.

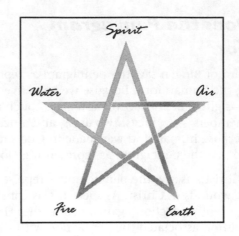

The following list explains what each point represents and lists the most common color associated with it. To find the correct point, face the pentagram as you read this list:

➤ **Fire.** The point on the left that slants down represents the element of Fire. If the pentagram is multicolored, the color of this point is red.

➤ **Water.** The point representing the element of Water is on the top left. The color associated with Water and this point is blue.

➤ **Earth.** The point on the right that slants down represents the element of Earth. Because the color associated with Earth is green this point is green.

➤ **Air.** The point representing the element of Air is on the top right. The color associated with this element is yellow.

➤ **Akasha.** The top point of the pentagram represents Spirit. If the pentagram is multicolored, this point will be white or purple.

Pick Your Pentacle

You can buy pentacles made from a variety of substances for your altar or to wear as jewelry. Sometimes the material from which they are made also has symbolic signifi-cance. Pentacles come in all sizes. Visit your local metaphysical store and see what they have. Here are some types of pentacles you may find:

➤ Silver to represent the Goddess.

➤ Gold to represent the God.

➤ Copper for drawing energy.

➤ Multicolored with each point bearing the color of its element.

➤ Inset with stones at the points. Each stone is the color of that point's element.

➤ Inset with one central stone. For example, amethysts represent healing or Spirit. Onyx is for protection. Hematite is for grounding. Moonstone represents the Goddess. And there are many more.

➤ Crafted with an image or figure of the Goddess in the center. Isis, the Egyptian Mother Goddess, is a popular incarnation.

➤ Crafted with an animal, such as a wolf, in the center.

You can buy pentacle pendants, pins, earrings, and rings. Some are so subtle that other people won't be able to tell what you are wearing. One discrete pentacle comes in the form of the Egyptian Cat Goddess Bastet (or Bast). She has a tiny pentagram drawn on her chest. To the casual observer, it will look like you are just wearing cat jewelry.

Webweaving

Scholars who have studied the development of modern-day Wiccan practices trace the drawing of invoking pentagrams back to Eliphas Zahed Levi, a Frenchman who had trained for a career in the Catholic Church. In 1854, Levi recommended that magickians make invoking pentagrams to call the quarters. Prior to this time, it is believed that magickians used banishing pentagrams to ward off demons, but did not use invoking ones to pull in positive energy.

The Path of the Pentagram

To truly understand the pentagram, many witches will walk the path of the pentagram. To do this you start with a given point on the pentagram—Fire, Water, Earth, or Air. You usually don't start with Spirit as this is the most difficult to truly understand. Decide at what point you are going to start and learn everything about that element, and work with it in ritual and in magick. Meditate with the element that you have chosen. Learn all about its aspects, colors, elementals, and power. This is not something you can do in a week. It can take up to a year to fully understand the element you are working with. When you feel you are ready to move on to a different element, move along the pentagram to the next one. Follow the same agenda with each element until you reach Spirit.

Spirit will be the most difficult. As humans, we will never fully understand the power and unconditional love that Spirit has to offer. Just remember that as long as you continue to work to understand the energy of Spirit then you yourself will continue to grow in a spiritual manner.

Pentagrams in the Air

The pentagram drawn in the air is an important part of consecrating your altar elements and other objects that you want to make holy. You make banishing pentagrams to remove all the negativity from the element. Then you can make an invoking pentagram to bring in positive energy.

For example, when you consecrate the elements on your altar you make a banishing Earth pentagram over the bowl of salt on your altar. You make a banishing Water pentagram over your bowl of water and a banishing Fire pentagram over the candle flames. Then you make a banishing Air pentagram in the incense smoke over your censer. Once you have done that, you have removed all the negative energy from your altar elements. As a final step, you can make an invoking Spirit pentagram so that Spirit infiltrates the elements on your altar.

Banish!

If you attend ritual with other witches and see them make the banishing or invoking pentagrams different from the way you've learned them, don't worry. There is some variation from tradition to tradition in the way that they are drawn. Similarly, if you are practicing ritual on your own and you make a mistake, never fear. If your intention was to make a banishing Earth pentagram but what you drew was closer to a banishing Fire pentagram, you have still made a banishing Earth pentagram. Spirit, unlike a computer, always knows your intentions.

At the beginning of ritual when you call in the quarters, you can make the appropriate invoking pentagram in the air for each quarter. For example, when you call in the East, or Air, make an invoking Air pentagram. When you call in the North, or Earth, make an invoking Earth pentagram. When you bid the quarters farewell, make the banishing pentagram for each one.

You can also use invoking pentagrams to help with your magick. If you are working a love spell, you might want to draw an invoking Fire pentagram to pull in the positive (and passionate!) energies of Fire. In addition, you might want to invoke Water to help promote the positive emotional side of the relationship.

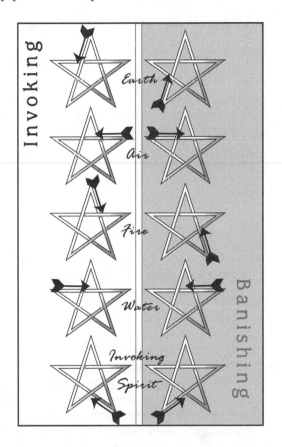

Invoking pentagrams and banishing pentagrams for Akasha, the Spirit, plus each of the Elements.

What About Inverted Pentagrams?

Typically a pentagram has one point at the top and two points at the bottom. The single point on top represents the idea that the Spirit rules over matter. An inverted pentagram has two points on top and one on the bottom. The inverted pentagram suggests that Spirit is subservient to matter. Satanists use the inverted pentagram to express their belief that that their immediate, physical needs are more important than any spiritual or moral value.

In the Gardnerian tradition of witchcraft (discussed in Chapter 3, "Practicing Wicca and Witchcraft Today"), the inverted pentagram has been used as a symbol of Second

Webweaving

In the Gardnerian tradition, a triangle with one point downward symbolizes First Degree Initiation. The inverted pentagram represents Second Degree Initiation, and the upright pentagram stands for Third Degree Initiation. Some Gardnerian witches use an upright pentagram with a small triangle on top of the single upward point, as if the pentagram is wearing a hat, to symbolize Third Degree Initiation.

Banish!

Resist the temptation to wear a pentacle simply to freak out your fundamentalist Christian relatives. Certainly you have the right to wear the symbol of your faith, but you also have to take their fear seriously. People who have been told their whole lives that witches are Devil worshippers and that the pentacle is a sign of evil can have strong, visceral reactions when confronted with this symbol.

Degree initiation. This symbol is used to remind the witch that she will have to learn to face her own internal darkness before attaining Third Degree Initiation. Because of its associations with Satanism, some Gardnerian witches have abandoned the use of the inverted pentagram.

To Wear, or Not to Wear ...

When you do ritual you should wear a pentacle as a sign of your faith and for protection. You don't have to wear one when you are out in the mundane world. But it is nice to have that kind of protection. There are many ways to wear a pentagram or a pentacle without anyone else having to know about it.

Remember the couplet from "The Rede of the Wiccae"?

> When misfortune is enow,
> Wear the blue star on thy brow.

You can visualize the blue star, or a pentagram, on your forehead or draw it with holy water or oil. When doing this, imagine that a white light surrounds you. The pentagram that you visualize will be just as potent a protection as one that you can actually see.

There are many varieties of jewelry that incorporate the five-pointed star. Some of them will not be obvious to the casual observer. Some witches choose to wear small, hidden symbols, while others go for more easily recognizable pentagrams and wear them under their clothing. You can always drop your pentacle pendant down your shirt if you feel uncomfortable with the idea of a certain person seeing it. Still other witches are quite public about their involvement with the craft and openly wear the pentagram and other pagan or Wiccan jewelry. How open you want to be is entirely up to you. Only you can decide how comfortable you will be with the multitude of people in your life. You may decide to wear a pentagram when at home and around the neighborhood, but to take it off when you go into town. Or, if you live in a small community, you might feel it necessary to do the exact opposite. Whatever you decide, know that you have made the right decision.

So Mote It Be

If you're going away on a road trip, bless your car before you leave. Imagine a big penta-gram on the roof of your vehicle. You can encircle your car in white light, too. You still want to drive carefully, but every little bit helps, right? You'll also want to leave a penta-gram to protect your house or apartment while you're gone. Imagine a huge pentagram on the roof. Let it keep your house safe from thieves and fire.

The Least You Need to Know

➤ The pentagram (a five-pointed star) and the pentacle (a pentagram surroun-ded by a circle) are powerful symbols of protection.

➤ The pentagram has become the symbol of witchcraft, Wicca, and neo-paganism. It does not represent evil; in fact, it banishes any and all negative energy.

➤ Draw banishing pentagrams in the air to banish negative energy. There are five types of banishing pentagrams—one for each element represented by the pentagram's points.

➤ Draw invoking pentagrams in the air to invoke positive energy. There are five types of invoking pentagrams as well.

➤ You should wear a pentacle during ritual; wearing one at other times is en-tirely up to you.

Part 4

Working Magick

Get ready to celebrate the Wiccan holidays. In this part, you'll learn about Esbats—the monthly celebration of the Goddess, and about the eight Sabbats—celebrations of the God. You'll also learn more about magick—when to use it, who will help you when you do use it, and how to make it more effective. Did you know that many objects found in nature have magickal properties? Read on.

Chapter 13

Esbats: Moon Magick

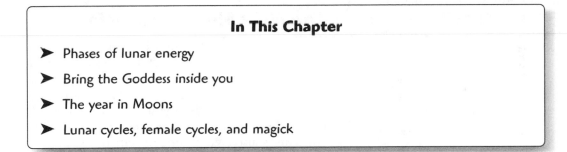

In This Chapter

➤ Phases of lunar energy

➤ Bring the Goddess inside you

➤ The year in Moons

➤ Lunar cycles, female cycles, and magick

Wicca has both religious and magickal elements, and an Esbat is a Moon ritual in which these two aspects are represented. Esbats are times of celebration of the Goddess and her energy; they are also great times for many types of magickal workings.

Many people believe that witches gather on the full Moon. Many witches do prefer to work with the full Moon, but, as a witch, you can work with any phase of the Moon you like. As a solitaire, you can plan your ritual and magick for any day of the month. If you are working with a coven, you will meet with the group at a prearranged time. You can also hold more than one Esbat a month, either on your own or with others.

Esbats: Wicca Celebrates Moon Magick

At least once a month witches honor the Goddess. One of the most traditional ways to do this is by celebrating an *Esbat*. During an Esbat, which is celebrated at night, you pay homage to the Goddess and you draw on her energy to do magick. You can celebrate the different phases of the Moon, depending on what kind of energy you want to draw on. Many witches prefer to honor the Goddess on the full Moon. (Remember the words from the Charge of the Goddess in Chapter 4, "Wiccan Deities: Homage to the Lord and Lady"? "Assemble in a place of secret, better it be when the Moon is full and give praise to the spirit of me.") Some witches will do their magick on the phase of the Moon appropriate for the magickal task at hand, and then formally honor the Goddess when the Moon is full. The full Moon is the time when you can ask for your heart's desire. There are usually 12 and sometimes 13 full Moons every year.

Book of Shadows

An **Esbat** is a Wiccan Moon ritual in which the Goddess is honored. Esbats are also great times to do magick. You can celebrate an Esbat on a full Moon or on any other phase of the Moon, but you should make sure to celebrate one once a month.

Webweaving

Some witches celebrate Diana's Bow—the first sliver of Moon visible in the sky. This usually occurs about three days after the Moon has been dark and is a great time for new projects that would benefit from a gradual increase in energy.

Working with Lunar Energy

The energy of the Moon changes depending upon the phase that the Moon is in. You've probably noticed that the energy of the full Moon is quite strong. On full-Moon nights, police departments and hospitals often have their hands full. In Wicca, each phase of the Moon is noted, because different kinds of Moon energy are used for different kinds of magick.

The New Moon: Initiation

The energy of the new Moon is great for new beginnings, initiating a new project, or the start of an adventure. Say you have just met a new love interest. This would be the time to do some magick to help the relationship to flourish. If you want to change jobs, now is the time to hunt for something new and different. This is also a good time to start trying to get pregnant if that is something you want to do. Under the new Moon, work with the new—the beginning of a new life, new career, new love, maybe even a new you.

The Waxing Moon: Growth Potential

The waxing Moon, when the Moon is growing larger in the sky, is a time of growth. Under this Moon you want to work with building on what you have started under the new Moon—getting money, developing love, or receiving love. If you have become pregnant, this would be the time to work to have the pregnancy develop in a normal and healthy way. You want to work to bring constructive and positive things into your life at this time. For example, you could do magick to bring yourself prosperity or health. The larger the Moon gets, the more powerfully you will feel the Goddess's energy.

The Full Moon: Your Heart's Desire Seek

Remember the ninth couplet from "The Rede of the Wiccae"? (We talked about it in Chapter 5, "So You Want to Be a Witch?") In case you haven't got the Rede memorized yet, here it is:

> When the Moon rides at her peak,
> Then your heart's desire seek.

This is the time to really go for what you want. When the Moon is full, her energy is very powerful and you can ask her to help you accomplish almost anything. The energy of the full Moon is great for magick involving divination, dreams, and love, and whatever else you want. Full Moon energy is available three days before the actual date of the full Moon and three days afterward.

Banish!

If you don't know what you want, resist the temptation to do magick under the full Moon just because it is a good time for magickal workings. You don't have to do magick at every Esbat. You can simply choose to do ritual to honor the Goddess and feel at one with her. And that can be a powerful enough experience on its own.

The Waning Moon: Taking Away

When the Moon is waning, or getting smaller, you want to work with banishing magick. This is the time to get rid of negative things in your life. You might do banishing magick to help take away an addiction, shed some extra weight, get rid of an illness, tumor, or hemorrhoids. You can also work to get rid of negative influences in your environment. You might work to banish stress from your office or banish the tensions that are causing you to have the stress.

So Mote It Be

Do you have a hard time telling if the Moon is waxing or waning? Here's a neat trick that Denise teaches her students. Notice how the Moon in the sky sometimes looks like a backward letter "C"? That's a waxing Moon. If you imagine a straight line dropping down from the top of the backward "C" to the bottom, you get a capital "D." The full Moon, because it is nice and round, looks like an "O," and the waning Moon looks like a "C." So, think of the phases of the Moon as "DOC"—waxing, full, and waning.

The Dark Moon: Take a Break

Many witches believe that you should not practice magick at all during the three days a month when the Moon is dark and is not visible in the sky. This is the time of the month when the Goddess is thought to have descended into the underworld. She is in mourning, and her energy is at its lowest point. During the Dark of the Moon, Hecate, the Goddess in her aspect as queen of the underworld, rules. Some witches have been known to call upon her dark powers to do negative workings at this time. But we think this time is best used to take a break. Meditation and relaxation are the order of the day.

Drawing Down the Moon

Many witches Draw Down the Moon during Esbats. When you Draw Down the Moon during a full-Moon ritual, you pull the energy of the Goddess into yourself. To do this, picture yourself standing in a field. Above you the full Moon is glowing brightly. (Or go out and actually stand in the light of the Full Moon.) Gaze at the Moon and assume the Goddess position—feet apart and planted firmly on the floor, arms raised up until they are over your head, elbows slightly bent. Picture white light streaming from the Moon down through the night sky and into you.

Raising the arms to assume the Goddess position during a full Moon to pull the Goddess energy into your being: Draw Down the Moon.

Everyone's experience of Drawing Down the Moon is somewhat different. But everyone agrees that it is a powerful experience.

The first time Denise Drew Down the Moon she had no idea what it was going to be like. She felt a strong tingling in her hands and feet and around her mouth. The sensation spread up her limbs, as if she had millions of ants crawling on her, and it intensified to the point where she became frightened. She took a little gasp of air, and in an instant the feeling vanished. For six months after that, every time she tried to Draw Down the Moon she was unsuccessful. She figures she just wasn't psychologically ready to feel that kind of intense energy. Now she still feels the Moon energy as an intense ant-like tingling, but she doesn't find it scary any more. Rather she feels intense connection to deity and a great spiritual high.

Other witches, when they have Drawn Down the Moon, feel the Goddess energy differently. Some feel it as an intense heat spreading through their limbs and body. Some get the tingling sensation that Denise experiences with a feeling of a cool breeze blowing over them. Most people get quite emotional, and some cry. Whatever the feelings are that you encounter, stand there with them and let the Goddess fill you up.

After you have Drawn Down the Moon and are filled with the Goddess's energy, you can do magick, or you can just enjoy the deep connection that you will feel with her. Afterward, you will feel cleansed and replenished. You probably won't need to Draw Down the Moon every month. But it's great to do it if you are feeling drained or empty. If you've been doing a lot of magick, helping people and healing them, you'll probably want to Draw Down the Moon to recharge and replenish your energy from the Goddess, the endless source.

In terms of ritual structure, you Draw Down the Moon after you have cleansed and consecrated your space, cast the magick circle, and called the quarters and the God and Goddess.

Webweaving

In addition to Drawing Down the Moon, you can Draw Down the Sun, although you probably wouldn't want to on an Esbat, because the Esbat is the celebration of the Goddess. When you Draw Down the Sun, you are calling the energy of the God into you. To do this, assume the God position. Stand with your feet together and your arms crossed over your chest with your hands up by your collarbones. In the same way that you did with the Moon, imagine the energy of the Sun pouring into you and filling you up.

In a coven, the High Priestess Draws Down the Moon. When she has done that, she is seen to have become the Goddess. (When you do this on your own, you, too, will be the Goddess incarnate.) Some High Priestesses will share the Goddess's energy with the coven members, and others will not. As a solitaire, you get to experience that direct connection with the Goddess that is reserved in many covens for the High Priestess alone. In some traditions, only the High Priestess, as opposed to the High Priest, can Draw Down the Moon. And Drawing Down the Sun is reserved for the

High Priest. As a solitaire, there is no reason that you can't pull down either one. If you are male, you have just as much right to pull down the energy of the Goddess as a woman does. And if you are female, you can pull down the energy of the God as well.

Once in a Blue Moon

You've probably used the expression "once in a Blue Moon," or heard someone else use it. But what does it really mean? A *Blue Moon* is the second full Moon that occurs during one calendar month. Because the Moon's cycle has 29$\frac{1}{2}$ days and some of our months have 31 days, sometimes you will see two full Moons in a month. This doesn't happen very often. In fact, it occurs only about every two and a half years. So, using the expression "once in a Blue Moon" to mean "rarely" makes sense. Interestingly enough, during the year 1999 two Blue Moons appeared in the sky. Perhaps this was nature's way of getting ready for the millennium?

In terms of magick, the Blue Moon is a special magickal Moon. You might want to save any really special magick you are planning and do it on the night of the Blue Moon. Some witches use the Blue Moon as a time to set goals for themselves. In addition, the Blue Moon is used for doing magick for something that you have never done before.

The Blue Moon is also known as the Wine Moon. The name Wine Moon is used because Wine is seen as a luxurious gift from deity. The "extra" Moon in the year is also seen as a luxurious, divine gift. So, you could say that Wine Moon means Luxury or Gift Moon. The Wine Moon is a Moon of love, goodwill, peace, and protection.

Book of Shadows

The **Blue Moon** (or Wine Moon) is a special full Moon that appears in the sky in a calendar month in which there has already been a full Moon. Blue Moons occur in the longer month of our calendar—January, March, May, July, August, October, or December. The Blue Moon isn't exactly rare, but neither is it common. We see Blue Moons every 2.2 years.

Seasonal Moons of the Lunar Calendar

Each full Moon of the month has its own name and its own qualities. Because Wicca draws from a number of folkloric traditions, you will probably see different names assigned to different months. Here we'll use some of the most common terms.

January: Wolf Moon

The Wolf Moon, also known as the Cold, Snow, or Winter Moon, is a time of protection and strength. While it is the first full Moon of the calendar year, in terms of nature it occurs in the middle of the cold winter season, a season of death and desolation. In these respects, the Wolf Moon can be seen as a time of both beginnings and endings. This is the time to start to consider what you want to plant and plan for the spring. You can do magick so that as the spring approaches your magickal goal will grow closer and closer to fruition.

February: Storm Moon

The Storm Moon, also known as the Death or Quickening Moon, is a time to do magick for fertility and strength. For most people in the Northern Hemisphere, February is a time of storms and bleak, short days. In the olden days, it was a time of true hardship.

This is a good time to do magick to help you face life's challenges. You could do a spell to help you with a particularly challenging project at work. Your spell could focus on helping you to accept the challenge, persevere, and make it through. You could concentrate on the idea of weathering the storm and giving yourself the extra stamina to succeed. This is also a time of cleansing both internally and externally. As such, it's a great time to get rid of physical things you don't need and any mental or emotional baggage you might be hauling around with you, too.

March: Chaste Moon

Also known as the Seed or Worm Moon, the Chaste Moon is a time to plant mental seeds—thoughts of success and hope. This is also a time of purity and newness. It's the time to bless the magickal herbs and plants in your garden and to start preparing the soil for the seeds that you will plant. It's also the time to mentally prepare yourself for new experiences, a new job, pregnancy, taking a trip, or bringing a new animal into your home.

April: Seed Moon

The Seed Moon signals a time of fertility, growth, and wisdom. This Moon is also known as the Egg, Grass, or Wind Moon. This is the time to sow the seeds of magick. If you are planting a magickal garden, you want to get out there now and put things into the Earth. This is the time to move from the planning phase into action. If you want to get pregnant, this is a great time to go for it. Fertility is in the air. This is also the time to bring that new puppy home, if that is what you have been planning. It's also a great time to empower some seeds to both help them grow and to do Earth magick. (See Chapter 24, "Easy Spells," for more about Earth magick.)

May: Hare Moon

The Hare Moon, also known as the Flower or Planting Moon, is a time of health, love, romance, and wisdom. This is a great time to plant the seeds that you have empowered. As the seeds begin to grow, the energy you have filled them with will start to manifest in your life. It's also a great time to rekindle the romantic spark and passion in a relationship. If you've been working magick to help your career, now will probably be the time to decide which of your job offers to accept. And you might want to do some divination magick to help you make that decision.

June: Lover's Moon

Also known as the Strawberry or Rose Moon, the Lover's Moon brings with it energy for love, marriage, and success. Is it any wonder that in some traditions this Moon is called the Honey Moon? This is a time to nurture your garden and marvel at its beauty and abundance. If you have taken that new job, now is the time to make sure you have everything running smoothly. And you might want to keep your eyes open to see how you can move into a more desirable position.

Webweaving

August 17 is the Festival of Diana, the Ancient Roman Goddess of fertility, hunting, and the Moon. Some witches celebrate this date with feasting, ritual, and magickal doings.

Book of Shadows

Wyrt is the Old English word for "plant" or "herb." Our word "wort"—as in St. John's wort, the popular mood-enhancing herb—comes from this Old English root. So, a Wyrt Moon is also a Plant or Herb Moon.

July: Mead Moon

The Mead Moon, also known as the Blessing, Lightning, or Thunder Moon, is a time of enchantment, health, rebirth, success, and strength. This is the time of the first harvests, when you begin to enjoy the fruits of your labors. This is also a time of celebration and magick. Remember that mead is the nectar of the Gods. Now is the time to gather your magickal herbs and do some prosperity magick so you get that raise you've worked so hard for.

August: Wyrt Moon

The *Wyrt* Moon, also known as the Wort, Barley, Corn, or Red Moon, is a time of abundance, agriculture, and marriage. This is the time to collect your magickal herbs and store them for the winter or share them with others. Remember to give an offering back to the Goddess for her generosity. At this time of the year, you might want to do magick to help someone else reap the benefits of the Earth's abundance. (With that person's permission, of course!) This is also a good time to make a move at work for that higher level position. If you have become pregnant, this is the time to concentrate your energies on having a healthy pregnancy.

September: Harvest Moon

Also known as the Barley or Hunter's Moon, the Harvest Moon is a time of protection, prosperity, and abundance. This is the time of year when the grains are being harvested, and it is a good time for magick involving your prosperity, abundance, and the nurturing of others. If you have had a long illness, this is the time to finally come back to full health again. This is also the time to obtain that higher paying position at work. The energy of the Harvest Moon will help along any magick that is geared to bring you or someone else abundance.

So Mote It Be

In Chinese culture, the Moon Festival is celebrated on the full Moon in August or September. This day is considered to be the Moon's birthday and is the occasion of feasts and toasts with wine. Many people compose poems to the Moon, and families give other families gifts of decorative Moon cakes. Why not throw a Moon party yourself? Write the Moon a poem, and look for beautifully packaged Moon cakes at Chinese specialty shops. (Vegetarians beware: Moon cakes are often made with lard.) Look for cakes with candied fruit or preserved melon filling—delicious sliced thin and served with tea.

October: Blood Moon

The Blood Moon is sometimes called the Falling Leaf or Hunter's Moon. It is a Moon of new goals, protection, resolution, and spirituality. The night of the Blood Moon is a great time for divination of any kind. At this time of year, all of nature is making ready for the winter. Animals that hibernate are gathering the last scraps of food. Birds are heading south. In human societies, this used to be the time when we turned from agriculture to the hunt as our means of sustenance. This is the time to reflect on what you did during the year and to evaluate your accomplishments.

You also want to check to see how you will survive the coming months. Make sure that you have enough money in the bank. If your work is seasonal, you might want to do some magick to find other ways to support yourself. If you work outdoors, do magick to help you survive the cold months ahead. You also want to check on things that are important to your safety and survival. How are the tires on your car? And what about that smoke alarm in the kitchen? Because the holidays are fast approaching, you also might want to do some work to remove stress and negative energy from your surroundings.

November: Snow Moon

The Snow Moon is also known as the Beaver, Mourning, or Tree Moon. This is a good time to work with abundance, prosperity, and the bonds of family and friendship. This is also an excellent time to use divination to get an idea of what is up ahead. Remind yourself that although winter is coming, it will not last forever. Do what you can to reduce your stress and to strengthen your bonds with family and friends. Back before the advent of grocery stores and central heating, people really counted on those bonds, which could be the difference between making it through the winter or perishing. So, know who is really there for you, and count your blessings.

Webweaving

Feminist witch Zsuzsanna Budapest has written an informative book called *Grandmother Moon: Lunar Magic in Our Lives: Spells, Rituals, Goddesses, Legends, and Emotions Under the Moon* (see Appendix A, "Resources"). She gives suggestions on how to tap into lunar energy to increase the energy, health, harmony, and balance in your life. She even includes 13 lunar Goddess meditations—one for each full Moon.

December: Oak Moon

Also known as the Cold or Long Night Moon, the Oak Moon is a time for hope and healing. This time of year the Moon has reign over the Earth, because there are more hours of night than day. Our thoughts turn to the rebirth of the light and the longer days that are promised after the winter solstice. Women who have become pregnant in the spring are about to give birth and will probably want to focus their energies on delivering a healthy baby. This is the time of year to complete something you have worked hard on and to make sure that the task is truly completed, all the details dealt with. It's also a great time to let go of old patterns or problems and start anew. If something has been eating at you for a long time, work to give it up at this time. Let go of the negative and let the light of longer days shine inside you. Working with children in a nurturing way can be very rewarding and healing.

Blood of the Moon

Many female witches celebrate and welcome the Blood of the Moon—their own bleeding phase in their monthly menstrual cycles. Many female witches feel that their cycles are tuned into the phases of the Moon. Some regard the days that they have their periods as Days of Power, especially if the periods coincide with the full or the new Moon.

Menstruation, Magick, and the Lunar Cycle

Have you ever noticed that a woman's menstrual cycle is about the same length as the Moon's 29$\frac{1}{2}$-day cycle? Many female witches pay close attention to the relationship between their own personal cycles and the phases of the Moon. Some witches have been known to use magick to synch their menstrual cycle to the Moon's cycle so that they will bleed on the full or the new Moon. You can do very powerful magick if you have your period on those nights.

Many witches feel that a woman's intuition is at its peak at the time of menstruation. Others feel that the days leading up to menses, the premenstrual phase, is one of supersensitivity and powerful intuition. They feel they have prophetic dreams and can better channel energy during those few days of the month than at any other time.

The Least You Need to Know

➤ Esbats are celebrations of the Goddess. An Esbat is a great time to do magick or to simply pay homage to the Goddess.

➤ The different phases of the Moon bring different energies. The new Moon is great for starting projects, the waxing Moon for building and growth, the full Moon for your heart's desire, the waning Moon for banishing, and the dark of the Moon for rest and meditation.

➤ When you Draw Down the Moon you take the energy of the Goddess into you, and, whether you are male or female, you become her. You can do magick while you contain this energy, or you can just enjoy your close connection with deity.

➤ The full Moon of each month has its own name, which varies from tradition to tradition, and its own special associations, energies, and qualities.

➤ The days when a female witch has her period can be Days of Power—times of special insight and access to magickal energy.

Chapter 14

Observing the Sabbats

Do you love holidays or loathe them? We think you'll probably like the Wiccan holidays. In this chapter, we'll tell you about eight of them. The good news? They don't involve long exhausting trips to the mall.

Wiccan holidays do involve Nature and the cycles of the Earth in her seasons. Most of the things that you'll need (besides your magickal tools) can be found in your backyard or in a local park. And if you want to exchange any gifts, they, too, can be crafted from Nature's gifts. The Wiccan holidays are truly a time when you tune in to the Earth and the changes she undergoes with the turning of the seasons.

All About the Sun

The Sun represents the God, the male spirit of the All. Like the Sun's, his energy is bright, vibrant, powerful, and protecting. He allows the plants to grow, warms the Earth, and provides the Earth and all her creatures with light and nutrients that are crucial to the flourishing of life.

As we've all noticed, there are many more hours of daylight during the summer than there are in the winter. Summer days are longer because the Earth's axis, the imaginary pole on which the Earth spins, tilts a little in relation to the plane of the Earth's orbit around the Sun. The fact that the Earth is tipped in this manner actually causes the seasons and causes there to be a longest day of the year and a shortest day. Because Wicca is a Nature-based religion, each of these changes, the heralds of the shifts of the season, is honored.

Book of Shadows

Most dictionaries define **Sabbat** as the witches' Sabbath. They usually go on to say that a Sabbat involves demons and orgies. But really a Sabbat is a Wiccan holiday. The word comes from a Hebrew word that means to rest.

What Are the Sabbats?

The *Sabbats* are holidays on which Wiccans celebrate the male energy of the All, which is represented by the God and the Sun. These are days of celebration of the God just the way the Esbats (as discussed in the previous chapter) are celebrations of the Goddess. There are eight Sabbats. Unlike human-made holidays, the Sabbats are naturally occurring events. They mark the equinoxes—the two days a year when daytime and nighttime are of equal duration. The Sabbats also include the longest day of the year, the longest night of the year—known as the solstices—and the midpoints between these occurrences.

As the Lord and Lady Travel the Wheel of the Year

In Wicca, the year is seen as a wheel that keeps turning. Once it has completed a rotation, it keeps going and turns around again and again. The Lord and the Lady, as manifestations of the All, play a major part in this continuous cycle. Many Wiccans look at the year as the continuing and repeating story of the Lord and the Lady.

Although Samhain is the Wiccan New Year, let's start with Yule. Here's a quick tour of the Wheel of the Year:

➤ At **Yule**, which occurs at the time of the winter solstice in December, the Lady gives birth to the Lord and rests from her labor.

➤ At **Imbolc**, in February, the Lord is seen as a small boy, and the Lady recovers from giving birth.

➤ **Ostara** marks the first day of spring and the awakening of the Earth. At this time, the Lord is seen as a growing youth.

➤ At **Beltane**, the Lord has grown to manhood. He falls in love with the Lady, and they unite, producing the bounty of Nature. The Lady becomes pregnant by the Lord.

➤ The **Summer Solstice** is the point in midsummer when everything in Nature is at its peak, growing and lush. The Lord and the Lady are both at the height of their powers.

➤ **Lughnassad** is the day in August of the first harvest. The first grains are cut, and the Lord begins to weaken.

➤ At **Mabon,** the second harvest, the Lord is coming to his end. The days grow shorter, and Earth readies for the slumber of winter.

➤ At **Samhain,** in October, the Lord dies only to be reborn of the Lady again at Yule.

When the Lord is born at Yule, he is the incarnation of the God of Light. From Yule onward, the daylight hours will be longer and longer until the Summer Solstice, when the balance tips the other way. After the Summer Solstice, as the days begin to grow shorter, he becomes the Dark God. At that point, the shortening of the days herald his coming death.

Quartering the Year: Greater and Lesser Sabbats

The Lesser or Minor Sabbats, which sometimes are also called Fire Festivals, occur at the quarters of the year. They include the vernal or spring equinox, the fall or autumn equinox, and the summer and the winter solstices.

The Greater or Major Sabbats—Samhain, Beltane, Imbolc, and Lughnassad—occur at the cross quarters, the midpoints between solstice and equinox. They mark the turning of the seasons and are considered to be very powerful days in and of themselves. Midpoints are considered to be times of great power because most things in Nature reach the peak of their strength when they are in the middle of their lives.

Here some dates you can put in your planner.

Sabbats: Quick Reference Guide

Date	Cycle of the Year	Holiday Name
October 31	Cross quarter	Samhain
December 21 (give or take a few days)	Quarter	Yule
February 2	Cross quarter	Imbolc
March 21 (give or take a few days)	Quarter	Ostara
April 30	Cross quarter	Beltane
June 21 (give or take a few days)	Quarter	Summer Solstice
August 2	Cross quarter	Lughnassad
September 21 (give or take a few days)	Quarter	Mabon

Because the summer and winter solstice and the autumn and spring equinoxes are actual astrological events and because the calendar that we follow was made up to approximate natural events in a standardized way, the dates of these events vary from year to year. To find the actual date of the solstices or the equinoxes for a given year, consult a witch's calendar or an almanac.

The Wheel of the Year.

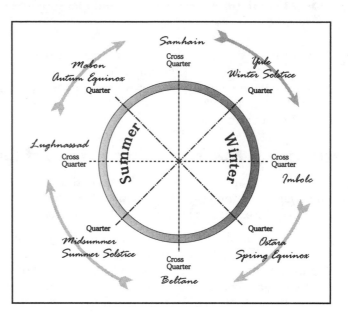

Natural vs. Human-Made Holidays

The Sabbats mark actual events in Nature, and people have marked these events of Nature since megalithic times. The boulders of Stonehenge form alignments with both the spring and autumn equinoxes and the winter and summer solstices. Such indicators of Nature also exist from ancient cultures in China, Egypt, and Peru.

Webweaving

In 1644, the English Parliament passed an act that forbade the celebration of Christmas. Apparently the Puritans in power did not like the popular character of the revels, which involved eating, drinking, and general merry-making.

Human-made holidays are celebrations that occur on certain dates because people decided to celebrate on that day, such as the Fourth of July, Labor Day, and Thanksgiving. There are no naturally occurring events underneath all the trappings of these festivities. The celebrations that people decide to engage in on such dates are the events themselves. Actually, Christmas is a human-made holiday, too. Many people believe that Christ was actually born in the spring. Church authorities decided to celebrate his birth in the winter because they could not stop the pagans from celebrating Yule. And those Pagans knew how to party!

Celebrating the Sabbats helps to keep you in tune with Nature and the cycles of the Earth's seasons. Living in cities, as many of us do, often leaves people feeling cut off from the cyclical Nature of life. Observing the Sabbats can aid you in realigning your rhythms and energies with the natural forces of the Earth.

Celebrate!

The Sabbats are holidays to celebrate deity. These holidays are not all about shopping and buying and other people's expectations. They are times for you to enjoy—with friends and family, if you like—but definitely with the Gods.

Light the Balefire: When to Celebrate

Some of the Sabbats are best celebrated at night and some are best enjoyed during the day. In olden times, many of these holidays were commemorated with *balefires,* which are very exciting, especially at night. Samhain, the Witches' New Year, the night when the Lord dies, is typically celebrated at night. Yule and the other cool-weather holidays also usually are celebrated in the evening.

The spring and summer Sabbats are often celebrated during the day and outdoors. This way you
can enjoy the Sun and all of Nature while you celebrate the holiday. And there are practical consid-
erations, as well—it's hard to put up a Maypole in
your living room!

Some witches try to celebrate each Sabbat on the
actual day of the Sabbat. At times, this can be difficult because these holidays can fall on workdays.
In case a Sabbat does fall in the middle of the
week, you can celebrate on the Saturday or Sunday
before or after the actual date. Even if you celebrate on a different date, you can still give reverence and recognize the holiday on the day or
night of the Sabbat. Because the Sabbats are naturally occurring events, they will happen with you
or without you.

Book of Shadows

A **balefire** is a bonfire or a smaller fire that is lit for magickal purposes. Some witches say that the balefire is traditional at Yule, Beltane, and Midsummer. Others list Beltane, Summer Solstice, Lughnassad, and Mabon. And, of course, the yule log is tradition-ally burnt at Yule.

As a Solitaire, or in a Group

You may want to celebrate the Sabbats one-on-one with the Lord and the Lady. You could write your own ritual and have a private experience, or you could ask a friend or two to come celebrate with you. It's your choice. Sabbats are just as meaningful celebrated quietly alone with deity as they are in a large, noisy group.

In a coven, the High Priest and High Priestess either select a ritual they have written or use one from a Book of Shadows that has been handed down from earlier generations. Sometimes the coven will put on a Sabbat play that explains the story behind the holiday that they are celebrating. Each coven member takes a part, so everyone is involved. Or the coven may practice a regular ritual and place on the altar symbols appropriate to the given Sabbat.

What's in a Wiccan Sabbat Ritual?

Often a Sabbat ritual is just like a regular Wiccan ritual. But during a Sabbat the altar might be decorated for the particular occasion. For instance, on Ostara you might put eggs on the altar, on Samhain you'd place pictures of those who have passed over on the altar, while at Imbolc you might pass out seeds to all the celebrants. And for Yule, people often light a lot of candles to symbolize the return of light and the Sun to the world.

Because Sabbats are usually occasions to honor the God, there is an emphasis placed on him and on his life cycle. Sometimes Sabbat rituals are built around him and his station in life as he grows from infant at Yule, to boy, to youth, to manhood, and then as he begins his decline as the days grow shorter.

So Mote It Be

Giving yourself a goal is a great way to celebrate the Sabbats. One way to do this is to relate the Lord's growth to your own. At Imbolc, set your mind on an idea or goal. Think about how to implement your idea. At Ostara, start to implement the idea. At Beltane, act on it, and your plans will start to manifest. You'll see some initial results. In June, at the Summer Solstice, your idea, like the Lord, will be at its peak, and when fall approaches it will come to fruition. At the end of the year, review your progress. If you have not achieved your goal, keep at it for another spin of the wheel.

The Wheel of the Year

The Wheel of the Year is the cycle of the seasons that turns from birth to death to rebirth again. This has been the way of the Earth through the seasons forever and ever. A plant grows, dies, and leaves behind its seeds that in turn give life again. In Wicca, people look at their own lives in the same way. Each time you are incarnated you have a lesson to learn. You live with that issue of spiritual growth, and you learn. After you die, you come back again, and you learn more until your spirit has reached enlightenment and becomes one with the All.

Samhain (October 31): Halloween, the Witches' New Year

Samhain (pronounced *SOW-wen* or *sah-VEEN*), one of the Greater Sabbats, is probably the witch's biggest holiday. And it is certainly the one that the public always associates with witches! For witches, this holiday has a rather different tone than it does for the population at large. Samhain, rather than being a festival of sugar overconsumption, is a profound and spiritually moving event. It marks the death of the Lord and also the start of a new year.

On Samhain witches hold celebrations to honor the dead. Some witches have a silent supper during which they relive a moment of life with a friend or loved one who has passed on during the year. If you were to celebrate at such a supper, with each bite you chew, you would think fondly of an incident that involved that person. When you swallow, you would let go of that memory and chose a new one for your next bite. Usually you would reflect on the life of someone, including a pet or animal, who has

died within the year. If you have not lost anyone during the year, you can give support to people who have. Or you can give reverence to all the people who have died that year and reflect on how their lives touched the lives of others. You can also think on your own life and on ways that you can grow to be a better person. Some witches eat a regular meal on Samhain, but set a place and leave food out for loved ones who have died.

Webweaving

Janet and Stewart Farrar, probably one of the best-known writing couples in the craft, wrote a whole book about the Wiccan holidays. The book is called *Eight Sabbats for Witches*. Now you can get it, together with another one of their books, in a large volume called *A Witches' Bible* (Phoenix Publishing, Inc., 1996).

On October 31, the veil between the living and the dead is said to be at its thinnest. This makes it a great night for communicating with the dead and the best night of the year for divination and scrying. The closer you get to midnight on that night, the thinner the veil becomes. Like most people, witches celebrate this holiday at night. It just seems fitting to commemorate a holiday about the dead when it is dark. Although the witches' New Year is a sedate holiday, witches also attend Halloween parties, but not on the night of October 31. That night is reserved for more solemn pursuits.

Yule (December 21): Winter Solstice

Many of the traditions that people observe at Christmas have their roots in *Yule* and other pre-Christian seasonal celebrations. The ancient Romans decorated their homes

Book of Shadows

In common usage the English word **yule** has come to mean "Christmas" or "the season of Christmas." The word comes from an Old English word that referred to a 12-day pagan feast. As we said before, those pagans knew how to celebrate!

with the boughs of green trees. The Druids also honored trees and collected and hung mistletoe. So, if you celebrated Christmas in the past, you can probably hang on to some of your traditions.

Yule (pronounced *YOOL*) marks the winter solstice, the longest night of the year. It is also seen as the time when the God is reborn and light begins to return to the Earth. Wiccans celebrate by exchanging gifts and by burning a yule log. The exchange of gifts symbolizes hope for the future and the gift that the Lady has bestowed upon the Earth by giving birth to the Lord who is also the Sun.

The yule log is burned in the evening in a fireplace or a cauldron. It symbolizes the Lord reborn and the return of the Sun. Every year, some of the log is saved and is used the following year to light that year's yule log. In this way, the fire of the yule log is symbolically reborn as well.

Imbolc/Candlemas (February 2): Rebirth of the Sun

Imbolc (*IM-bolk*), which is often called Candlemas, is the time when Wiccans celebrate the renewing fertility of the Earth. The Goddess is seen as recovering from childbirth, and the God is a small child. This is also the time of "fire in the belly." There is the feeling that spring is coming, but a certain restlessness or cabin fever can set in. This can also be the bleakest time of the year when we start to fear that spring will never arrive. It's no coincidence that many people celebrate Ground Hog's Day on this date. What is Ground Hog's Day but a way to let Nature reassure us that spring really will come? Sometimes, even though it is still cold, you can see early buds on trees on this date. This is another way that Nature reminds us to hang on; life is getting ready to burst forth.

Imbolc is a time to celebrate with seeds, with a newly germinating idea. Some covens like to initiate new members at this time of year. Imbolc is a holiday of purification and of the renewed fertility of the Earth. It's a great time for some early spring cleaning, too. Get rid of things you don't need. Get ready for the spring season to come.

Ostara (March 21): The Spring Equinox

Many of the symbols of Ostara (*oh-STAR-ah*) are also common to Easter. Eggs have been a symbol of renewed life and fertility since the time of the ancient Egyptians and Persians. In fact, in both cultures people dyed eggs and ate them in honor of the returning spring. The Egyptians also saw hares, or rabbits, which were associated with the Moon, as symbols of fertility and rebirth.

In the Wiccan tradition, the Lord and Lady are seen as young and innocent at this time of the year. The day and night are of equal duration at the spring or vernal equinox. In the days that follow, the hours of light grow longer, spring blooms in the air, and the Lord and Lady, as do all the creatures of Nature, begin to wonder about one another.

A Wiccan celebration of Ostara might include boiled and decorated eggs. Some Wiccans even do egg hunts and eat chocolate bunnies. If you can celebrate at the exact moment of the vernal equinox, you can even balance a raw egg on one end because of the change in the Earth's tilt. In ritual, witches might bless seeds for future planting. This is also a good time of year to buy a new ritual broom for sweeping out negative energies.

Beltane (April 30): Handfasting of the Lord and Lady

At Beltane (*BEL-tayne*), one of the Greater Sabbats, the Lord has reached manhood, and he and the Lady unite in a *handfasting*. In this act they help the Earth to burst forth with life and new growth. To celebrate Beltane, which sometimes is called Cetsamhain or Walpurgisnacht, Wiccans dance around the Maypole, which is a phallic symbol that represents the Lord. Some Wiccan focus on the cauldron, the symbol of the Lady who becomes pregnant at Beltane. Celebrants wear flowers in their hair or wreaths of green foliage. This is also a great day for spring-cleaning and to bring flowers into the house so everything feels bright and new and fresh.

Summer Solstice (June 21): A Midsummer Dream

The Summer Solstice (also known as Litha, pronounced *LEE-tha*) marks the longest day of the year. The Lord and the Lady are at their peak, and all is green and growing. Wiccans give reverence at this time of the year, but don't usually hold large celebrations. In the past, this Sabbat was celebrated with large bonfires that were burned to promote purification, fertility, and love. People were even said to jump over the fires to encourage these

qualities in themselves. The fire, of course, also represents the Sun at the height of his powers. (Today, though, setting bonfires can be against the law, and is certainly a potentially dangerous fire hazard—both to property, and to human life.)

While this can be a joyous holiday, celebrating the triumph of the Sun, it is also tinged with sadness because, after the longest day of the year, the days will continue to grow shorter and shorter. Midsummer Night's Eve has traditionally been a great day to perform love and healing magick. It's also a good time to communicate with fairies and forest sprites.

Lughnassad (August 2): The Early Harvest

Lughnassad (*LOO-nus-uh*), also called Lammas, is one of the Greater Sabbats and marks the beginning of the fall harvest, the day on which the first grain is cut. As fall approaches and the hours of sunlight begin to shrink, the God also starts to lose his strength. But the Goddess is already pregnant with the God, who will be reborn again at Yule.

Lughnassad is also referred to as the Feast of Bread, because it is traditional to bake on this day. The name Lammas, by which this holiday is also known, comes from an old English festival, the loaf mass, which was held on this date. Wiccans often hold feasts in honor of the holiday because everything is so plentiful at this time of the year. You can decorate your house for the holiday with a wreath and place fruits and vegetables on your altar while you do ritual.

Mabon (September 21): Harvest Festival

Mabon (*MAY-bon*), one of the Lesser Sabbats, is the second harvest festival and is held on the autumn equinox to celebrate the last fruits of the year. Some people call this holiday Harvest Home. Night and day are of equal duration on this date, and you can feel the approach of winter and darkness. The Lord is preparing for his death at Samhain, and the Lady is beginning to mourn his loss.

Rituals to honor this Sabbat might include late-season vegetables such as squash, nuts, and sheaves of late wheat and corn. A cornucopia, a symbol of prosperity and plenty, is a nice addition to your altar at this time of the year. Some witches like to hold feasts or do food magick on this holiday.

Banish!

Avoid using the Sabbats as occasions to be hard on yourself. (Don't we have enough of those?) You don't have to celebrate each Sabbat perfectly. It's nice to have all the right symbols and decorations on your altar, but if you can't come up with a cornucopia, which can be found at craft stores, the Lord and Lady will understand. What's really important in celebrating the Sabbat is that you are really there with the Lord and Lady. And if you're worrying about your decor, then clearly your mind is elsewhere.

The Least You Need to Know

➤ Wiccans celebrate eight Sabbats.

➤ The Sabbats occur at the time of natural events associated with the change of the seasons.

➤ Celebrating the Sabbats helps keep you in tune with the natural energies of the Earth and her seasons.

➤ While both the Lord and Lady can be honored at these holidays, the Sabbats follow the life cycle of the Lord.

➤ Celebrating alone with the Lord and the Lady, with a small group of friends, or with a coven can all be profound experiences. And the Sabbats can be fun, too.

Chapter 15

Summon, Stir, or Call

In This Chapter

➤ How to ask various entities to ritual

➤ Bringing in the big guns

➤ From the Realm of Fairy

➤ From the Realm of Spirit

We've talked about the various pantheons of Gods and Goddesses that you can work with in the Wiccan religion. You can also work with a number of other entities. Some of them you've probably heard of. Others will be less familiar, and still others you will be meeting for the first time.

When you work with these entities and with deity, it's important to show the proper respect. Treat them as honored guests in your home. These beings are very old and very wise, although their intelligence is quite different from human intelligence. So, don't expect them to act the way a person does. You must be very specific and clear about what you respectfully ask them to do.

Summon, Stir, Call, Request, or Invite— Which Is Right?

In Chapter 7, "Observing Ritual the Wiccan Way," we discussed ritual etiquette—how to behave toward fellow celebrants during an actual ritual. You also want to give the proper respect to the entities from other realms that you invite to your ritual. One way to show that respect is in how you ask them to ritual.

You can *summon* certain entities—the four elements, fairies, and the Elementals, for example. Other larger, more powerful entities are stirred. You *stir* them because they are sleeping and need to be awakened before they can attend your ritual. If you want the God and Goddess to attend your ritual, you *call* them respectfully, and they will come. When you *invite* entities to your ritual, you ask them to be present, but not to join you inside the circle. You can *request* the presence of any of the four winds and of your spirit guides. You also need to tell the entities you have asked to ritual what you want them to do. You can ask them to protect you, observe, or help you to carry out your magick.

Book of Shadows

Summon, stir, call, invite, and **request** all mean close to the same thing, but these terms are not all the same in magick. You summon the entities that are close by and all around you, such as the elements and the elementals. Stirring implies a higher level of respect and is used for larger, more powerful beings—the ancestors, dragons, and Watchtowers. You call to angels and to the Lord and Lady. You invite your familiar to join you in ritual (although you probably won't need to ask). Finally, you request the presence of the winds and of your spirit guides.

Here's an invocation named "Summon, Stir, and Call" that Denise uses when she calls in the quarters in ritual:

> I call to the Lord and Lady fair
> I summon to us the Element of Air
> I stir the Ancients with knowledge of old
> Be here this night our spirits you hold.

> Lord and Lady protect us, keep us from harm
> Air empower us with communication and charm
> Ancient Ones give us knowledge that lasts
> Provide us this in the circle that's cast.

> I call the Lord and Lady to hear your sons and daughters
> I summon to me the Element of Water
> I stir the Ancients with truth from the past
> Be here this night, be here at last.

Lord and Lady protect us, keep us close to your side
Water empower us with emotions of pride
Ancient Ones give us patience that lasts
Be here this night in the circle that's cast.

I call the Lord and Lady who gave us birth
I summon to me the Element of Earth
I stir the Ancients to be here this night
To travel upon their spiritual light.

Lord and Lady protect us, surround us with love
Earth empower us as below so above
Ancient Ones give us wisdom that lasts
Provide us this in the circle that's cast.

I call the Lord and Lady with loving desire
I summon to me the Element of Fire
I stir the Ancients, the old ones, the wise
To comfort our fears, our yearning, our cries.

Lord and Lady protect us with your strength of healing
Fire empower us with passionate feeling
Ancient Ones give us understandings that last
Provide us this in the circle that's cast.

Notice that this invocation calls the Lord and Lady, summons the Elements, and stirs the Ancients, or Ancestors. In addition, the invocation spells out what each entity should do.

The Elements: Fire, Water, Earth, and Air

Names: Fire, Water, Earth, and Air

Where from: Elemental Realm

How to invite them to ritual: Summon

You can summon the elements to attend your ritual. Many witches call them in when they call in the quarters. Ask the elements to stand outside your magick circle and guard it, or just have them witness your ritual and any magick that you do. Depending on the magick that you are doing you might want to call upon one particular element. For example, if you were working with issues of love and sex or transformation you might want to summon Fire to your ritual and draw on that intense Fire energy. Alternatively, if you were working with issues having to do with the emotions and adaptability, you'd want to draw on Water. You'd contact Earth energies for stability, growth, or giving birth, and you'd want to use Air for any magick dealing with communication or ideas.

Dragons

Types: Fire Dragon, Water Dragon, Earth Dragon, Air Dragon, and Spirit Dragon

Where from: Elemental Realm

How to invite them to ritual: Stir gently. You never want to make a dragon angry.

There is some disagreement among witches about the nature and characteristics of dragons. Some see them as noble beasts. Other witches, Denise included, see them as the awesome powers of the elements. The Earth Dragon possesses all the strength of the Earth itself. If it is provoked to anger, it will cause earthquakes and geological plate shifts. The Water Dragon wields all the power of the ocean—a tidal wave that could sweep away a city in an instant. The Dragon of the Air commands forces equal to the jet stream and those of a devastating tornado, while the Fire Dragon represents lava and the molten core of the Earth. The Spirit Dragon is the essence of the God and Goddess, the spirituality of everything on Earth.

For special occasions such as a Wiccaning, a handfasting, or an initiation, you would stir the dragons. You also might invite them to attend ritual if your group, community, or coven were facing a major issue that affected everyone. You probably should invite the dragons only under unusual circumstances. They are very powerful and are not for everyday situations. Whatever you do, treat them with tremendous respect.

The Guardians of the Watchtower

Names: Guardian of the Watchtower of Fire, Guardian of the Watchtower of Water, Guardian of the Watchtower of Earth, Guardian of the Watchtower of Air

Where from: Elemental Realm

How to invite to ritual: Stir gently

The Guardians of the Watchtowers are the guardians of the Elemental forces of each direction. Because they guard entities of such enormous force, they themselves possess tremendous power. Some witches are afraid of them and won't use them in ritual. They are to be invited only when what you are doing is important. You can have them observe, guard, or protect you during ritual.

If you were doing an initiation, you might ask them to watch and protect you. Inviting the Watchtowers to an initiation ceremony is a distinct advantage for the initiate. If they have been to your initiation, then they'll know your name, protect and watch over you, and be aware of who you are if you ever need them to guard your circle again. You also might invite the Watchtowers to a Wiccaning or handfasting or if strife or some major conflict is occurring in your community. You could also ask them to deliver your magick in cases of life or death, if someone were very ill and you needed your healing magick taken to that person. The Watchtowers should be stirred only for important workings. And remember, if you invite them, you must create your magick circle inside of a square so that the Watchtowers have corners to sit on. You'll find a Watchtower call that you can use in Chapter 24, "Easy Spells."

Winds

Names: South Wind, Wind of the South, or Notus; West Wind, Wind of the West, or Zephyrus; North Wind, Wind of the North, or Boreas; East Wind, Wind of the East or Eurus

Where from: Elemental Realm

How to invite them to ritual: Request their presence politely

The winds are great for taking your magick and delivering it quickly and forcefully. When you ask the winds to carry your magick for you, you are doing Air magick. Keep in mind that each wind has its own elemental correspondence. The South Wind is associated with the element of Fire. So, if you were sending out a love spell, the South Wind would be a good choice for its delivery. You would call upon the North Wind for its Earthy aspects, upon the West Wind for its Watery qualities, and upon the East Wind for its Air associations.

The winds are mighty forces. They will help you communicate by taking your energy where it needs to go. You can also use the Winds in weather magick. You might ask the South Wind to blow up some warm weather from the South or to blow a storm away from your house. If weather magick is something that interests you, look for the weather spell in Chapter 22, "More Ways to Work Magick."

A Little Help from Your Friends

You can have friends in the Realm of Fairy, but you need to be careful with them. Be really sure that you want them in your life before you ask them to help you.

Fairies

Names: Flower fairies, mermaids, mermen, little people, sprites, and pixies

Where from: Realm of Fairy

How to invite them to ritual: Summon

You're probably familiar with the concept of fairies. You may think of them as cute little creatures. Well, they are little—much smaller than you are, in fact. Fairies can take lots of different shapes and forms. They can appear as miniature humans or they take the form of an elf because that is how people expect them to look. They can change their shapes to match their environment.

Webweaving

Fairies do not like to be constantly thanked. They expect payment for their services. If they have helped you, leave a bowl of sweetened milk out for them or give them silver coins and shiny trinkets and save your pretty words.

You can summon fairies to ritual, but as a novice it's not a good idea to invite them into your magick circle. If you do, they might cause some mischief with the energy you have raised. The best times to contact fairies are at dawn, dusk, noon, and midnight and on the equinoxes and solstices. You'll know that the fairies have arrived when the flames of your candles start to dance all around. Sometimes you can even feel a crawling sensation on your skin as if bugs were walking on you.

Fairies are skilled in the healing arts, metalworking, and all artistic pursuits. They will enhance your magick and help you make it happen quickly. They may inspire you or literally guide your hand. You can also work with fairies to control the weather and instill sleep or altered states of consciousness.

So Mote It Be

If you have an infestation of fairies, you can get rid of them. Fairies dislike the metal iron. To discourage fairies from taking up permanent residence in your abode, hang iron pots around your house. You can even paint one and hang it as a "decoration" on your front door. According to some people, iron makes fairies incapable of magick. So, because fairies don't want to be powerless, they will go away and leave you in peace. Now, are you sure that it was fairies that kept losing those house keys?

If you have called fairies into your home, they will guard the house and make sure that nothing goes wrong. Be forewarned, however. They are extremely mischievous. They might wake you up in the middle of the night to let you know that the coffee-pot is still on, but they will borrow your earrings. Or hide your keys just as you are about to leave the house. The other down side to fairies is, once you have invited them in, they're really hard to get rid of. So, make sure you really want their help before you ask for them. They may stick around and mess with your stuff for a long time.

The Elementals

Names: Salamanders, undines, gnomes, and sylphs

Where from: Realm of Fairy

How to invite them to ritual: Summon

You can summon the Elementals to your ritual, but you don't want to invite them into your magick circle. You can have them guard your circle, observe, or carry your magick to the place it needs to go. Some people believe that we each have a salamander, undine, gnome, and sylph assigned to watch over us from birth. Elementals have a very basic mentality and are not compassionate little creatures. Just like fairies, they don't like to be thanked a lot and will get irritated if you do so. Instead of thanks, you should leave them gifts of milk, honey, coins, or small shiny objects.

Salamanders inhabit any place where there is Fire—from the molten core of the Earth, to a candle, to the Sun. They also are associated with our fiery aspects. They are great to summon if you need to work with issues of sexuality or love and will help you build up your passion, vitality, enthusiasm, and spirituality. Their king is named Djinn, and they influence our emotions, metabolism, and sense of idealism. Their energy is one of transformation; they destroy and then rebuild. They also can help to heal and detoxify the body. Salamanders, because of their great energy, can be difficult to control.

Undines exist in any place where there is Water—from the depths of the oceans, to rivers, to drops of rain. They are also associated with our watery, or emotional, aspects. You might want to call them if you were dealing with healing, purification, creativity, or emotional issues. They usually take a female form, and their Queen is called Niksa. They influence our dreams, creative expression, and artistic performance. They can help to awaken our empathy, imagination, and intuition. They also help to regulate the water balance in the body.

Gnomes are of the Earth. They maintain geological structures and are associated with our Earthy

Book of Shadows

Salamanders are the Elementals of Fire, while **undines** are the Elementals of Water. **Gnomes** are the Elementals of Earth, and **sylphs** are the Elementals of Air.

nature—sensations and fertility. You might call Gnomes to help you work with issues involving growth, nurturing, abundance, fertility, or prosperity. Gnomes and their kind, who is called Ghob, guard the treasures of the Earth and can help you to find such treasures. They give each rock and crystal its own unique energy and are skilled craftspeople. They can lend us endurance and persistence.

Sylphs are a force of Air, from gentle breezes, to gusts of wind, to tornadoes, and in fact, they help to make Air. They are also associated with our thoughts and mental development, and they help us to breathe and metabolize air properly. The King of the sylphs is called Paralda. You might want to summon him, or his subjects, to help give you inspiration, heighten your intuition, or digest a lot of information. Sylphs can spur and activate your imagination and can also carry a message from you to another person's sylph.

Tree Spirits

Names: Tree spirits

Where from: Realm of Fairy

How to invite them to ritual: Summon

Each tree spirit has its own personality, depending on the kind of tree. You might want to work with the spirit of a willow tree to learn to become more bending, forgiving, and adaptable. You'd go to an oak for strength, wisdom, and steadfastness. And a redwood could help you with longevity, wisdom, and issues of aging.

In the Company of ...

The Lord and the Lady are all around us all the time. So, too, are all the many varieties of angel. The ancestors ... well, they dwell in the Realm of Spirit too, but they are sleeping.

Deities

Names: The Lord and Lady, the God and Goddess, the All, and many others

Where from: Realm of Spirit

How to invite them to ritual: Call

As we discussed in Chapter 4, "Wiccan Deities: Homage to the Lord and Lady," there are many, many different names and aspects of the All. You can think of the All as the Lord and Lady, the God and Goddess, Apollo and Venus, or Shiva and Kali. You'll want to be quite familiar with a given aspect of deity before you invite it to your ritual. You can call the Lord and Lady to ritual to protect, guide, or support you. They will help you carry out your magick, if it is positive. They will also heal, nurture, and love you.

Angels

Names: Many and various (see the following list)

Where from: Realm of Spirit

How to invite them to ritual: Call

There are three different levels of angels:

➤ **Level 1.** Seraphim—angels of pure love and thought; cherubim—spirits of harmony and the wisdom of the All; thrones—spirits of will and justice

➤ **Level 2.** Dominions—angels of wisdom and intuition; virtues—angels of choice and movement; powers—angels of form and space

➤ **Level 3.** Principalities—angels of personality and time; archangels—Michael, Gabriel, Uriel, and Raphael; angel messengers; guardian angels

Webweaving

Silver RavenWolf has written a whole book about angels and magick from a witch's perspective. If this is a topic that interests you, check it out. It is called *Angels: Companions in Magick* (Llewellyn Publications, 1996).

You probably don't want to deal directly with the highest level of angels. They are very intense and can be rather frightening. The guardian angels and the archangels are more accessible. However, you might want to call upon some of the higher-ranking angels if your community is experiencing strife.

So Mote It Be

Many people believe that we each have a guardian angel (or several of them) assigned to us at birth. Your guardian angel watches out for and gives you hints and clues that can help you improve your life. You can get to know your guardian angel better thorough meditation. Sit quietly for a few minutes with your eyes closed, then ask your guardian angel to come to you. Stay very still and listen to the sound of your own breathing. You'll probably have to try this a few times before you get a sense of your angel's presence.

You can ask angels to help or enhance your magick or to carry it up to deity. They can also help to have your magick manifest. They are great to work with on spiritual issues and health matters. They can help to heal you from physical and psychological pain. You might call them if you've been hurt in a love relationship or if your child has died. They will also protect you any time you need them. But don't call on angels for day-to-day matters such as money issues or doing magick to get a job. Angels like to deal more with the spiritual plane.

Ancestors

Names: Various

Where from: Realm of Spirit

How to invite them to ritual: Stir

The ancestors are figures from the past who held great wisdom and knowledge. You don't have to be related to such a person to consider him or her an ancestor. Many witches consider historical figures who were well versed in the magickal arts—Merlin, Aradia, some of the ancient kings of Egypt, Socrates, or Pythagoras, for example—to be ancestors. If your own relatives were particularly wise, you could look to them as your magickal ancestors. You might want to do some research into your own ancestry. Who knows, you could be related to a famous witch! If you have a deceased grandmother or other relative who has passed on who possessed unusual knowledge, insight, and the wisdom of an old reincarnated soul, and whose decisions you respected, you could consider her an ancestor. But remember, just because someone is dead does not automatically make that person wise. You can stir the ancestors and ask them to attend your ritual to aid your creativity and wisdom. They will give you good guidance and help you make decisions.

Tapping into the Power of ...

We are still in the Realm of the Spirit. Now you are going to meet some more allies who can help you—spirit guides, spirit animals, and familiars. Does any of this sound familiar to you?

Spirit Guides

Names: Varies from individual to individual

Where from: Realm of Spirit

How to invite them to ritual: Request their presence

Like guardian angels, spirit guides are assigned to us at birth, and we can have as many as seven of them. Sometimes a spirit guide is a soul who doesn't need to incarnate again. Your Spirit guides help you to learn your spiritual lesson. They also watch over you and often will quite literally guide you on your path through life. In addition, your Spirit guides will sometimes set up learning situations to help you evolve spiritually. Often Spirit guides come to us in our dreams.

Once you learn to work with your spirit guides, they will send you messages or warnings when something is wrong. They might even block you or smack you on the back of your head when you are about to do something stupid. When your work is going really well and just seems to flow out of you, that is often an indication that your spirit guides are working through you and that you are doing the right thing.

When you do ritual, you'll want to invite your spirit guides to come into the circle with you. Actually, you probably won't need to ask—they will already be there with you. You can ask from them the same kind of help you would ask from deity—to help carry out your magick, and to protect, guide, and support you. The more you work with spirit guides the more aware you will become of their presence. Some people can feel them. Others smell them. Sometimes you can catch a glimpse of them out of corner of your eye. If you meditate regularly, you may start being able to see them. They usually present themselves in a form that is comfortable for you. Some people's spirit guides appear in the form of an animal. They can even look like big, human babies.

Spirit Animals

Names: The species of animals

Where from: Realm of Spirit

How to invite them to ritual: Summon

A spirit animal represents the spirit of a particular species of animal, not of an individual animal, such as your dog who died when you were eleven. Spirit animals possess all the knowledge and habits of their species. Many people have one particular spirit animal—a wolf, raven, otter, or bear, for instance. They feel that this spirit animal represents them, and they will ask the animal for help.

Even if you are not in touch with your own spirit animal, you can ask one to help you. You can ask spirit animals to carry messages or magick to their destinations. When you ask a spirit animal to take something somewhere for you, keep in mind that it will perform this action in the manner characteristic of its species.

If You Want Your Message Delivered with ...	Pick This Spirit Animal
Aggression	Badger
Beauty	Cardinal, deer
Bravery	Elk
Cunning	Fox, coyote
Docility	Cow
Friendship	Butterfly
Gentleness	Rabbit
Grace	Flamingo
Helpful energy	Donkey

continues

continued

If You Want Your Message Delivered with …	Pick This Spirit Animal
Independence	Cat
Intelligence	Pig
Joy	Canary, hummingbird
Loyalty	Dog
Optimism	Chickadee
Playfulness	Otter
Protective or defensive energy	Armadillo, porcupine, skunk, meadowlark
Resourcefulness	Squirrel, beaver, woodpecker
Sexual energy	Bull
Strength	Bear
Wisdom	Lizard

So Mote It Be

If you don't have a familiar, you can create one. All you need is a box with a lid and your imagination. Sit down with the box, take the top off, and get quiet. In your mind's eye, see your familiar sitting in the box. You will see your familiar in the form in which it wants to present itself. Imagine that the box is his or her comfortable home. Welcome your energy familiar, put the top back on the box, and put it away. When you are ready to do ritual, take your energy familiar out and he or she will aid your magick. Make sure to put your familiar away again after ritual.

Familiars

Names: Various

Where from: Realm of Spirit

How to invite them to ritual: Invite

Familiars are individual animals (not whole species of animals) that are inhabited by spirit. A familiar works with a witch to help with his or her magick. Typically a familiar seeks you out, and not the other way around. Familiars have more dignity than regular pets because they are able to communicate with you telepathically, and they tend to be drawn to ritual. When you start ritual, they will show up so you usually don't have to ask them to attend. And you would never want to force an animal to attend. Familiars can enter and exit your magick circle at will. You don't need to cut a door in the circle for them to go in or out.

It's also possible for a familiar to be a living organism other than a particular animal. Some witches have plant familiars! If your familiar is a plant, you can bring it into your circle for ritual.

While you are doing ritual your familiar will give you confidence. It will warn you if you have made a mistake or if you are about to have an accident with a candle. The presence of a familiar will also enhance your magick.

Webweaving

In the 1600s in England, many women accused of witchcraft were convicted because their judges found "witches' teats" on their bodies. A witch's teat was a small protuberance, such as a large mole, from which the witch's familiar was imagined to suck her blood. Now that sounds like one demanding animal!

The Least You Need to Know

➤ When you ask the various entities to come to ritual, you can summon, stir, call, or invite them, or you can request their presence. Show your respect when you issue your invitation by asking them in the proper way.

➤ The elements, dragons, Watchtowers, and Winds are all large and awesome powers from the Elemental Realm. Many witches call upon the elements when they practice ritual. You want to invoke the dragons and the Watchtowers only for special occasions and in cases of real need.

➤ Fairies and Elementals inhabit the Realm of Fairy. They will help you with your magick, but you must be careful with them. As a beginner, you should not invite them into your magick circle because they can be very mischievous and might mess with your magick.

➤ Deities, angels, ancestors, spirit guides, spirit animals, and familiars are all from the Realm of Spirit and also will help you. And some of them will help you without you even asking.

Chapter 16

Why Do Magick?

Magick is something that people have done for thousands of years. But in modern times, most of us have been taught that magick is evil, so we have suppressed our magickal abilities. Adding the element of magick to your life can make you feel whole and complete. Doing magick can help raise your consciousness and bring you luck. Through magick, you will have new experiences, and you may even have your fantasies come true!

Magick is fun and interesting. It can help you heal or can smooth out a bumpy life path. It can help you control bad habits, build your self-esteem, give you piece of mind, and help you achieve your goals. So, why *not* do magick?

Are You Ready for Magick?

Are you ready to change your life and yourself? Have you thought about what your needs are and what your wants are? Do you know the difference between your needs and your wants? Are you ready to control your life? Are you willing to take full responsibility for all of your actions? If you answered yes to these questions, then answer this next set. Have you tried other methods to achieve your goals? Have you really considered all the implications of using magick to achieve your goals? Are you sure that your magickal action will not cause harm to others? If you can answer "Yes" to all of these questions, you are ready for magick!

What Is Magick?

Magick is the direction and application of energy using psychic forces in order to create change for a specific, desired outcome. Magick is also a system of symbols, which are programmed in your mind, that help you achieve your magickal goal. As such, it is a form of mental training in which you can alter a situation by using your will. Magick can also take the form of change and growth within yourself. In this respect, you change how you look at things or how you feel about a given situation. Magick can be a wonderful addition to your life. Or you can manipulate magickal energy to negative, destructive ends. It's your choice.

Magick, Magic, and Prayer

Magick with a "k" is what witches do. Witches use the elements—Earth, Air, Water, and Fire—and other forces of Nature, along with their will and their good intentions, to create change. This kind of magick can be slow in happening, but sometimes you can see the results in a day or two. It really does work. People have used it for centuries.

Magic without a "k" is what performers do on stage. A magic act is a theatrical production of illusions where stage magicians make you see something that does not really exist. They trick you with their tricks. Because this type of magic does not create real change and is only illusion, its effects are immediate.

So Mote It Be

Because your own energies and the outside energies you pull in are what you use to do your magick, you want to learn to focus as best you can. One way to practice this is to meditate for 10 minutes a day. Turn off the phone. Sit comfortably in a chair with your feet on the floor and your spine erect. Close your eyes and listen to your breath as it moves in and out of your body. If you find yourself distracted by a thought, just bring your attention back to your breath. At first, you probably won't notice much, but after practice (and daily practice is best) you'll probably start to feel that your little sessions leave you refreshed and less distracted.

If you ask for something in prayer, it is not the same as doing magick. Prayer is a form of communication with deity. Sometimes it is nice just to have a little chat! This is the time for you to get closer to deity, to feel the love deity has to offer, and to connect in your spirit. In prayer you can ask for something, but that is not magick because you are asking deity to do something for you (though we know that all prayers are not just requests for favors!). In magick, you put forth effort by using your energy to get what you need. In this way, you work along with deity instead of just asking from them.

Where Magick Starts

Magick starts within yourself. Once you begin to change and enable yourself by recognizing your magickal potential, things start happening for you. The magick allows you to open up to new ideas and experiences. It can help you know yourself, and that in turn can help you to know and relate to other people and situations. Magick starts within the person who is contemplating using his or her power along with outside energies. Because it is *your* energy (in addition to outside energies that you will control), the magick starts with you. Once the change of recognizing your magickal potential has happened inside you, the rest will start to fall into place naturally.

How Magick Works

Just as there are laws of physics, there are laws in magick. There are four magickal laws:

1. **The Universe abounds with energy.** As you may remember from your high school physics class, everything is energy. Objects that appear to be solid are actually mostly empty space. They consist of tiny subatomic particles bound by pure energy. According to the brilliant theoretical physicist Albert Einstein, even the particles themselves can be seen as energy instead of as solid matter. A rock is energy. Water is energy. Wood is energy. The various tissues of your body are energy. Because we are part of the huge energy field of the universe, sometimes it is hard to see. But there is energy all around us all the time. You can use this energy any time you want.

2. **Everything is connected to everything else.** Remember the metaphor of throwing a stone into a pond and watching the ripples move away from the spot where the stone had splashed down? The ripples move out in concentric rings, just as the repercussions of your actions do. If you actually do toss a stone into a pool of water, you see these ripples form because all the water molecules in the pool are connected. If you move one, or in this case a few, you move them all. In esoteric teachings, you're taught to see the Universe as a network of fine threads called "Indra's Web." The web connects us all to one another and connects each individual to all things. Besides connecting us to physical, material things, the web also connects us to the higher realm, to spirit. As the witches say, "As above, so below." In other words, a movement in the heavens will cause a corresponding movement down here on Earth.

3. **There are an infinite number of possibilities.** Have you ever looked at the stars on a clear night and seen them go on and on and on? Well, they do. (If you haven't done this recently, try it!) Just as there are an infinite number of stars, there are an infinite number of events that might occur. Your possibilities really are limitless.

4. **The path is within you.** In order to do magick, you have to tap into your subconscious mind. Your normal waking mind is used for gathering together all the things you need for the magick you are going to do. In fact, you use your conscious mind to decide what it is you are going to do. But once you have begun the actual act of magick, itself, you are communicating your purpose to your subconscious. Your subconscious then increases the energy that you raise in the process and sends it to your higher self, your superconscious, and to spirit. At that point, the energy is ready to create the desired result.

In other words, when doing an act of magick, you use the connectedness of all things plus part of the huge supply of naturally occurring energy to turn possibility into reality by following the path within.

Magickians and Witches: Highs and Lows

Magickians practice high magick, while witches do low magick. Low magick consists of taking your raw energy and emotion and channeling them in order to achieve a goal. While engaged in an act of magick, a witch chants, sings, dances, says spells, and plays drums to build up internal energy. Once the energy has been built up, the witch releases the energy to affect change. Low magick is a fairly simple type of magick, but it is extremely effective. Even though most witches practice low magick, there are those witches who do perform high magick.

In contrast, the magick of the high magickian is complex and time consuming. High magick involves long, complicated rituals for the sole purpose of doing magick and not for religious or spiritual reasons. High magickians use many different tools in their magick and have to memorize huge amounts of material. Many of them—the ceremonial magickian, for example—tend to wear expensive, ornate costumes when they work.

Throughout history *alchemists*, a type of high magickian, even exposed themselves to physical dangers in pursuit of their craft. Alchemists, who often were supported in their work by kings and other nobles who

Book of Shadows

Alchemy is a traditional practice in which the alchemist mixed various materials to try to make a Philosopher's Stone. The Stone was said to turn base metals, such as lead or copper, into gold or silver; act as a panacea—the cure for all aliments; and prolong life. The word "alchemy" comes from a Late Greek term that means the "art of transmutation practiced by the Egyptians."

hoped to get rich, often dealt with toxic substances such as lead and mercury. As a result, they frequently suffered various symptoms of poisoning. Through their study of chemical reactions and processes, alchemists not only worked to change material reality, but strove to transform their own souls.

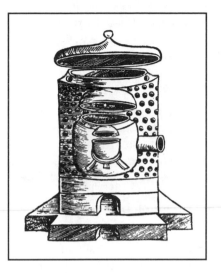

A Renaissance depiction of the alchemist's oven (1529).

While high magick can be a formal system that often uses a lot of ceremony or smelly chemical concoctions, a witch might pick up a handful of dirt, say a spell, cast the dirt over her shoulder, and her magick is done!

Sometimes high magickians will conjure up other entities to work their magick for them. Witches don't usually do this; they tend to direct their own energy toward their goals. Because it is so formal, high magick takes years and years to learn. Low magick is much more accessible. In fact, most of us probably do it on a daily basis without even realizing it! With the proper training, anyone can practice either form of magick. Although many witches are Wiccan, you don't have to be of any particular religion to do magick.

Magickal Ethics

Remember the law of three-fold return? Whatever you do will come back to you three times. Keep

Webweaving

Aleister Crowley was a famous—some would say *infamous*—magickian. He was involved with a group in England called the Hermetic Order of the Golden Dawn. In the early 1900s, he split off from that group and formed his own. One of the reasons that he left the Golden Dawn was that he liked to summon demons. In his autobiography, he claims to have seen 316 of them in one evening!

this law in mind when you are contemplating doing magick, and do no harm. If you do, you will get three times as much harm coming back at you. Ouch!

But there's more. If you are thinking of doing magick for someone else, stop and get that person's permission first. Even if the magick is completely for that person's benefit, you must have that person's permission before you act. Why? Because your magick will affect change in someone else's life. If you do this without a person's permission you could be impinging on that person's free will. Maybe deep down your friend, who always gripes that she can't stop smoking, really likes having this insoluble problem to complain about! If she asks for your help, go for it; but without her permission, any magick for her benefit is a no-go.

What about love spells? (We knew you were going to ask about that!) Again, any magick that involves another person must not in any way manipulate that person's free will. So, you can't make the amazingly cute guy (or girl) you see on the bus every day fall in love with you. But here is what you *can* do—you can do a love spell to increase your own powers of attraction. You can also do a spell to attract the person who is right for you without focusing on any particular individual. Who knows? That spell might just cause you to attract the attention of your object of affection. Or you might attract someone even better!

Parents, in their roles as caretakers, can do spells for their young children. But once the child is old enough to make his or her own decisions, the parent should ask the child if it is okay first. You want to do a spell for your sister's baby who is in the hospital? Ask your sister first! If she does not agree for whatever reasons (maybe magick scares her or is against her religious beliefs), don't do it.

Working with Magickal Energy

Magickal energy is real, and it is powerful. You need to respect it. Before you do magick, you need to try to resolve whatever the problem is by mundane means. If all else has failed, only then should you turn to magick. You also need to know your intent—are you 100 percent clear on what you want? Are you really sure that you want it? Is getting what you want going to hurt anyone?

Working with magickal energy requires time, patience, and planning. No witch just wiggles her nose and achieves her goal. Because magick works with natural energies, you want to select a good time to do the particular type of magick that you are planning. You want to be sure that the Moon is in a phase conducive to your plans. You might also want to check an almanac or witches' calendar for any significant planetary movements. (See Chapter 20, "Magick's Astrological Correspondences," for more information about the planets and planning your magick.) You also need to be aware of the advantages of working magick at different times of the day or night. (For information on this topic, see Chapter 21, "Magickal Timing.")

You shouldn't try to do magick when you aren't feeling well. Remember, magick comes from within you. It is your energies that are going to be put out there. So, don't wipe yourself out! Wait till you're over that icky cold before you cast your great new spell.

Banish!

Resist the temptation to do magick when you are angry. Wait until you have calmed down and had a chance to think because you may feel different in a few hours. If you've already done some magick, you can't take it back without a lot of work, and maybe even then your spell will cause the change you'd asked for anyhow. Be careful what you wish for, you just might get it! Witches, unlike computers, don't come with "undo" keys. And remember, what you send out comes back to you three times.

The Magick Circle Revisited

As you learned in Chapter 11, "Cast a Magick Circle," you work in a magick circle when you are doing magick. You can think of it as your magickal office or workshop. Your magick circle is not just a two-dimensional area described by a line on the floor. Your circle goes through the floor. Using the powers of your mind and creative visualization, you will create a sphere or bubble around yourself. Imagine that you are in the center of this bubble. Inside your circle, you are protected from any negative energy so you can do your work. The circle will also protect you from outside distractions and will keep any other entity from changing your magick.

Building a Cone of Power

Once you are safe inside your magick circle with all your tools, begin to build up your energy to form a *cone of power*. After grounding yourself and preparing your work area and magickal objects, start out with your magickal intent—what do you want to have happen? Concentrate on that positive outcome. See it happening in your mind. Then start to build your energy by chanting, swaying, and drumming. Put your intent into your activities and increase their volume, pace, and intensity.

Book of Shadows

The energy raised by you while you are doing magick takes the form of a cone. That's where the term **cone of power** comes from. In your mind's eye, visualize the cone of power, which is made of your energy, so that its peak points toward your desired goal.

199

Directing a Cone of Power

When you feel the heat from all the energy you have built up, you are ready to direct your cone of power into a magickal tool or another object that will hold it for you. If you are using a candle, grab the candle and channel all that energy into the wax. When you light the candle, all that stored energy will be sent out to do your work. Or, if you are working with air magic, you can direct your cone of power out into the air. In either case, focus on your intent, visualize the magick happening, and know that it will happen.

Protect Yourself

The best way to protect yourself when doing magick is to do positive magick. If you don't mess with negative stuff, it won't come bothering you. You want to call upon positive forces to protect you and help you to get your magickal work done. And when working magick, stay inside your protective magick circle. That's what it's there for.

That Ol' Black, White, and Gray Magick

Magick in itself doesn't really have any color. What matters is a person's intent. If you intend to harm, you are doing negative, or black, magick. If you intend the greatest good for all, then you are working positive, or white, magick.

In the popular imagination black magick might sound sexy and cool—Frank Sinatra sang a song about "That Old Black Magic." In fact, many things use the name "black magic," including a rock group, a girls' soccer team, a restaurant in California, and a popular alcoholic drink. But what is black magick really? Doing black magick is using negative energy to cause harm. And we know you know about negative energy. Have you ever walked into a room where two people were arguing? You can feel it right away. As people say, "The tension was so thick you could cut it with a knife." Well, that tension is negative energy. Doesn't feel good, does it? And why work with what doesn't feel good?

Webweaving

In 1995, a yacht from New Zealand called "Black Magic" raced in the America's Cup off the coast of San Diego. Despite the name, the boat made it into the finals and did very well indeed.

Positive, or white, magick is the kind of magick that witches usually do. It helps you with everyday things without causing anyone any harm.

Gray magick is the kind of magick that falls in between black magick and white magick. The wrong spell done for the right reason would be an example of doing gray magick.

What Magick Can Do for You

Magick is a wonderful healing tool. In this respect, it can help you psychologically, physically, and spiritually. It can help you become strong and confident in your body. It can also help you to break bad habits. Do you tend to come home from work and binge on junk food? Do you feel worse and worse every time you do it? You could try using cord magick on the waning Moon to bind your negative behavior. You could then try losing the extra weight you've gained by giving yourself willpower on the waxing Moon. (For more on cord magick see Chapter 22, "More Ways to Work Magick.") The period in which the Moon is waning, or appearing to get smaller in the sky, is great for ridding yourself of things you don't want—bad habits, addictions, or illness. The period when the Moon is getting bigger in the sky, or waxing, is the time to bring things to you like willpower, health, and prosperity.

Does the Witch Have to Harm to Heal?

If you think about it philosophically, everything has the right to live. This includes parasites, viruses, bacteria, or cancer cells. When you heal someone of a disease, you destroy the cause of that disease, the bug that is making the person sick. Killing off some rhinovirus cells will probably not cause any repercussions, even though what you are doing may be bad for that pesky cold bug.

But what if you just have to do something about your very noisy and crazy neighbor? It's okay to stop him, but don't harm him. What you want to do is treat the behavior, not the person, by binding his negative behavior. Is he keeping you up all night by screaming out the lyrics to an old Bee Gees song? If you've tried everything else—talking to him, your landlord, and the police—then you can do magick and get some peace and quiet. We discuss binding spells in Chapters 23, "Spellcraft," and 24, "Easy Spells."

From High Ritual to Everyday Magick

The magick that you do can involve a lot of formalized ritual or it can be more casual. Some covens use high ritual, meaning they follow a very detailed plan in casting the circle and in building and directing the cone of power that is raised. High rituals, because they are so detailed, can take a lot of time. Often, they feel kind of solemn and serious. (Wiccans also use high ritual for religious ceremonies that are distinct from magickal work.)

But magick can be as simple as making a bowl of soup or throwing a handful of dirt over your

Webweaving

Many of the herbs and spices that we use to flavor our food have magickal and healing properties. Basil, that staple of summer pasta dishes, will help you attract money. Allspice is also good for drawing money to you, and it can also be used to improve your luck and for healing.

shoulder and mumbling a spell. If you are a solitary witch, the amount of ritual that you use depends on what feels comfortable and what works for you. For some people the more ritual they use, the more effective their spells. Others don't like ritual and try to avoid it. As a solitaire, you can do whatever you want. So, play around. Try using a complex ritual or two out of a book. Or write your own. See how they feel, and if you like them, use them.

So Mote It Be

Here's a tip that Denise gives her students to help strengthen their creative visualization skills. (Remember, you have to see the magick happening in your mind's eye.) Get a cardboard gift box that comes apart. Disassemble the box and put it back together again. Do it a few times so you are really familiar with the necessary actions. Now close your eyes and imagine yourself going through each step. See it in your mind. Feel it in your fingers. Hear the sounds the cardboard makes as you bend it into shape. If you get frustrated, don't worry. Put it down and try it again later. Remember, practice does make perfect.

Book of Shadows

Sex magick!? Yup, there is some sex in witchcraft. When doing **sex magick,** you raise your cone of power, either alone or with a partner, by stimulating your sexual energy. All the while, you must concentrate your mind on the magick and not think about the sex. Actually, it's really hard to do right. But it sure is fun trying!

All Kinds of Magick

There are many kinds of magick that fall within the category of low magick. And all of them are accessible to you. Here are some of the different kinds you will probably encounter:

➤ Color magick

➤ Candle magick

➤ Poppet magick

➤ Elemental magick

➤ Herbal magick

➤ Crystal and gem magick

➤ Food magick

➤ Knot magick

➤ Powder magick

➤ Healing magick

➤ Weather magick

➤ Binding magick

➤ Protection magick

➤ *Sex magick*

➤ Glamour magick

➤ Dream magick

➤ Scrying magick

➤ Angel magick

As you can see, you have lots of different magickal choices! The type of magick you decide to work with on a given day will depend on a lot of things, among them your magickal intent, your personal preferences, and what kind of tools you have at hand. We'll tell you more about all the types of magick we've listed later. We promise.

Webweaving

You still want to know what is in the drink called Black Magic? Okay, but we're not going to tell you how to make one. It's vodka, coffee liqueur, and lemon juice. Just thinking about it is giving Katherine a headache!

The Least You Need to Know

➤ Magick, the direction and application of energy, is a powerful tool for change and self-discovery. Magick can help you reach your goals, know yourself, and achieve a deep and meaningful spirituality.

➤ Be sure that your reasons for using magick are truly positive. If you harm someone, that harm will come back to you multiplied by three.

➤ Doing magick for another person's benefit without that person's permission is unethical. You must obtain the person's permission first; otherwise you will be impinging on that person's free will.

➤ Using magick requires effort on your part. First you must try to reach your goal by mundane means; then, once you have decided to do magick, you still must work at it.

➤ You have many different types of magick available to you. Choose the kind you want to do based on your personal preferences, your goals, and your intuition.

Chapter 17

Enhancing Your Magick Power

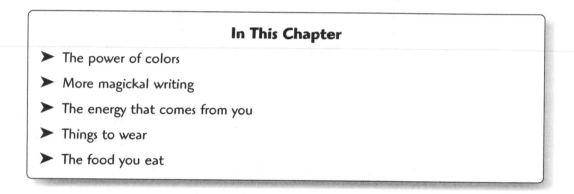

In This Chapter

➤ The power of colors

➤ More magickal writing

➤ The energy that comes from you

➤ Things to wear

➤ The food you eat

Witches use many different means to enhance their magick. Some are as simple as selecting the color of the object you will work with, or getting dressed in special clothes for ritual. Others involve a little more knowledge and understanding of magickal correspondences.

When you first start using magick, you'll want to begin with one or two simple enhancements so you don't get frustrated. As you gain more practice with your magick you can add more. How elaborately you design your spells and how many magickal objects you use is up to you. The important point with magick (and with so many other disciplines) is to practice, practice, practice!

Working with Magickal Colors

Because our ability to perceive colors is dependent upon the light waves that bounce off objects, colors really do have their own energies. The energy of each color, or its light-wave vibration, has an affect on the human body. Colors have been scientifically proven to affect our moods and to aid in healing. In magick, colors help you fine-tune your intent, focus your energy, and help your magick work.

You can use colors in every aspect of magick. To use the energy of colors in your magick, you simply select magickal objects—candles, powders, material, or string, for example—of a color appropriate to the work you plan to do.

Banish!

Avoid getting hung up on details. Worried that you don't have the absolute right color fabric for your poppet? Don't fret! What's important is to do what works for you, and you can always substitute white for a color that you can't find or reproduce. Remember that color is a tool to help you define your intent. Your intentions are more important than the actual hue of the cloth. You don't want to become an obsessed perfectionist about your magick.

Colors have many associations. Some of your own associations about a given color will be purely personal. Maybe you dislike green because, as a child, you were forced to wear an itchy, green dress that you hated. Even so, if you listed all the thoughts and images that occur to you about green, you would probably write down "money."

Here is a list of colors and their magickal associations.

Colors and Their Magickal Associations

Color	Magickal Association
Black	Divination, banishing, absorbing negative energy, protection, binding
Blue	Truth, tranquility, protection, hope, honor, change, psychic ability
Brown	Stability, integrity, justice, sensuality, endurance, animals, concentration, grounding
Gold	The God, vitality, strength, success, action, courage, confidence
Gray	Vision, neutrality, absorbs negativity
Green	Abundance, growth, healing, prosperity, fertility, employment, luck, jealousy
Indigo	Insight, vision, change, flexibility, psychic abilities
Magenta	Intuition, change, spiritual healing, vitality
Orange	Courage, pride, ambition, enthusiasm, energy, friendship, communication, success, opportunities
Pink	Compassion, tenderness, harmony, affection, love, romance, spiritual healing

Color	Magickal Association
Purple	Growth, self-esteem, psychic ability, insight, inspiration, spirituality, success in business
Red	Sexual love, lust, passion, fire, willpower, courage, energy, strength, anger
Silver	The Goddess, spiritual truth, intuition, receptivity, psychic ability, stability, balance
Turquoise	Creativity, discipline, self-knowledge, honor, idealism
Violet	Success, intuition, self-improvement, spiritual awareness
White	Cleansing, peace, protection, healing, truth, divination, tranquility (white can be used in place of any other color)
Yellow	Joy, vitality, intelligence, study, persuasion, charm, creativity, communication

If your loathing of green is so strong that it does not mean abundance, growth, prosperity, and employment to you, then you don't have to use it for those purposes. Say you are working a spell with candle magick to get a new job that will bring you more money, and you hate green. You could use a purple candle for growth and success in business, an orange candle for success and opportunities, or a white candle, which can substitute for any other color. Or you could pick the color of your candle based on your own preferences and personal associations that say money to you. The point is to do what works for you.

Magickal Signs and Symbols

You know that the pentacle and the pentagram are both powerful magickal symbols of protection. Wiccans use a whole host of other symbols as well. There are even magickal alphabets that you can use for writing anything magickal—from spells to your craft name.

Magickal Alphabets

In Chapter 8, "Dedicate Yourself to the Craft," we introduced you to Theban Script. There are several other alphabets you can use, too. Using a magickal alphabet can help tell your subconscious that it is time to get to work to do magick. Because the magickal alphabet you choose is not something that you use every day and are surrounded by everywhere you go, it can make your magickal workings feel more special. Its very unfamiliarity can also help you to focus your intent, because, when

Webweaving

Some witches use ancient languages such as Latin or Greek for their spells. Others like the way spells sound in German, French, or Italian.

writing in a magickal alphabet, you'll have to pay attention to the formation of every letter, instead of dashing something off the way you could if you wrote normally. An added benefit to writing your spells in a special alphabet—no one else will be able to read them!

		Ancient Greek	Egyptian Hieroglyphs	Phoenician
A	as in "cat" / as in "frame"	Λ		K
B		Β		
C	sound of "s" / sound of "k"	Σ / Κ		
CH		χ		
D		Δ		Δ
E	as in "let" / as in "sweet"	E / H		E / H
F		V		
G	as in "grimoire" / as in "german"	Γ / Z		
H		Γ		
I		Ι		
J		Z		
K		Κ		
L		Λ		
M		Μ		
N		Γ		
O	long / short	Ω / ο		long & short
P		π		
PH		φ		
Q		φ		
R		Ρ		
S	as in "sand"	Σ		
SH		Σ		
T		Τ		+
TH		θ		⊕
U	as in "ugly" / as in "unicorn"	V		Y
V		V		Y
W		V		Y
X		Ξ		
Y	as in "yang" / as in "superbly"	Y / Ι		
Z	as in "zany" and "knees"	Z		I

Magickal alphabets.

Magickal Symbols

You can put magickal symbols on any of the tools or objects that you use for magick. You can even wear magickal symbols on your clothing. Like a magickal alphabet, magickal symbols speak to your unconscious. You can use symbols to make a statement. For example, a Goddess symbol on your wand could stand for your dedication to the Lady and your commitment to use magick for the good of all. You can also use symbols to further define your magickal intention—carve them on a candle for candle magick, sew them on a poppet, or draw them on paper and place them inside your poppet. You can even use magickal symbols when writing in your Book of Shadows. If you don't feel like writing the word cauldron, you can draw the symbol instead.

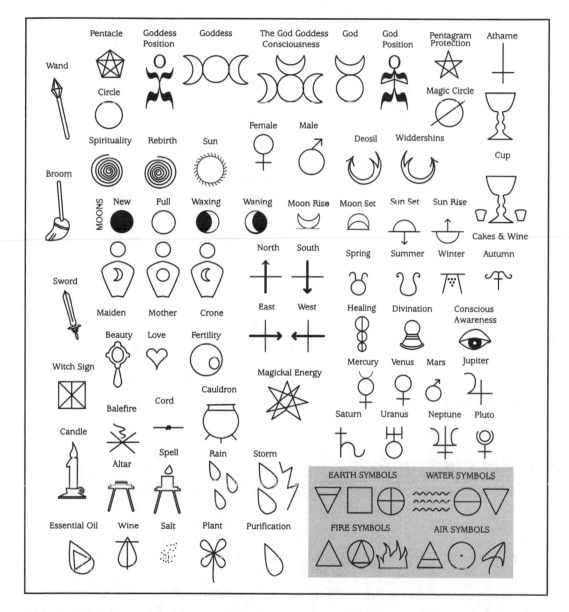

Magickal symbols.

Many witches use the magickal symbols we've just shown you. Others use *runes*, and some use a combination of both. A rune is a character in an ancient Germanic alphabet. There are several different types of runes—Anglo-Saxon, Danish, and Swedish-Norwegian, for example. The word "rune" comes from a Middle English word that means "secret writing." In addition to being a system of writing, runes are also used as tools in divination and magick. Each individual rune has its own meaning.

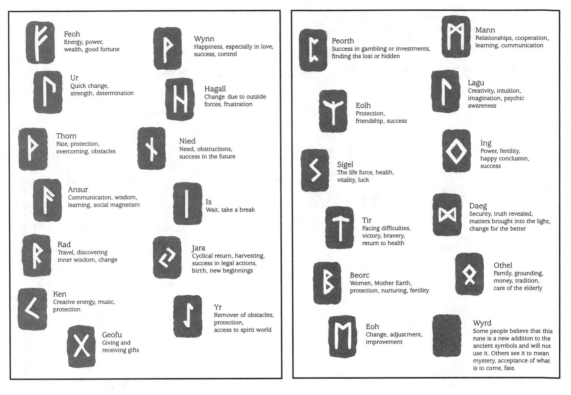

Feoh
Energy, power, wealth, good fortune

Ur
Quick change, strength, determination

Thorn
Fate, protection, overcoming, obstacles

Ansur
Communication, wisdom, learning, social magnetism

Rad
Travel, discovering inner wisdom, change

Ken
Creative energy, music, protection

Geofu
Giving and receiving gifts

Wynn
Happiness, especially in love, success, control

Hagall
Change due to outside forces, frustration

Nied
Need, obstructions, success in the future

Is
Wait, take a break

Jara
Cyclical return, harvesting, success in legal actions, birth, new beginnings

Yr
Remover of obstacles, protection, access to spirit world

Peorth
Success in gambling or investments, finding the lost or hidden

Eolh
Protection, friendship, success

Sigel
The life force, health, vitality, luck

Tir
Facing difficulties, victory, bravery, return to health

Beorc
Women, Mother Earth, protection, nurturing, fertility

Eoh
Change, adjustment, improvement

Mann
Relationships, cooperation, learning, communication

Lagu
Creativity, intuition, imagination, psychic awareness

Ing
Power, fertility, happy conclusion, success

Daeg
Security, truth revealed, matters brought into the light, change for the better

Othel
Family, grounding, money, tradition, care of the elderly

Wyrd
Some people believe that this rune is a new addition to the ancient symbols and will not use it. Others see it to mean mystery, acceptance of what is to come, fate.

Runes.

Magickal Inscriptions

You can carve inscriptions on your magickal tools. For example, you could use the inscription to dedicate the tool or you could simply inscribe it with your magickal name. Some witches create a *sigil* for themselves or make magickal monograms out of their names. When you make a magickal inscription, concentrate on the intent of the words or symbols you are forming. Your concentration will help to empower the object with your energy and good intentions.

Try creating a magickal sigil or symbol for yourself. Play around with your initials or the letters of your magickal name either in our regular Roman alphabet or in another alphabet; or, use a combination of letters and magickal symbols. Once you've come up with your sigil you can use it on your tools. You can even use it as a seal on your magickal correspondence.

That Something Extra

Your tools and magickal objects aren't the only things that can be enhanced with color or symbolism. Because what you wear on your body can also have an effect on your magickal workings, you'll want to consider your ritual outfit carefully.

Magickal Clothing

Your magickal clothing is another way you can add power to your magick. When you wear your magickal clothing it lets the subconscious know that there is work to be done. Your magickal clothing can also carry magickal symbols or messages. This too will help empower the clothing. You could make a robe for yourself and add embroidery or appliques. As we mentioned in Chapter 6, "What You Need to Do Magick," you should wear your magickal clothing only for magickal purposes and ritual. Don't wear your magickal clothing for everyday activities. If you do, your outfit will cease to be magickal. And please wear clothing made of natural fibers. Synthetics are highly flammable and as a result can be dangerous in ritual. There's nothing worse than the thought of a flaming witch!

Book of Shadows

A *sigil* is a magickal sign, seal, or image. The word comes from a Latin word that means "little distinctive mark, small seal, or signal." You can use sigils for just about anything—from inscribing your tools to letter writing to empowering a poppet.

Magickal Jewelry

Jewelry is another way in which witches enhance their magickal powers. Again, remember that you should wear your magickal jewelry only when performing ritual or doing magick. Some witches own more than one pentacle necklace—one for every day and one for magical purposes.

The metals used in jewelry have their own energies and symbolic significance. Gold represents the God, and silver represents the Goddess. Many witches will wear a combination of both metals when doing ritual so as to have a balance between the male and female energies of the All. The stones and gems used in jewelry also have powers. We'll talk about the properties of the various minerals in Chapter 18, "Magick Powers of Nature."

Energy and Attitude

When you do magick you focus your intent and your energy on your desired goal. Obviously, in order to do this, you must be able to concentrate and focus your energy. Because the quality of your energy can affect your magick, you want your energy to be as clear and strong as it can be. And your attitude toward your goal, your magick, and yourself will also affect your energy and the outcome of your magick.

Channeling Chakras

The seven chakras are energy centers in the body that lie along your spine. Each chakra picks up and sends out a specific type of energy. Imagine them as wheels of spinning energy.

➤ The root or base chakra, located at the base of the spine near the tailbone, is all about survival and our basic physical needs for food, sleep, and shelter.

➤ The second chakra, the sacral or spleen chakra, which is just below the navel, is the center of sexuality, sensuality, and emotions.

➤ The third chakra, located at the solar plexus is the seat of the will. The energy of the third chakra helps you make decisions, be responsible and creative, and carry out your plans.

➤ The fourth chakra, the heart chakra, concerns itself with giving and receiving love.

➤ The fifth chakra, the throat chakra, deals with our energies of communication both in the mundane world and on the spiritual plane.

➤ The sixth chakra, located in the middle of the forehead just above the eyebrows (where the third eye—the organ of spiritual perception—is located) is the seat of psychic visions and clairvoyance.

➤ The seventh chakra, the crown chakra, is at the top of the head. This last chakra is our spiritual door, our connection to spiritual wisdom and the All.

The seven chakras also have color correspondences. Each chakra has a color associated with it. The root chakra is red. The second chakra is orange, and the third is yellow. The heart chakra's color is green. The color of the fifth chakra is blue, while the sixth is indigo or violet. The seventh chakra, the crown chakra, is white.

(Drawing by Wendy Frost)

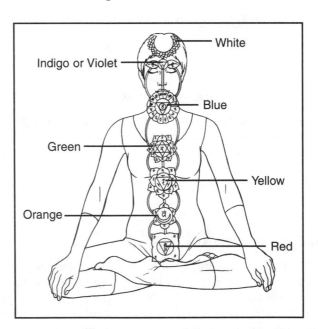

212

If you have energy blockages in any of your chakras, they will negatively affect your magick by making it difficult for you to send or receive certain types of energy. You can work to open and balance your chakras by meditating on the area of the chakra in your body. Color meditations can be particularly helpful in chakra work. You can also use specific gemstones to open each chakra. A blockage in a chakra usually has physical manifestations. For example, if you have chronic problems with receiving or giving love, you may have a problem in your fourth, or heart, chakra. For information on how to balance your chakras with gemstones, see Melody's book *Love Is in the Earth* (Earth-Love Publishing House, 1995).

Magickal Attitude

Because your magick comes from you and is a product of your energies, keeping the right attitude is crucial. You must be absolutely clear on your magickal intent. You must know that you have tried all the mundane means at your disposal to get what you want. You also must know that your magick will not harm any other living thing. And you must have thought out how your magick is going to affect everyone involved, including you!

When you send out your energy to do magick, you must be able to see the desired result happening. Visualize yourself reaching your goal. Give the image in your mind as many concrete details as you can. You have to know that your magick is going to happen. Just hoping it will come true is not enough.

By the same token, you don't want to get cocky about your magick and start taking it for granted or just using it for fun. What you do with magick is work. That's why we use the phrase "magickal workings." Keep the proper respect for your powers and the powers of other entities that you draw on, and magick will serve you well. Yes, the energy of your magick comes from you, but you are only a tiny little part of the Universe. Without the aid of other larger entities, your magickal work would not get done. You may be the catalyst for the changes that you affect through magick but you are not the sole operator. Respect and give thanks to all the entities, beings, and energies that aid the manifestations of your magickal work and your magick should continue to work for you throughout your lifetime.

Talismans, Amulets, and Charms

Wearing or carrying talismans, amulets, or charms can enhance your magick and protect you from negative energy. All talismans, amulets, and charms are charged and blessed before you put them on.

Sometimes *talismans* look like the thing that you want to draw to you. For example, a money-drawing talisman might be round like a coin. Alternatively, your money-drawing talisman might be square but have symbols or runes for money or prosperity inscribed on it. A horseshoe that brings good luck or protection would be another example of a talisman. Some witches define talismans as man-made objects that have been imbued with power, and amulets as naturally occurring objects that have been so charged.

Book of Shadows

A **talisman** is an object that has been empowered to draw something to you. An **amulet** is an object that has been magickally empowered to protect you from a specific type of negative energy. A **charm** is an object that a person associates with luck or some other form of protection. It is usually very personal to him or her.

Amulets are worn for protection. Alligator teeth are considered to be amulets that will protect you against danger. You wear or carry the charged amulet or talisman until the magick that you have charged it for is done. For example, if you had a friend who was going into the hospital, you could make a healing talisman for him or her. You might want to use a piece of rose quartz, a stone that has healing energy of its own to do this. During ritual, build up a cone of power, then focus it and all your healing energy into the piece of rose quartz. After you have done this, the quartz will be a healing talisman for your friend.

Charms are usually personal possessions that are not designed as magickal objects, but with which you have a special relationship. This relationship imbues the object with power. You might be wearing a particular pair of green socks the day that your softball team wins for the first time. After that win, you might feel that wearing those socks or having them near you will bring you either luck or protection. You may then wear those socks whenever you play sports.

Webweaving

Hospitals are required by law to respect your religious beliefs. So, if you want to bring healing charms or crystals into the operating room with you, the hospital will let you. The staff at many hospitals now understands that the spirit plays an important role in healing. They no longer just tolerate your ideas, but they respect your beliefs and may even encourage you to use alternative methods that may help you heal faster.

Magickal Recipes

You can turn your favorite dish into a magickal dish by empowering one or more of the ingredients with magick. Remember in Chapter 16, "Why Do Magick?" how we talked about building a cone of power and directing the energy into a magickal tool such as a candle? Well, you can do the same thing with food. You can turn your favorite oatmeal raisin cookies into special cookies used for ritual, sometimes known as Sabbat cookies, by directing concentrated energy into the raisins or other ingredients.

Once you have baked these empowered cookies, you want to treat them properly. Keep them in a special tin. You can make the tin special by cleansing and consecrating it and then marking it with magickal symbols. Make sure to store it in a special place, too.

You should eat these magickally empowered cookies, along with a special ritual tea, only while preparing yourself for ritual or during ritual when you do the cakes and wine. Whether you eat the cookies as a part of your preparation for ritual or have them during ritual, will all depend on what magickal intent you put into the cookies. While you eat your magickal cookies, meditate on the magick that you intend to do and give thanks for the enjoyment of the grains that the Goddess has provided for us. Or reflect on the magick you have just done. With each bite, see the magick coming to pass.

Some foods have magickal correspondences. You could use such a food as an ingredient, or you could base a whole recipe on one of these foods. Here are some foods and their magickal correspondences:

Banish!

Use caution when using herbs. Never ingest herbs that you are unfamiliar with. Before adding an herb to a recipe or making a tea from it, double-check that the herb is indeed edible. Many magickal herbs can be toxic, and some can be harmful if you are pregnant or nursing. Get all the facts before you partake. It's better to be safe than sorry!

➤ Apples attract love, healing, and aid in divination.
➤ Almonds bring money and wisdom.
➤ Avocados help bring love and lust.
➤ Bananas are for fertility, potency, and prosperity.
➤ Barley helps with love spells and healing and can also be used for protection.
➤ Blackberries promote healing and prosperity and help draw money.
➤ Beets draw love.
➤ Carrots promote fertility and lust.
➤ Cashew nuts can help draw money.
➤ Celery promotes mental and psychic powers.
➤ Corn is used for protection, drawing luck, and promoting divination skills.
➤ Cucumbers are good for healing and fertility issues.

215

➤ Grapes promote fertility and mental powers.

➤ Leeks are useful for protection and can be used in love spells.

➤ Lemons are used for purification and as an aid to mental clarity.

➤ Oranges promote prosperity and luck.

➤ Mustard is used for strengthening mental powers and fertility.

➤ Pineapples bring love and money.

➤ Pomegranates help with divination and can bring wealth.

➤ Rice promotes rain and fertility and can be used to draw money.

➤ Strawberries bring love and luck.

➤ Turnips are good for protection and help end relationships.

➤ Vanilla helps attract men and promotes mental energy.

Another way to prepare magickal recipes is to use herbs and spices with the appropriate magickal properties. You might drink mugwort tea before ritual to help open up your psychic awareness. Peppermint tea will also help increase your psychic abilities. Or you might want to add some cinnamon to those oatmeal raisin cookies to draw money or success to you. We'll talk more about magickal herbs in Chapter 18, "Magick Powers of Nature."

The Least You Need to Know

➤ Because colors have their own energy, they can help your magick. But use only colors that work for you. Don't feel that you must use a certain color that you hate because it is supposed to be good for the magick you are planning.

➤ Using magickal symbols and alphabets can help you fine-tune your magickal intent and enhance your magick's power.

➤ Your energy will flow best through open chakras. If your chakras are blocked, work to open them before you try doing magick.

➤ Amulets and talismans can be charged to help you with a given task or situation. Amulets will deflect negative energy from you. Talismans will help to bring things you want to you. Charms usually develop on their own and are objects that you associate with instances of good luck.

➤ Many common foods and herbs have magickal properties. If you are unfamiliar with a magickal herb, do not ingest it. While many herbs are edible, some are poisonous.

Chapter 18

Magick Powers of Nature

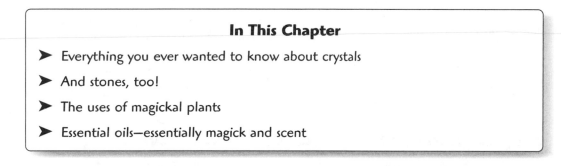

In This Chapter

➤ Everything you ever wanted to know about crystals

➤ And stones, too!

➤ The uses of magickal plants

➤ Essential oils—essentially magick and scent

Flowers open in the spring, and plants grow toward the Sun. Nature has its own magick. You can harness some of that energy when you do your magick.

Crystals, plants, and stones all have their own individual vibrational frequency. In that respect, you might say they are very similar to humans. When you first start working with these materials, you may want to think about them as new colleagues and learn as much as you can about them. You may find that you migrate toward a particular crystal, plant, or stone just as you migrate toward certain people. Call it the coming together of two minds.

In Harmony with Nature

Witches honor and respect Nature. Doing so is part of the Wiccan religion. To truly give Nature her due, you have to understand her awesome power. Witches cultivate their knowledge of all aspects of Nature's energy and work in concert with that endless supply to pay homage to deity and to heal themselves, their loved ones, and the Earth herself.

Working Magick with Crystals and Stones

Crystals and stones contain their own energy. You can use the crystal or stone's energy for yourself or to enhance your magick. Rose quartz, for instance, has a healing and loving energy. You could wear a piece of rose quartz to help heal a broken heart. Or you could build a cone of power and put your specific intent into the piece of rose quartz. Probably you would want to use a crystal or stone with an energy that "goes with" your intent and will amplify it. So, it would make sense to put a loving or healing intent into rose quartz, while you might want to use malachite or bloodstone if your intent were to build wealth and a successful business.

Book of Shadows

A **crystal** is a stone with a particular, regular molecular structure. For magickal purposes, you don't really need to make a distinction between crystals and other minerals.

When you first get a stone you should cleanse it and energize it. You can do this by washing it in salt water, seawater, or holy water. Then take it out into the light of the full Moon. The Moon does two things—it cleanses and energizes the stone. You might say it wakes it up. You can also awaken it by tapping it gently on sand after washing it, or giving it a gentle slap with your fingers. This action gets the stone's attention.

Magickal Properties of Crystals and Stones

Which crystal or stone you use for which magickal purpose will depend on your own feelings and intuitions. If you are drawn to a particular stone, try it out. It may be just what you need. The following crystals and stones are generally considered to have the properties listed.

Crystal or Stone	Magickal Properties
Agate	Courage, strength, love, protection
Alexandrite	Luck, love, spiritual transformation, joy
Amazonite	Success, joy, self-expression; awakens the heart and throat chakras
Amethyst	Courage, psychic energy, dreams, healing addictions (especially to alcohol), peace, happiness, love; opens crown chakra
Aquamarine	Courage, purification, peace, psychic awareness, self-expression; balances all the chakras
Aventurine	Money, luck, mental agility, visual acuity, peace, healing; opens heart chakra

Crystal or Stone	Magickal Properties
Azurite	Psychic energy, dreams, divination (the art of looking into the future), healing, concentration, transformation
Beryl	Energy, love, healing, psychic awareness, protection (especially from the weather and water)
Bloodstone	Courage, strength, victory, wealth, self-confidence, business and legal affairs, stops bleeding; helps regulate the first four chakras
Calcite	Centering, grounding, purification, money, peace; calms fears
Carnelian	Courage, sexual energy, verbal skill, peace; alleviates jealousy, apathy, fear, and rage
Celestite	Verbal skill, healing, compassion, calming; aids growth
Clear quartz	Intensifies energy (both positive and negative)
Chrysocolla	Wisdom, peace, love, communication, vitality
Chrysoprase	Prosperity, luck, happiness, friendship, protection, healing
Citrine	Psychic powers, protection, creativity, sexual energy; deflects nightmares
Diamond	Courage, strength, healing, protection, spirituality, mental and sexual abilities
Emerald	Prosperity, mental and psychic abilities, dreams, meditation, visual acuity, love, peace, balance; opens heart chakra
Garnet	Strength, physical energy, healing, protection, purification, compassion; opens the root and crown chakras
Geode	Fertility, childbirth, meditation, freedom of spirit, psychic ability, dreams, astral travel
Hematite	Grounding, calming, healing, divination, intuition, physical strength; aids restful sleep
Jade	Healing, protection, wisdom, prosperity, love, long life, fertility, courage, peace
Jasper	Healing, protection, health, beauty, energy
Kunzite	Creativity, communication, peace, balance, relaxation, grounding
Lapis lazuli	Courage, joy, love, fidelity, psychic abilities, protection, healing, beauty, prosperity
Lepidolite	Peace, spirituality, physical strength, luck, protection, psychic ability, emotional balance; deflects nightmares
Malachite	Power, energy, protection, love, peace, success in business, vision quests, gardening

continues

continued

Crystal or Stone	Magickal Properties
Moldavite	Psychic abilities, mental and emotional balance
Moonstone	Grounding, love, divination, sleep, gardening, protection, youth, sleep, harmony, magick, peace, travel
Obsidian	Grounding, divination, protection; deflects negativity
Onyx	Emotional balance, self-control (especially in sexual matters), binding, protection (especially against someone else's magick), strength
Opal	Beauty, prosperity, luck, power, psychic abilities, visual acuity, emotional balance
Peridot	Protection, prosperity, sleep, health, emotional balance, intuition
Rose Quartz	Love, peace, happiness, healing (especially of the emotions)
Rhodochrosite	Energy, peace, calm, love, mental activity, emotional balance; balances the root chakra
Rhodonite	Peace, mental clarity, memory, confidence; opens the crown chakra
Ruby	Prosperity, power, courage, integrity, joy; deflects nightmares
Sapphire	Psychic abilities, inspiration, love, meditation, peace, healing, power, prosperity, protection
Smokey quartz	Healing, directing and absorbing energy, altered states
Sodalite	Healing, meditation, wisdom, calm, grounding, stress reducer
Sunstone	Protection, energy, health, passion, sexuality
Tiger's Eye	Courage, prosperity, protection, energy, luck, judgment and common sense, honesty, divination; eases depression
Topaz	Protection, healing, dieting, prosperity, love, emotional balance, tranquility, creativity
Tourmaline	Love, friendship, prosperity, business, peace, sleep, energy, courage, protection, inspiration; opens the third-eye center, or sixth chakra
Turquoise	Courage, protection, prosperity, luck, friendship, healing, communication, happiness, emotional balance, astral travel; strengthens all the chakras
Zircon	Protection especially from theft, beauty, love, peace, sexual energy, healing, mental alertness, emotional balance

As you can see, all the stones have more than one magickal use and there is a fair amount of overlap in terms of which stones you can use for which purposes.

Finding, Buying, and Storing Crystals and Stones

Experts say you do not find a crystal or stone; it finds you. Most crystals and stones find their people in stores, although sometimes they hook up in quarries, riverbeds, forests, or beaches. If you are interested in crystals and stones, you probably should start exploring them at New Age, metaphysical, or rock and mineral shops. You can also attend rock and mineral shows.

When shopping for a crystal or stone you should look at a lot of them. Pay close attention to which ones attract you most strongly. The crystal or stone that pulls your attention might not be the prettiest one in the bunch. If you are attracted to an ugly stone, just know that it is the stone you are meant to have. You may not need the stone right at the moment, but you will need it in the future. Pick up the stone and see how it feels.

If you're looking at crystals, unless you intend to use it for scrying, you don't have to seek out the clearest, most translucent one. Crystals that have cloudy "ghosts," inclusions of other minerals, and other crystals inside of them carry a lot of energy. Buy the stone that feels right to you, and try not to worry too much that you could have bought a cheaper one. A cheaper stone that you can't relate to really is no bargain at all.

Sometimes a stone to which you are attracted will turn out to be something that a person you know needs. When this happens, you'll usually be able to tell because you'll have the urge to give that stone to the person in question.

Stones and crystals are best stored in a cool, dark place. You can keep all of your stones and crystals together in one bag and store it in your magickal tool chest. You'll need to cleanse your stones of energy periodically, especially if other people have been handling them. Because stones and crystals are so sensitive to energy, the people who touch them will affect them. And you don't want someone else's negative vibe hanging around your stones. So, cleanse your stones regularly with sunlight, moonlight, saltwater or holy water.

Webweaving

Some witches make crystal tinctures or extracts by soaking their stones in oil or distilled water. After a few days, they remove the stones and use a few drops of the liquid essence of the stone in tea or as anointing oil. Of course, they always check to make sure that their crystals are completely nontoxic before they ingest any such tincture.

Webweaving

If you find a stone with a natural hole through it, hang on to it. Such holey stones, or holy stones, are rare. It's said that if you look through the hole, you'll be able to see into the Realm of Fairy.

221

So Mote It Be

If someone you love brings you flowers (especially roses), dry them after you are done en-joying them. You can do this by tying them together and hanging them upside down in such a way that air can circulate around them. The dried petals will hold the loving en-ergy of the giver. Use the petals in any magick having to do with love, and your energies will be amplified by the love that is already in the flowers.

Learning More

There are many books about the magickal properties of crystals and stones. *Love Is in the Earth,* by Melody (Earth-Love Publishing House, 1995) is one of the books that Denise recommends to all of her students. You also might want to locate a copy of *Cunningham's Encyclopedia of Crystal, Gem & Metal Magic,* by Scott Cunningham (Llewellyn Publications, 1988).

Banish!

Resist the temptation to touch someone else's crystals without that person's express permission. An acquaintance may be wearing a tempting, sparkly crystal pen-dant, but keep your hands to yourself. If you pick it up, you could affect the energy of the stone and might even ruin your friend's magick.

Experts will tell you that you will also learn a lot from the stones themselves. In order to do this, you need to develop a relationship with a crystal or two. Try medi-tating with a crystal and keep an open mind. Crystals communicate in subtle ways. Because they have been around for hundreds of years, their energy can seem very slow. After some time, you may start to receive messages from your crystal in the form of hunches or intuitions.

Working Magick with Herbs and Botanicals

You can use herbs and botanicals in many ways. If, for instance, you are working with love, you can choose an herb or botanical that is associated with love and sew it into a poppet or a dream pillow. Or you can place it in a small bag and wear it around your neck, or hang some of the herb in your bedroom. Some herbs can be burned, and others can be added to the water of your ritual bath. If you suffer from allergies, be aware that even in dried form herbs can be powerful allergens. You might want to try using herbal extracts instead.

Magickal Herbs and Botanicals

Here are a few herbs (plants used for seasoning or medicinal purposes) and botanicals (other plants) commonly used in magick.

A word of caution: Many magickal herbs and botanicals can be toxic. Never ingest an herb unless you have checked it out with an herbalist first. You should know both the magickal and the medicinal properties of an herb. You should also be aware of any interactions an herb could have with another herb, with any medication that you are taking, or any possible allergic reactions it could cause. If you are thinking of making your own herbal tea, stop by your local herb shop first. Read to someone on staff a list of your ingredients to make sure what you are planning is safe. There are also many excellent books that can tell you whether an herb is edible or not.

So Mote It Be

Before there were doctors, people went to their local witch for healing. Hearing the witch use plant names such as deer's tongue, people began to believe that witches maimed or killed animals to do their magick. Not true! Deer's tongue is a plant that resembles the tongue of a deer. (It's good for developing lust and psychic awareness.) Still, there's no herb we know of called "eye of newt."

Herb or Botanical	Magick Properties
Angelica	Protection, healing, visions; removes hexes
Balm of Gilead	Love, manifestations, protection, emotional healing
Burdock	Protection, healing, happy home
Carnation	Protection, strength, healing, vitality
Celery seeds	Lust, mental and psychic powers
Dandelion	Divination, calling spirits, favorable winds
Dill	Money, love, lust, protection (especially of children)
Elderberries	Prosperity, protection, sleep, banishing of negative entities
Fenugreek	Money, mental powers
Frankincense	Spirituality, protection, banishing of negative entities, consecration
Gardenia	Love, peace, healing; enhances spiritual connections
Ginseng	Love, lust, vitality, wishes, healing, beauty, protection
Horehound	Protection, healing, mental powers, banishing of negative entities

continues

continued

Herb or Botanical	Magick Properties
Hyssop	Purification, protection, prosperity
Irish moss	Money, luck, safe travel
Jasmine	Love, money, sleep, dreams
Juniper	Protection (especially from thieves), love, health, banishing of negative entities
Mugwort	Divination, clairvoyance, psychic powers, dreams, protection, strength, astral projection
Mustard	Fertility, money, protection, mental acuity
Nettle	Protection, healing, lust, banishing negative entities
Orris	Long-lasting love, divination, protection
Parsley	Purification, protection, lust, fertility
Passion flower	Peace, friendship, popularity, sleep
Pennyroyal	Protection, peace, strength (especially during travel), anti–sea sickness
Pine	Healing, protection, fertility, money, banishing negative entities
Poppy	Fertility, love, money, luck, sleep
Raspberry	Love, protection of the home; alleviates labor pains
Rose	Love, beauty, luck, psychic powers, protection
Rue	Mental powers, healing, love, curse-breaker
Sage	Wisdom, prosperity, healing, longevity, money
Slippery elm	Stops gossip, aids verbal development
Star anise	Psychic and spiritual powers, luck
Valerian	Love, sleep, purification, protection, peace
Vetivert	Love, luck, money, protection against theft
Violet	Spiritual protection, luck, love, lust, wishes, peace, sleep, healing
Willow	Love, divination, protection, healing
Witch hazel	Protection, chastity, healing of broken heart
Wormwood	Psychic powers, protection, safe car travel, love, calling spirits

Finding, Buying, and Storing Herbs and Botanicals

You can grow your own magickal herbs and botanicals or you can buy them at a metaphysical or herb shop. If you grow your own, you can consult an almanac to find good planting and harvesting times. You should also read up on the best methods and necessary precautions for drying your herbs. Know that some herbs are toxic and can give off a noxious vapor while drying. There are many books available about growing and preparing plants for magickal purposes. If herbs are new to you, you're probably better off buying what you need. As you gain experience, you can begin to forage for herbs or cultivate your own magickal garden.

You'll want to store your dried herbs in a cool, dry place and keep them out of the light. Sunlight will bleach your herbs and pull the energy out of them. You should also make sure that insects or mice don't get into your herbs. If you find that your herbs have become infested, don't use them. Your herbs should keep for a long time, but once they do begin to deteriorate, dispose of them and get new ones. When you need to throw herbs away, because they are old or you have discovered bugs in them, don't toss the herbs in the trash. Rather, take them outside and give them back to the Earth.

It is probably best to keep your herbs in glass jars, because plastic can start to breakdown and contaminate them. Use big labels so you can clearly mark each container. In addition to the herb's name, put the date of purchase on each label.

Banish!

Many herbs, such as the hallucinogens that were used in flying ointment—a toxic preparation that, when rubbed on the body, caused witches in the historical past to feel as if they were flying, are readily absorbed through the skin. So, when you work with fresh herbs before you dry them, it's a good idea to wear gloves to protect you from any toxins and safeguard your skin in case you turn out to be allergic to any of the plants you are using.

Learning More

Many Wiccan books present information about the magickal uses of herbs. *Cunningham's Encyclopedia of Magical Herbs* (Llewellyn, 1985) is an excellent illustrated resource for information about the magickal properties of herbs and botanicals. But you should also learn about the medicinal properties of herbs. A thorough knowledge of herbs will make you a better witch. And witches throughout history have always held knowledge of plants, magick, and herbal healing. It's also a good idea to take a class on the medicinal uses of herbs. Many metaphysical shops offer such classes, as do herb shops. If your local herb store does not have classes, you should at least be able to ask questions of the herbalist on staff.

Working with Essential Oils

Essential oils have a number of magickal uses. You can use them for healing, cleansing, blessing, banishing, empowering, anointing, and consecrating. And, of course, you can enjoy them for their great scents! When working with pure essential oils, you should wear gloves, because the oils are very potent and can burn your skin. Because they are so strong, essential oils are usually cut with a *carrier oil*. This way they won't damage your skin. In addition, carrier oils help to stretch your essential oils and your dollar. When you're dealing with an essential oil that can cost as much as $90 a dram (the equivalent of 0.0625 of an ounce) you'll want to stretch it as much as you can!

Book of Shadows

Carrier oils such as grapeseed, apricot, jojoba, almond, or vegetable oil, are used to dilute essential oils. The carrier oil helps you stretch your essential oil and helps prevent the essential oil from burning your skin.

After they are mixed with the carrier oil, essential oils are blended together according to your magickal purpose. When designing a mixture you'll also want to pay attention to how well the different scents combine and your own preferences and associations. You can also mix in the energy of plants and stones by adding herbs or crystals to your essential oil mixtures.

When blending oils, you should concentrate on putting energy and your magickal intent into the mixture. You can do this by saying a chant or incantation, such as ...

> With this magick oil I mix,
> Another magickal spell I'll fix.
> Fire, Water, Earth, and Air,
> To know, to will, be silent, and dare.
> As this magick is sent out to thee,
> Let it grow and set it free.
> This is my will so mote it be!

Or you can mix your oil and then charge it during ritual by raising a cone of power and directing all of that energy into the oil. One easy way to do this is to stand before one of the elements in your magick circle. If you were working with love, passion, or sexuality, you should face Fire in the south. Repeat over and over the name of the element that represents your intent. Start out softly and slowly and increase the speed, volume, and intensity until you feel ready to burst with all the energy. Grab your vial of oil and send the energy into the oil. Once you've done that, your oil is charged with the power of the element and ready to use. Many witches like to dress candles for candle magick with essential oils. You can also use it to anoint your body, your magickal tools, or other objects.

So Mote It Be

Another great way to use essential oils is to put a few drops of them in an oil burner. The oils don't actually burn, but are heated to the point of evaporation, and their scent fills the air. The scent will affect you psychically and physically. You can use certain oils to stimulate a meditative state during ritual or use them as part of your routine to prepare for ritual. Either way you can't go wrong. And your nose, surrounded by great, natural smells, will be happy, too!

All About Essential Oils

Consult the following list of essential oils and their magickal correspondences before making a blend. Pick your oils based on your magickal purpose and your sense of smell. But, however delicious they may seem, never, never take essential oils internally! In addition, camphor oil has been known to cause toxic reactions in some people even at a dilution of 4 percent essential oil to a base of carrier oil. For safety's sake, don't use camphor oil on the skin even in a blend.

Essential Oil	Magickal Properties
Basil	Money, harmony; promotes sympathy, happiness, peace
Benison	Increases power, awakes the conscious mind, peace
Bergamot	Money, protection
Black pepper	Protection, courage, banishing; spices up a romance
Camphor	Purification, healing (particularly of respiratory problems), chastity
Cardamom	Love, lust, sexual energy
Cedar	Balance, spirituality, courage, dreams
Chamomile	Meditation, peace, dreams
Cinnamon	Money, psychic awareness, lust, purification
Clove	Courage, protection, sexual attractiveness, lust; adds spice to any situation
Coriander	Love, health, and healing
Cypress	Consecration, protection, healing (especially of psychological pain), longevity
Eucalyptus	Health, healing (especially of respiratory problems), purification

continues

continued

Essential Oil	Magickal Properties
Geranium	Protection, happiness, love
Ginger	Sexuality, love, courage, money, prosperity
Grapefruit	Purification; banishes a sour disposition
Jasmine	Love, psychic awareness, dreams, peace, sex
Juniper	Protection, meditation, purification, healing, communication
Lavender	Health, peace, relaxation, sleep, purification, love
Lemon	Energy, mental clarity, wit, cleansing
Lemon grass	Psychic awareness, purification, lust
Lemon verbena	Love, purification
Lime	Purification, cleansing, protection, fertility, love
Magnolia	Meditation, psychic awareness, love, fidelity
Myrrh	Spirituality, meditation, healing, blessing
Neroli	Happiness, protection, purification
Oak moss	Money, prosperity, fertility
Orange	Purification, heightened awareness, luck
Palmarosa	Love, healing, protection
Patchouli	Money, physical energy, attraction, protection, sex
Peppermint	Purification, mental energy, psychic powers
Pine	Purification, money, healing, cleansing
Rose	Love, peace, sexual desire, beauty, maternal love
Rosemary	Love, healing, energy; breaks hexes
Sandalwood	Spirituality, meditation, sex, healing, psychic awareness
Sweet pea	New friends, love, happiness
Tangerine	Strength, power, vitality
Tuberose	Calm, peace, love, happiness, psychic powers
Vetivert	Money, prosperity, attractiveness; breaks hexes
Yarrow	Courage, love, psychic awareness; banishes negative entities
Ylang-ylang	Love, peace, sex, healing

Finding, Buying, and Storing Essential Oils

When you first start out using essential oils, you'll probably want to buy the blends that a shop has already made up. For example, it is often cheaper to buy a small bottle of House Blessing oil than it is to acquire all the ingredients to make the blend. Whether you're buying blends or pure essentials, you should make sure that what you're getting really are essential oils and not fragrance oils. Fragrance oils, synthetics that are designed to smell like the real thing, often trigger asthma attacks in people who are susceptible. Although many witches don't like to use fragrance oils, sometimes a substitution is necessary. Essential rose oil can cost upward of $100 a dram!

If you do decide to start collecting oils, buy only the few that you will need the most. There's no sense in buying a bottle of each kind of oil if you're not going to use them.

Keep your oils, whether they are blends or not, in a dark place, preferably in a dark glass bottle, because heat and light will cause your oils to go rancid. Most blended oils will keep for about six months. Remember to label and date all of your oils before you put them away. And smell them before you use them—you don't want to work magick with rancid oil.

Learning More

To learn more about essential oils, look for Scott Cunningham's *The Complete Book of Incense, Oils, and Brews* (Llewellyn, 1989). You also could take a class on aromatherapy. Such a class won't get into the magickal uses of essential oils, but it will teach all about the physical properties of the oils and how to handle them properly. An aromatherapy class will also teach you about the medicinal uses of the oils—important knowledge for any witch. Remember, all witches are healers.

Webweaving

If you put a few drops of essential oil into your bath, they will dissolve in the water and give you a lovely, scented soak. Fragrance oils will not dissolve, but will float on top of the water. Another reason to go with the natural choice!

The Least You Need to Know

➤ Crystals and stones have their own inherent energy. You can use those forces on their own, or you can charge stones to aid your magick.

➤ Herbs and botanicals have magickal properties as well. You can use dried herbs as stuffing, make teas or tinctures from them, burn them, or add them to bath water. Always make sure that an herb is nontoxic before ingesting it or exposing your skin to it.

➤ Essential oils have many magickal properties and uses. You can use them for anointing, to perfume your ritual room or in your ritual bath, or for medicinal reasons. Never ingest an essential oil, and don't apply a full-strength oil to your skin.

➤ You can add crystals, herbs, and botanicals to your essential oils to achieve the right balance of energies for your magickal work.

Part 5

Any Time Is the Right Time for Magick

Is this the right time for you to be doing magick? We'll talk about the issues involved. Then we'll look at the stars and discuss the importance of astrology in witchcraft. Although you can do magick at any time, we'll look at how to determine the best times to do the magickal work that you have in mind.

Chapter 19

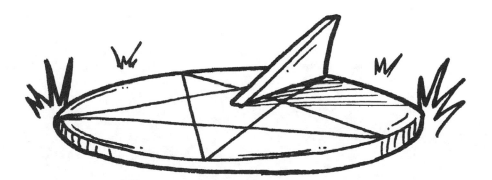

To Know, to Dare, to Will, to Keep Silent

In This Chapter

➤ What you should know about being a witch

➤ Do you dare?

➤ The importance of willpower

➤ Silence is golden

You have come this far. You've learned a lot about Wicca and witchcraft. Now is the time to decide if you are really ready to get serious. Do you really want to become a witch? And if so, is this the right time for you to do it?

To protect their magick, most witches follow the conditions expressed by the witch's pyramid. They make sure that they know, dare, will, and keep silent about their magickal acts. You can also use the witch's pyramid to formulate a lifestyle. This is perhaps the toughest challenge of all. But without the firm base of strong convictions a witch cannot grow. The stronger and richer the soil of your conviction, the stronger and better witch you will grow to be.

To Know ...

This is the first building block of the witch's pyramid. Before witches do magick they must know what they are going to do, what magickal tools they will need, what their intent is, and what the karmic repercussions of their actions will be. And finally they must know that their magick is going to happen. Are you ready for the magick that will happen inside when you decide that you want to be a witch?

If Wicca Is Right for You

Most people who come to the craft have always marched to the tune of a different drummer. Or, as Denise puts it, they've felt like round pegs in square holes and have not found the right answer in other religions. Maybe as a kid you hugged a tree and felt there was life and something really precious inside it. Or maybe you have always had a special feeling for animals. Many Wiccans were plagued by a sense of dissatisfaction when they practiced more conventional religions that don't take into account the central role of Nature and the Earth. If God created both humankind and Nature, how is it possible, they ask, that He cares only about humans? Isn't Nature equally His creation? Doesn't He care about it, too?

Most Wiccans don't like to be told what to do or to hear stock answers from their religion. They find their truths for themselves and define their own inner spirituality. Many have found great joy and fulfillment in the independence of working one-on-one with deity. Wiccans are also open to new ideas, to the existence of other realms, and are true seekers on the unconventional path of the spirit.

Have you always felt a spiritual hunger? Are you starting to feel from what you have experienced since you picked up this book that you're getting satisfied? Then Wicca may be the path for you.

So Mote It Be

Get out your notebook and turn to a blank page. Starting at the top of the page write down a list of numbers from one through 20. Now, fill in the list by jotting down beside each number one thing you have learned about Wicca. Read over your list. We bet you didn't know that you knew so much!

Turn to a clean sheet of paper. Number from one through 20 again. This time put down 20 things that you want to learn about the craft. Let this list guide you. If you ever feel at a loss for what to read about next, look at your list and pick a topic. Soon you'll start transferring topics from your list of things you want to know to a list of those your already understand.

Where to Start

You have to start within yourself. After you have determined that you want to try Wicca, you need to start listening and gathering information. Open your ears and pay attention to what people are talking about in New Age shops. Visit libraries and bookstores. Surf the Internet, and read everything you can get your hands on about the craft. The more you read, the more it all starts to make sense and form comprehensible patterns. The ideas that you have heard and sort of believed will fall into place. But you have to be hungry for it because it does involve work, searching, and study on your part.

You also should start by trying simple rituals. See how practicing ritual affects you. Does ritual fulfill you or bore you? If ritual leaves you cold, then maybe Wicca is not for you. But if it makes you feel good and as if change is happening in your life, then continue.

When to Advance Yourself in the Craft

Before you start to practice magick, it is really important that you take the time to learn the basics first. Learn all you can about deity, the elements, and ritual. Only when you really understand what magick is should you try to work with it.

Start with a beginner's book, such as the one you're holding in your hands right now, and use it as the outline for your course of study. Learn all about the various aspects of the craft, but don't limit yourself to this book alone—read several books about each area. Acquaint yourself with as many different authors and viewpoints as you can. Unlike in some other religions, in Wicca there is no single approved way of explaining the various aspect of the faith. You have to come to your own understandings. To do that, you'll need to read widely. One book might explain the steps of ritual in a way that both appeals to you and makes sense. When reading another book, you might suddenly understand the elements. Gather knowledge from wherever you can get it. You need to know a lot before you commit yourself to the Wiccan path.

Webweaving

Most covens won't allow a prospective witch to dedicate until he or she has studied for a year and a day. You might want to spend a year and a day learning and absorbing before you make the decision to become a witch.

The Responsibilities of Being a Witch

There are many responsibilities that come with being a witch. One of the major responsibilities is to understand what you are doing. If you practice magick without a firm base of knowledge and an understanding of your own actions, you can make your life miserable. And you can make the lives of other people miserable as well.

When you become a witch you literally take on responsibility for the care of Earth. Because witches work with the Earth and her natural energies you will want to protect her, heal her, and nurture her. As a witch, you will view the whole Earth as your temple. It is your responsibility, and it is a big one, to take care of your temple. For many of you, that may mean looking at the Earth in a whole new way. You'll take Nature into consideration with everything you do. In concrete terms, you will want to recycle everything you can. For example, you'll find out how to properly dispose of potentially toxic items, such as dead batteries, instead of just sneaking them into the trash that gets dumped into a landfill.

Sharing what you have is part of the bond that you have made with the Goddess. In keeping with your promise, you'll want to put food out for the local birds, squirrels, raccoons, and other animals that live in your area.

As a witch, you also have to take responsibility for yourself and your own power. That may mean looking at different ways to handle situations in your life and learning to control your temper and your feelings of self-pity. Witches don't scream and yell about situations they don't like. They act. By the same token, you will no longer be able to mope when things don't go your way and indulge in a case of "oh poor me." As a witch, you control what happens in your life, so you can no longer blame things on other people. You have to accept the responsibility for everything that occurs in your life. So instead of blaming your financial problems on others, you will take control and fix them. Witches don't expect to be taken care of. Once you become a witch, you will probably find you will take care of other people, but most of all, you will take care of you.

Banish!

Don't cram your newfound knowledge of Wicca down the throats of your friends and relatives. It's only natural to want to share something that is new and exciting in your life. But trying to convert others runs counter to the tradition of the craft. So, don't go knocking at your neighbor's door, bent on conversion. Remember that Wicca is not the path for everyone.

What to Do with the Responsibility

The responsibility of being a witch is not a burden. It is part of what it means to be empowered. When you shoulder your responsibilities instead of avoiding them, you become empowered. The more you are willing to take on the stronger you will become. And the more empowered you are the more able you will be to empower others and to change the world. In helping to change the world, you want to make sure that you do not force your beliefs on anyone. You may believe fervently in the Wiccan path, but you cannot try to convert your friends and relatives. You have to maintain respect for their beliefs even if they are counter to your own. If you live with other people this may mean that you have to be discreet and not rock the boat by discussing your personal beliefs.

To Dare ...

We've reached the second level of the witch's pyramid. When it comes to magick, you have to determine if you have the guts to go through with it and cause change to happen. Do you dare, in your life at the present time, to make the necessary changes in yourself to become a witch?

To Take the Challenge

Becoming a witch is an immense challenge. It could require that you change your entire lifestyle and will probably spur you to look at the world and yourself differently. For one thing, you'll have to confront your dark side. A lot of us would rather not have to look at and examine the truth about ourselves. Neither do we wish to contemplate what we have done and are doing with our lives. But we need to confront these issues squarely and change the aspects we don't like.

Choosing to walk the Wiccan path is also a challenge in terms of your stamina. To be a witch, you need the mental stamina to study for years. No one will hand you pat answers on a plate. You must seek out your own truths.

You also need the stamina to get involved in what is going on around you, in this realm and in other realms. Do you have the courage to confront what is happening to animals all over the world? Can you accept the challenge to protect Nature and her creatures? That may mean speaking out against neighbors who mistreat their pets, puppy mills, hunting, or protesting the opening of a new shop that sells furs.

You may face the challenge of losing friends or having family members stop speaking to you as you begin to change. If you're a woman and are part of a family in which the women are very dependent, you will seriously disturb the family dynamics when you begin to stand on your own two feet, as all witches must do.

To Confront the Issues of the Day

As a witch, and as an informed citizen, you need to read the newspaper and listen to the news. Keep abreast of politics on the local, national, and worldwide levels, because the decisions made by political leaders affect what happens to our planet. The people in office may facilitate the destruction of wetlands or they may help to protect ecologically sensitive areas. You need to pay attention to what is going on and get out and vote. If you keep your head in box of sand, many acres of land and many species of animals could be lost. We all have the responsibility to look at the big picture. Yes, it might be really convenient for you if a developer built a new shopping mall just one mile from your home. However, you need to be aware that the developer is planning to build it on the only wetlands in your county.

If we don't look out for Nature's creatures, pretty soon they won't be here at all. Because of strong beliefs in protecting Nature and animals many Wiccans are involved with environmental organizations such as Greenpeace, or with animal rights groups such as People for the Ethical Treatment of Animals (PETA). As a witch you have to be brave enough to face the issues of the day, get involved, and help bring about change for the better.

Webweaving

Since 1971, Greenpeace has worked to protect wildlife and the environment. The organization has an informative Web site (www.greenpeaceusa.org) that will get you up to speed on the issues of the day.

PETA campaigns against animal abuse in its many forms—from animal testing in labs, to the mistreatment of circus animals, to the hideous conditions in puppy mills where dogs are treated like machines that produce a product. Their Web site (www.peta-online.org) will let you know how you can get involved.

To Get Involved in Your Community

On the local level, there are so many things you could do to make the world a better place. Check out your local community service center and see what's happening in your community. If you love animals, you might volunteer at an animal shelter to help care for the cats and dogs and find homes for them. You could help educate people to control the pet population by working with a spay-and-neuter program. Perhaps someone needs your skills to help fundraise for a program to help low-income people get their animals fixed. Or you could devote some time to helping wild animals by collecting money for a wild organization or volunteering at a wildlife center.

If you'd rather work with people, visit an assisted living community or nursing home and take the time to listen to the residents—you'll probably hear some great stories. You might want to volunteer at your local homeless shelter or shelter for battered women. Or you could organize a crime-watch group in your neighborhood. Most people say they don't have the time to do volunteer work. Most witches just do it. Typically in a coven you are required to put in a certain number of hours of community service. But you do it, not because you have to, but because you want to make a difference. So, find an organization for which you have an affinity and help them make a change.

So Mote It Be

Make a list of all the community projects you have thought about joining. No ideas? Look under Social and Human Services in the Yellow Pages. And don't forget about organizations that are devoted to animals. Or check to see if your area has a volunteer workers' placement service. Get information from four different organizations about their volunteer needs. If their needs fit your skills and temperament, pick one of these organizations and go check it out. Don't sign up for volunteer work that is impossible for you to do. Find something that works for you and give of yourself. When you do, it brings you increased energy and a sense of empowerment. Yes, you really can make a difference in the world!

To Will ...

"To will" is the third level of the witch's pyramid. When working magick, this is seen as gathering the will to form a cone of power and focusing the will so that you can see the magick happen as you send the energy out. Can you muster sufficient will-power to become a witch? We can see it happening, but can you?

To Follow Through

Most people start their study of witchcraft with all the good intentions in the world. They run out and buy all these wonderful new toys—athames, cauldrons, pentacles, and candles—but they don't know what to do with them. They sit down with a book, discover how much work is involved, and everything gets put in the box with the old knitting. Yeah, they think, I sill want to be a witch, but ...

If you want to be a witch, you've got to have willpower on several fronts. First off, don't run out there and buy all the magickal toys you see. If you do, they will sit around your house while you are learning what they are for and they will stop feeling new, interesting, and magickal to you. Wait until you have some real knowledge before you start making the serious shopping trips.

You're also going to need the willpower to get up and go to class, network, and meet people—even if it is cold and drizzling outside. Of course, it would be easier to curl up on the sofa and watch *Charmed* on TV, but if you want to be a witch, you need to go out and take that class on magick or tarot or essential oils. Focus your energies and muster the willpower to make yourself do it. Lots of people want to do it, but wanting isn't enough. You have to act on that want.

And willpower comes into play with your ritual as well. You will need willpower to make sure you say a devotion to the God and Goddess each night before you go to bed. You'll also need to exert your will to keep ritual special. The first time you take a ritual bath it will be fun. The fifth and sixth time will also probably be fun, but after awhile you might begin to take shortcuts; say, when you reach your 132nd bath .... It's not easy, and it involves work.

Banish!

Resist the temptation to just give up without having really tried. Yes, being a witch is a challenge, but challenges have their own rewards. And the more accustomed you become to facing and meeting challenges, the more you will feel able to do so. Think of it as if it were an exercise. The first day you decide to go running you wouldn't force yourself to enter a marathon. You'd start with a short distance, right? So, start yourself on the Wiccan path slowly. Don't expect instant change. Remember that real magick takes time.

To Make a Change in the World

Having the will to create change in the world will probably cause you to rearrange your schedule. You may want to stay home and watch your favorite TV show, but there's a meeting at the library to discuss how to deal with local stray dogs and cats. You may have to miss your show. But which is more important, watching TV or helping the animals? Or you may have to ask yourself, which is more important, going to your daughter's soccer game or attending a meeting at the library to discuss the deer population? As a witch, you are responsible not just to your family but to the community, Nature, and animals. It takes willpower to keep that commitment, just as it takes willpower to get a group together to clean trash from the local stream when it's a beautiful day and you could be having a cookout.

Witches are strong-willed leaders who keep at it. As a leader in your community, you will come up with creative ways to get your neighbors involved. You'll motivate them to care for the Earth and take on community projects as well. Sometimes it takes a witch to grab the broom by the handle and get things started.

To Stand Firm in Your Beliefs

Some people, when they find out that you are witch, will try to save your soul. They may talk about you behind your back, ridicule you, and they will probably fear you. Some of these people may even be individuals you had counted as your friends. It can be very difficult when people are questioning you and your beliefs all the time. What makes matters worse, many of your questioners will be angry with you because they don't understand what you are doing, and they are frightened.

People may challenge you by quoting from their religious texts. When they do this, you need to exercise your will and stay calm and firm in your beliefs. Don't let others deter you from your path. But you also don't want to lose your temper. Be kind and gentle, but stick to your guns. Allowing your anger to spill out in nastiness will only give them more ammunition to fire at you. Exhort your will to stay cool and polite while you stand firm with what you believe. Watch out for your own frustration as well. Because Wicca is a complex and highly individualized religion, doubters may throw you questions that you can't answer. Be patient with them and with yourself, and don't let the absence of a sound-byte answer sway you in your commitment to the path.

To Keep Silent ...

We have reached the fourth and final level of the witch's pyramid. When practicing magick, witches keep mum about what they have done. You should never brag about how effective your magickal workings have been. Many witches think this is often the hardest part. During the process of becoming a witch, silence is still golden.

To Listen and Learn

If you talk too much, chances are you are not really listening. And listening is the best way to learn. Any witch who feels he or she knows everything is his or her own worst enemy. There is always someone who knows more than you do about a given subject. You can feel proud of what you have learned, but don't be a show-off. You also don't want to babble about craft subjects to non-witches. Doing so could be construed as *proselytizing*.

You should discuss the craft and what you know only when you are working with your teacher or when you, yourself, are teaching. You can also talk about your knowledge if someone asks you a question. You should speak in a gentle and nurturing manner, and remember that yours is not the only

Book of Shadows

To **proselytize** means to convert someone from one belief to another. However fervently you believe in Wicca, it is not okay to try to change someone else's mind. If it is right for them, people will come to Wicca when the time is right.

answer. Within the tenets of Wicca there is only one hard and fast rule: An it harm none, do what ye will. There are many ways to honor this law. There is no one right answer. Each individual must find his or her own truth.

And Walk the Walk

You've probably heard the expression, "If you're going to talk the talk, you have to walk the walk." Well, in the craft it is better to just walk the walk and not to talk the talk. As Denise likes to say, "Be a witch by example." Your good actions will serve as an example to others who then may decide to do good works or even investigate the Wiccan path for themselves.

Some of the most amazing people in your community may be witches and you wouldn't even know it. They work with kids in scouting programs. They're involved in the issues that affect your neighborhood. They support national and international organizations that lobby for environmental issues. These people always seem to be there when you need them. And on top of all that, they are kind and friendly and seem to have their lives together. Things go well for them, but they never flaunt their successes. All that positive energy just makes you want to hang around them. These people are living the life of the witch. They don't brag. They have inner peace and they serve as great examples of how to live in our complicated modern world.

So Mote It Be

We all live noisy, hectic lives. Many of us are constantly surrounded by sound. We put on music. We turn on the radio or the TV first thing in the morning. In some homes, the TV is on all day—a steady stream of background noise. With all this noise it can be difficult to hear our own thoughts. That small voice inside that knows what you need and what you want can get drowned out by the media frenzy. Try going one week with no TV or radio, no background noise of any kind. Listen to yourself. See what you learn in the silence. You may feel fresh and more relaxed, or you may be sad, restless, or bored. Write about your experience in your notebook.

Anyone can put on a black robe, adopt a funny hairdo, and say, "I am a witch. Look at me." But what does that really say about that person? It says that what they want is attention. There's nothing wrong with having an individual style, but that is not the point of being a witch, and often outward outrageousness can detract from your real responsibility as a witch. If people are afraid of you, it will be a lot harder for you to work to improve conditions in your community. And making change for the better is what witchcraft is all about. So, save your robes for ritual. As you develop a satisfying relationship with the God and Goddess, you'll no longer feel the need to make your private life public. You'll keep many subjects just between you and deity.

To walk the walk as a witch you don't have to look the part. You may appear to be an ordinary citizen. Not everyone will recognize what you are doing or why you are doing it, but by your good actions, you will set an example. To be a witch means that you work for change and don't need to talk about the craft, because actions really do speak louder than words.

The Least You Need to Know

➤ The magick of becoming a witch requires that you know a lot. You must study and learn about your new responsibilities.

➤ Becoming a witch takes guts. You may have to confront frightening or unpleasant aspects about yourself, your family, and your community.

➤ Choosing the path of the witch takes willpower, because Wicca is not the easy road. Creating real change takes real effort.

➤ Bragging or showing off your knowledge of the craft is not only uncool, it is counterproductive. The point is not to look or act different, but to create change for the better.

Chapter 20

Magick's Astrological Correspondences

When you practice magick, you need to be aware of what is going on around you. And that includes what is happening in the stars. Remember that phrase, "As above, so below"? So, let's look up into the sky and get an idea of what is going on up there.

You probably know a little about astrology. You probably know your Sun sign. Maybe you check out your horoscope in the paper on a regular basis. But there is more to astrology than the 12 signs of the zodiac. As a witch, you should familiarize yourself with several metaphysical disciplines, astrology among them, and you will probably want to have your chart drawn up by a professional astrologer. Astrology will help you to understand yourself—your potentials and challenges—and the personalities of the people around you.

Astrology: The Cosmic Muse

Astrology was the first science. People have studied the heavens since the Sumerians built their temples from which to watch the skies in 2900 B.C.E., and they probably started observing the stars even before that. Prior to the 1600s, astrology was taught in universities all over Europe. Astrology explores the relationship between the position of the Earth and the positions of the heavenly bodies. By noting the movement of the planets, you can make note of the potential energy that will be around you on a given day at a specific hour. If these energies correspond with the kind of magick that you want to do, then you have a good time to work that magick. In addition, by examining your birth chart, you can use astrology to understand yourself and the kinds of energy you will respond to best.

Webweaving

Many famous and well-educated people have used astrology, among them Sir Isaac Newton, the mathematician, scientist, and philosopher; kings and queens throughout history, including the current British royal family; and Nancy Reagan, who managed to keep her presidential hubby's poll ratings high despite his sometimes unpopular actions.

The Zodiac Wheel of the Year

From an astrological perspective, you can see the year as a wheel, just the way we described it in Chapter 14, "Observing the Sabbats." A coincidence? We think not. If you think about it, the year is cyclical, so what better way to see it than as a wheel?

The zodiac is the name of the path that the Earth takes in its revolution around the Sun. It takes one year for the Earth to go around once. The signs of the zodiac are actually constellations in the sky that the Sun appears to pass through as we go around it. Using the preceding illustration, find where your birth date falls on the zodiac wheel—that's your Sun sign.

The wheel of the zodiac.

Zodiac Signs and Their Energies

Okay, so if you didn't already know your Sun sign, you do now. Each sign of the zodiac has a different energy, either *yin* (indirect) or *yang* (direct). These energies are sometimes described as female or feminine for yin, and male or masculine for yang.

Here are the signs and their energies.

Zodiac Signs and Their Yin/Yang Energies

Yin	Yang
Taurus	Aries
Cancer	Gemini
Virgo	Leo
Scorpio	Libra
Capricorn	Sagittarius
Pisces	Aquarius

Yin signs tend to work through indirect action. Yin is also seen as the negative electrical charge, receptive, and internally oriented. Yang, on the other hand, tends toward direct action. Yang is the positive electrical charge, outgoing, and externally oriented.

Because Aries, Gemini, Leo, Libra, Sagittarius, and Aquarius are all yang signs, they tend to share those traits in common. Similarly, all the yin signs—Taurus, Cancer, Virgo, Scorpio, Capricorn, and Pisces—tend to share those traits in common.

The ancient symbol for the balance of yin and yang energies in the Universe.

Zodiac Signs and Their Qualities

Zodiac signs have qualities—cardinal, fixed, and mutable. Each quality represents a different stage of each season—beginning, middle, and end—and a different kind of activity—beginning, preserving, and changing.

Here are the signs and their qualities.

The Zodiac Signs and Their Qualities

Cardinal	Fixed	Mutable
Aries	Taurus	Gemini
Cancer	Leo	Virgo
Libra	Scorpio	Sagittarius
Capricorn	Aquarius	Pisces

Book of Shadows

The terms **yin** and **yang** come to us from Chinese Taoist philosophy. They are archetypal opposites—the negative, passive, and female versus the positive, active, and male. In Mandarin Chinese, yin means the Moon, shade, or femininity, while yang means the Sun or masculine element.

People born under cardinal signs, at the beginning of each season, tend to be independent. They like to move ahead, start projects, get things going, but can sometimes be impatient. Individuals born under fixed signs, during the middle of a season, are consistent, reliable, determined, and persistent, but can sometimes be stubborn. Those born under mutable signs, at the end of a season, are flexible, resourceful, quick to learn, and can adapt easily to change, but can sometimes lack perseverance.

Zodiac Signs and Their Elements

Each sign of the zodiac also is associated with one of the four elements—Fire, Earth, Air, or Water—which are the basic building blocks of all life. Each element represents a distinct personality trait or temperament.

Here are the signs and their elements.

Zodiac Signs and Their Elements

Fire	Earth	Air	Water
Aries	Taurus	Gemini	Cancer
Leo	Virgo	Libra	Scorpio
Sagittarius	Capricorn	Aquarius	Pisces

Notice that there are three Fire signs, three Earth signs, three Air signs, and three Water signs. If you compare this table to the one for energies, you'll also notice that all of the Fire and Air signs are yang, while all the Earth and Water signs are yin.

Fire signs tend to be energetic, idealistic, assertive, and courageous. People born under these signs are often active, stimulating, creative, and passionate.

Earth signs are usually practical, skillful, and down-to-earth. People born under these signs are often good at dealing with physical things and financial matters.

Air signs tend to be social and intellectual. People born under these signs often operate on a mental plane and concern themselves with ideas, communication, and social interrelationships.

Water signs are usually sensitive and emotional. People born under these signs are often intuitive and romantic and seem to think with their emotions.

Planets, Their Symbols, and Energies

There is more to astrology than Sun signs. The planets, in which group we will include the Sun and the Moon, represent various energies. In your birth chart, the planets describe your desires, soul, will, vitality, and your mental and emotional nature. They also represent the people in your life.

Here are the planets with their symbols and energies.

The Planets and Their Symbols	Energies
Sun ☉	Self, creativity, life spirit, willpower
Moon ☽	Emotions, subconscious, instinct, memories
Mercury ☿	Communication, mental activity, intelligence
Venus ♀	Love, beauty, art, sociability, harmony, money, resources
Mars ♂	Action, desire, courage, physical energy, ego
Jupiter ♃	Abundance, luck, wisdom, learning, philosophy, exploration, growth
Saturn ♄	Responsibilities, limitations, perseverance, discipline, structure
Uranus ♅	Change, originality, radicalism, liberation, the unexpected, intuition
Neptune ♆	Idealism, spirituality, intuition, clairvoyance, subconscious
Pluto ♀	Regeneration, destruction, rebirth, transformation, power

When preparing to do magick, you may decide you want to pull on the energy of a certain planet. The planet might be one that has special significance in your chart, or it might represent the particular energies you'd like to have help you on a given day. Before you call on a planet, be sure you know all you can about that planet's energy. You also should know where in the sky the planet will be located on the day you plan to do ritual.

Zodiac Signs and Their Planetary Rulers

Each sign of the zodiac is ruled by a planet (or two). One way to determine which planets have significance for you is to look at the planetary rulers. Here are the signs and their planetary rulers.

Zodiac Signs and Planetary Rulers

Zodiac Sign	Planetary Ruler(s)
Aries ♈	Mars ♂ and Pluto ♀
Taurus ♉	Venus ♀
Gemini ♊	Mercury ☿
Cancer ♋	Moon ☽
Leo ♌	Sun ☉
Virgo ♍	Mercury ☿
Libra ♎	Venus ♀
Scorpio ♏	Pluto ♀ and Mars ♂
Sagittarius ♐	Jupiter ♃
Capricorn ♑	Saturn ♄
Aquarius ♒	Uranus ♅ and Saturn ♄
Pisces ♓	Neptune ♆ and Jupiter ♃

Banish!

Resist the temptation to throw up your hands and give up in the face of all this new information. You will get it! And if it is not all 100-percent clear to you immediately, that does not mean you are stupid. Remember astrology is an ancient art and the first science. No one, including you, should expect you to get it all overnight.

A sign shares certain characteristics with its ruler. For instance, Libras are usually concerned with harmony and balance and so, too, is Venus, the planetary ruler of Libra. Some signs have more than one planetary ruler. Both Pluto and Mars, for instance, rule Scorpio. People born under the sign of Scorpio tend to exhibit characteristics of Pluto—the planet of power, destruction, and regeneration—and of Mars—the planet of physical energy, boldness, and warrior ways.

The Houses

An astrological chart is divided into 12 houses. On a chart, the houses look like slices of pie. Each house represents an area of the sky at the time of your birth. Imagine that the circle in the center of the chart is the Earth. The horizontal line that divides the pie in half is the horizon. Everything above the horizon was visible in the sky at the hour of your birth. The planets below the horizon could not be seen (but that doesn't mean they aren't important).

Each house also represents an area of your life. As you can see, the houses are numbered starting on the left below the horizon line and moving counterclockwise (that's widdershins for you witches).

The 12 houses.

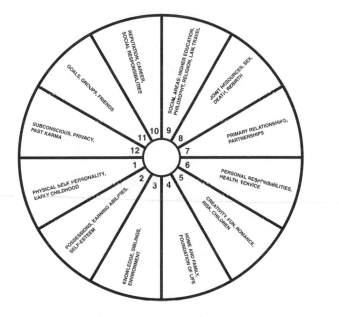

Each of the houses have planets in them on your birthchart. Each house in your chart also has its own sign.

Natural Planets and Natural Signs in Their Houses

Okay, now things start to get tricky. Remember how each sign has a planetary ruler? Well, each house has a natural planet and a natural sign.

You can think of the natural planets and natural signs as the landlord of a given house. They own the house, but they might not live there. The fact that Aries is the natural ruler of the first house will have an impact on the sign that appears in *your* first house on your birthchart.

It can get complicated, but astrology is a great tool to help you learn about yourself. Just as you would if you looked at yourself under a microscope, you

Webweaving

The ancients knew of seven "planets"—Sun, Moon, Mercury, Venus, Mars, Jupiter, and Saturn. Uranus was not discovered until 1781. Neptune was not discovered until 1846, and Pluto not until 1930.

will be able to see things with astrology that you probably wouldn't see with the naked eye. And if you should find trouble within one of your 12 houses, you could use magick to work on correcting the situation.

Natural planets and natural signs in their houses.

So Mote It Be

You might want to get your astrological chart drawn up by a professional astrologer. You can probably find one at your local metaphysical store. Don't be afraid to ask about that person's qualifications, though. You don't want just anybody doing your chart. Try to find a certified astrologer, one whose knowledge has actually been tested by others in the field. It's probably best to avoid the telephone hot-line astrologers. When you engage the services of a professional astrologer, you can simply have that person print out your chart, or you can have a consultation with the astrologer. A consultation, of course, costs more, but in it the astrologer will tell you a lot about your chart and about you.

Lunar Correspondences for Wiccan Rituals

When planning ritual, in addition to paying attention to the phase of the Moon (waxing, waning, new, or full), you also want to look at what sign the Moon is in. Because the Moon travels around the Earth quite fast, the Moon usually passes through all the signs of the zodiac in one month. That means that in a given month, the Moon spends a day or so in each sign. Each sign of the Moon has a different vibe, and that energy will affect your ritual. If you know the Moon's sign, you can plan your ritual so that lunar energy aids you in your endeavors.

Energy: Moon in Aries

With the Moon in Aries, the time is right to start new things. An Aries Moon promotes energy and ideas. It's also great for leadership, willpower, spiritual conversions, and general get-up-and-go.

Dependability: Moon in Taurus

When the Moon is in dependable Taurus, you might want to work on issues involving love or prosperity. The energy of the Taurus Moon is about love, money, and material things—not surprising when you consider that Venus, which represents love, rules Taurus.

Communication: Moon in Gemini

A Gemini Moon is great for communication, writing, and travel. Because Gemini is ruled by Mercury—the planet of communication, writing, and travel—this should come as no surprise. Want to do ritual to improve your communication skills or get that writing project done? With the Moon in Gemini is the time.

Nurturing: Moon in Cancer

A Cancer Moon has a nurturing, feminine energy. This is a good time for working on issues regarding your home, domestic life, and emotional support network. Did you remember that Cancer is ruled by the Moon? So, when the Moon is in Cancer, we get a strong dose of that nurturing energy.

Courage: Moon in Leo

When the Moon enters the sign of Leo, that brave lion, the vibe is about courage, showmanship, physical arts such as acting, fertility, and power over others. Do you need to increase your own courage? Ask the Moon for help when she is in Leo. She'll have plenty to spread around.

Self-Improvement: Moon in Virgo

When the Moon is in detail-oriented Virgo, you might want to start that self-improvement project. The Virgo Moon energy is concerned with matters of the intellect, employment, health, and, of course, details.

Balance: Moon in Libra

When the Moon is in Libra, the energies that surround us are conducive to balance—especially emotional balance. Other areas that are good to work on at this time include artistic and spiritual work, karma, and justice.

Desire and Transformation: Moon in Scorpio

A Scorpio Moon has an intense energy that hones in on matters of transformation and desire. It's a good time to work on making real changes in your life. This Moon is also concerned with sexual fantasies, which can be transformative in their own right, and psychic growth.

Exploration: Moon in Sagittarius

When the Moon is in Sagittarius, you can use that energy to explore. This is a great time for ferreting out the truth, which often involves some serious exploration. It's also a good time for work that concerns legal matters or publishing.

Webweaving

Are you fascinated by all of this? Can we recommend a book you might enjoy reading? Check out *The Complete Idiot's Guide to Astrology, Second Edition,* by Madeline Gerwick-Brodeur and Lisa Lenard (Alpha Books, 2000). It's chock full of astrological insights that can help you to better understand the important people in your life, starting with you.

Achievement: Moon in Capricorn

The Moon in Capricorn is an achievement-oriented Moon. This energy is associated with careers, political matters, and recognition. This is also a great time to get yourself organized because isn't organization the key to most success?

Revolution: Moon in Aquarius

Under an Aquarius Moon you'll feel revolution in the air. As such, this is a great time for work that involves freedom, creative expression, or problem solving. This is also a good time to cultivate your extrasensory abilities and friendships.

Compassion: Moon in Pisces

The energy of a Pisces Moon is one of compassion. In that respect, this can be a good time for healing. It's also excellent for working with dreams, clairvoyance, telepathy, and music.

Void of Course Moon

As the Moon travels around the Earth through the signs of the zodiac, it "goes void" between each sign. The period between the times when the Moon leaves one sign and enters the next one is called the Void of Course Moon. During this time, it's as if the Moon were in a tunnel. Much the way you lose the station you were listening to on your car radio when you drive through a tunnel, the Moon's energies don't do what they usually do. The Void of Course Moon or Moon Void period is best for nonmaterial, passive activities—play, yoga, psychotherapy, prayer, mediation, and sleep. While you can do ritual at this time, this is not a good time to start on magickal workings. It's also not a good time to make decisions, start a business, or buy things.

Planetary Positions for Wiccan Rituals

When you're preparing to do ritual, besides noting the position of the Moon, you want to be aware of the positions of the planets. Ideally, you'll plan your ritual so that the natural planetary energies in the atmosphere will help, rather than hinder, your work. To keep track of the location of the planets you'll probably want to buy a witches' calendar or you could get the information you need from an *ephemeris*.

Figuring out the best time for your ritual and magickal workings is a bit like doing word problems. Say you wanted to work some magick to improve communication between you and your spouse or lover. You decide you want to work with Mercury, the planet of communication. You might want to plan your ritual for a time when Mercury is in Taurus, a sign ruled by Venus, the planet of love. There are many different ways to work with the planets as they move through the signs of the zodiac. We'll give you some examples, but make sure to keep records of ritual you do. Fill out a Magickal Record each time you work (see Appendix B, "Magickal Record"), and you will start to see what works best for you.

Book of Shadows

An **ephemeris** is a book that shows where the planets are every day of the year. The book will tell you the exact position of each planet at noon and at midnight Greenwich Mean Time. (Greenwich Mean Time is five hours later than Eastern Standard Time.) Before the advent of computers, astrologers used an ephemeris and a lot of brainpower to calculate charts.

Where's the Sun?

Knowing the location of the Sun is the most widely available astrological information you'll need to find. The energy of the Sun is also probably the most powerful of all the "planets." In terms of ritual, this may mean that you want to start things when the Sun is in Aries, the first sign and the sign of new beginnings. Of course, you can begin a project at other times, but isn't spring a great, energized time for new work? Keep in mind the characteristics of each sign and it's planetary ruler and the pieces will start to fall into place. You remember that the Sun rules Leo, right? So if you were going to draw on the energy of the Sun, which is the energy of the God, you might want to do that while the Sun is in Leo.

Where's the Moon?

The Moon is the second major influence on the energies that you feel here on Earth. We've already gone into the characteristics of the Moon in all of the signs. And we've talked about the importance of the Void of Course Moon. When you're just starting out, you might want to focus on the position of the Sun and Moon first and worry about the other planets as you gain experience. (Do remember to record the positions of the other planets because they may tell you something important about your magick later on.) Keep in mind that as you add in the energies of the other planets and your "word problem" gets more complex it also gets more subtle and focused. If the Sun were in Libra and the Moon were in Cancer …. Could be a good time for nurturing your sense of balance or balancing your nurturing energies.

Book of Shadows

A planet is said to be **retrograde** when it appears to move backward in the sky from the point of view of the Earth. Of course, the planet does not move backward. It just looks that way because we are moving through the sky as well. All the true planets have retrograde periods. (The Sun and the Moon do not.) Because Mercury is fairly close to Earth, it's retrograde period can have a big impact down here. When a planet is retrograde, its energy is reversed, reconsidered, or turned inward.

Where's Mercury?

Mercury is the planet of communication so it's not a surprise that it travels fast. Mercury is also in charge of thinking, logic, reason, intelligence, and education. And remember that Mercury rules the signs of Gemini and Virgo.

Because astrologers look at the planets from the Earth and because the planets revolve around the Sun, there are times when the planets appear to be moving backward in the sky. When a planet is seen to be moving backward it is *retrograde*. In the case of Mercury, this retrograde movement happens three times a year for periods of about three weeks each.

During a Mercury retrograde, communications go awry—letters are misdelivered or arrive late, answering machines malfunction, and computers break down. In addition, travel plans fall through with flight delays, cancellations, and overbookings. In terms of your magick, you probably shouldn't try to increase communication with your lover or contact the spirit of a newly discovered ancestor during a Mercury retrograde period. This is also a bad time to buy high-tech devices—computers, cell phones, digital satellite receivers for television reception. And it's an inauspicious time for signing legal papers. Use this time to reflect, reconsider, and review your magickal workings.

Where's Venus?

Just like Mercury, Venus can go retrograde. During these times, the energies associated with the planet can be harder to work with. If you're looking to increase love, harmony, or balance in your life, probably better to do it when Venus is moving direct, or forward through the sky. But it's a great time to reconsider your relationship and personal possession needs. Want to add some enthusiasm to your love life? Try working on that area when Venus is in Aries, the sign of new beginnings and fresh energy.

Where's Mars?

Mars is the planet of action, desire, courage, physical energy, and ego. If you want to work with these energies when they are intense, you can plan to do ritual when Mars is in Aries, the sign that the planet rules. Or you could get a super hit of Mars's energy when the Sun is in Aries and Mars is in Aries. Watch out for the retrograde period, though. During this time old resentments can resurface. It's a good time to sit back and look at your motivations and develop new strategies for dealing with your issues and anger.

Where's Jupiter?

Jupiter is associated with abundance, luck, wisdom, learning, philosophy, exploration, and growth. Since Jupiter moves slowly in the sky—it takes a whole year for it to pass through one sign of the Zodiac—you won't be able to time rituals using this planet the way you would with the faster moving ones. The Jupiter retrograde period lasts for about four months and is best used for internal growth and preparation for the opportunities that will come when the planet goes direct. Concentrate on developing your understanding so you can tell if the things being offered to you are what you really want.

Where's Saturn?

Saturn is concerned with responsibilities, limitations, perseverance, discipline, and structure. It takes Saturn $29\frac{1}{2}$ years to orbit once around the Sun. During a Saturn retrograde, which lasts for four and a half months, try to become aware of your own power and how it fits into the structure of society. You also might want to examine how you fit into society and try to gauge to what extent you are letting its rules limit you and your potential.

Where's Uranus?

Uranus is the planet of change, originality, radicalism, liberation, the unexpected, and intuition. Uranus, another one of the slow-moving planets, is retrograde for five months out of every year. The retrograde period is a time to look at the changes being made in the world and your part in them. Are you really contributing to the betterment of the planet, or are you making things worse? Try to see the connections between your personal shifts and those in the world around you.

Where's Neptune?

Idealism, spirituality, intuition, clairvoyance, and the subconscious are all the province of Neptune. The retrograde period, which lasts about five months every year, is time best spent tuning into the collective unconscious. How are your fears, illusions, and spiritual development connected to the situation of humanity at large? Think about whether you are using your energies to develop faith and spirituality or if you are following a path of escapism.

Where's Pluto?

Slow-moving Pluto, concerned with regeneration, destruction, rebirth, transformation, and power, takes about 248 years to orbit the Sun. The retrograde period lasts for about five months of every year. This is a time to step back and look at how you are contributing to the evolution of humankind and the Earth. Try to become more conscious of how you impact the Earth and the other creatures that live here, too.

Webweaving

Ever wonder why our week has seven days? The ancients decided that there should be seven days in a week because that was how many planets or celestial bodies they could see. Each day is named after one of these seven.

Planetary Rulership of Hours

Now you know about Sun signs, the impact of the Moon in the various signs, and the movement of the planets. There's even a way to determine what hour of the day is best for your magick. As you may know, different days of the week are associated with different planets.

Here are the days of the week and the planets that rule them. If you look at the Spanish names for the planets, it's easier to see which planet rules which day.

Planets and Days of the Week

Sunday	Sun ☉
Monday	Moon ☽
Tuesday (*martes* in Spanish)	Mars ♂
Wednesday (*miércoles* in Spanish)	Mercury ☿
Thursday (*jueves* in Spanish)	Jupiter ♃
Friday (*viernes* in Spanish)	Venus ♀
Saturday	Saturn ♄

And on each day, every hour also has its own planetary rulership. The planet whose day it is rules the first hour of that day. In other words, the Sun, the planet of Sunday, rules the first hour after sunrise of Sunday; and the Moon, the planet of Monday, rules the first hour after sunrise of Monday, and so on. The remaining 23 hours in each day are ruled by different planets throughout the day. The following table details all of the hours of the week and the planets that rule them.

Planetary Rulership of the Hours

Hours	Sun.	Mon.	Tues.	Wed.	Thurs.	Fri.	Sat.
1 (sunrise)	Sun	Moon	Mars	Mercury	Jupiter	Venus	Saturn
2	Venus	Saturn	Sun	Moon	Mars	Mercury	Jupiter
3	Mercury	Jupiter	Venus	Saturn	Sun	Moon	Mars
4	Moon	Mars	Mercury	Jupiter	Venus	Saturn	Sun
5	Saturn	Sun	Moon	Mars	Mercury	Jupiter	Venus
6 (midday)	Jupiter	Venus	Saturn	Sun	Moon	Mars	Mercury
7	Mars	Mercury	Jupiter	Venus	Saturn	Sun	Moon
8	Sun	Moon	Mars	Mercury	Jupiter	Venus	Saturn
9	Venus	Saturn	Sun	Moon	Mars	Mercury	Jupiter
10	Mercury	Jupiter	Venus	Saturn	Sun	Moon	Mars
11	Moon	Mars	Mercury	Jupiter	Venus	Saturn	Sun
12	Saturn	Sun	Moon	Mars	Mercury	Jupiter	Venus
1 (sunset)	Jupiter	Venus	Saturn	Sun	Moon	Mars	Mercury
2	Mars	Mercury	Jupiter	Venus	Saturn	Sun	Moon
3	Sun	Moon	Mars	Mercury	Jupiter	Venus	Saturn
4	Venus	Saturn	Sun	Moon	Mars	Mercury	Jupiter
5	Mercury	Jupiter	Venus	Saturn	Sun	Moon	Mars
6 (midnight)	Moon	Mars	Mercury	Jupiter	Venus	Saturn	Sun
7	Saturn	Sun	Moon	Mars	Mercury	Jupiter	Venus
8	Jupiter	Venus	Saturn	Sun	Moon	Mars	Mercury
9	Mars	Mercury	Jupiter	Venus	Saturn	Sun	Moon
10	Sun	Moon	Mars	Mercury	Jupiter	Venus	Saturn
11	Venus	Saturn	Sun	Moon	Mars	Mercury	Jupiter
12	Mercury	Jupiter	Venus	Saturn	Sun	Moon	Mars

Say you were planning some candle magick to help you feel more attractive. You might want to light that candle on Friday, the day of Venus. Or you could light the candle at the hour of Venus on another day, or, to increase the Venus energy, you could light the candle at the hour of Venus on Friday. If you wanted to communicate your love better, you could light a candle on Wednesday, the day of Mercury (the planet of communication) at the hour of Venus.

The Least You Need to Know

➤ Astrology is a great way to learn more about yourself and the people around you.

➤ Each Sun sign is associated with a planet (and in some cases two). That planet is the ruler of its sign. A planet and its sign share certain characteristics.

➤ The houses on an astrological chart have natural signs and natural planets. These are like landlords who own each house. In addition, each house in your chart will be ruled by one of the planets, depending on which sign is on the cusp of the house.

➤ With a little knowledge of astrology, you can work your magick at times when the stars can help you achieve your goals.

➤ Astrology can even help you pick the hour at which to begin ritual for a given purpose.

Magickal Timing

There is a right time for every action. After reading the last chapter, you know about the major astrological issues involved in choosing when to do ritual and magick. But there's more ....

Even though magick can be done at any time, it's important for you to know that there are optimum times for every type of magick. If you coordinate your magick with the proper time of day, movements of the planets, and season, you can make it stronger. Of course, you don't have to engage in a lot of elaborate planning. You can use magick in an emergency with little or no planning and you'll probably still get results.

When there is something important coming up in your life (and you have tried all the mundane solutions at your disposal), why not plan ahead and give your magick an energy boost? All you have to do is select a good time for the kind of magick you plan to do. Picking the best time for your magick ritual may seem a little tricky at first, but with practice, you'll catch on quickly. Make sure that you write down what you've done and the circumstances under which you've done it so you can compare magick that has been planned to what happens when you don't plan.

Magick All Day Long

Different parts of the day have different energies, and you'll need to consider the inherent energy that surrounds us at these various times. Remember that you can do your magick any time you want. So, if you are not free to practice ritual at 2 P.M. on a Wednesday during the Full Moon, when the time might be perfect for you, don't worry. However, your magick will be even more effective if you do your workings at the time of day that is most conducive to the energies you are using. The great things about working with daily magickal timing is that you'll always get another chance tomorrow.

Morning Magick: Sunrise

The Sun is up. The birds are singing. Doesn't this seem like a good time to start something? Well, it is! Even if you are a late sleeper (like Katherine), you are fresher in the morning when you first get up and so is your energy. You can channel that extra energy into your magick and start something new with the new day. This is also a great time to get rid of any negativity that might be hanging around you from the previous day. If you've had a fight with a spouse or a lover and gone to bed mad or have run into aggravating issues at work, now is a good time to chase away those bad feelings so you can start your day with a clean slate.

So Mote It Be

Most people start their workdays in the morning. People also start their diets in the morning. So, to help yourself get rid of that extra weight, why not do magick when you first get up, on an empty stomach? Do this when the Moon is waning and you'll have the willpower to get rid of the weight.

First thing in the morning is also a good time to work with addictive behaviors and bad habits. For example, if you overeat compulsively, you could do a spell in the morning to make that day a binge-free day.

The start of the day is also good for magick having to do with business, school, or anything else that gears up in the morning. You might want to work with employment issues—getting a job, receiving that raise or promotion—early in the day. If you're looking for a job, magick at this time could help hook you up with the right people who have the job for you.

Midday Magick: Sunshine

During the middle of the day the Sun is at its strongest. This is a good time to call on that strength. You might want to work on overcoming a weakness that you have, and the energy of the Sun can help you to do just that. Most people take a break from working in the middle of the day. This is a great time to reset yourself. Have some lunch and do some magick to help you see the project of the day through. This is also a great time to ask for guidance or inspiration to rethink something that needs to be started all over again. Do some magick for the success of your project at noon, and you'll know that this time you are on the right track.

Evening Magick: Crepuscular Light

The light of the Sun fades in the sky and evening is drawing nigh. You might get home feeling tired and cranky from your long day. Although lots of people come home and have a drink or raid the refrigerator, why not arrive home, take a hot shower, and do ritual instead? This is great time to do magick to break up routines or banish bad habits. If you do ritual one night when you come home, it may stop you from eating that bag of chips. And the next night you'll be more likely to reach for a piece of fruit. This is a great time to work magick to boost your willpower, to help you relax, and to give yourself calmness and serenity.

Nighttime Magick: Resonating in Tune

After the Sun has set, we are better able to feel the energy of the Moon and the Goddess. This is a great time for divination and working with psychic energies. You might also want to work with issues involving love, lust, or beauty. And, of course, this is a good time to reflect on what has happened during the day. By the time you reach night, you may be pretty fed up with your work, school, or family. Doing magick at this time, can help you re-member that things are not always the way they appear. Getting some clarity on the events of your day can help you to banish the negativity around you. That way you can start the cycle again in the morning with a fresh outlook and renewed energy.

Magick All Week Long

You can also look at the cycle of the week when planning your magick. Remember in the previous chapter we talked about each day of the week being named for a different planet? Well, the days of the week also have genders based on their planetary associations. You'll want to keep this in mind too when planning the optimum time for your magickal workings.

Banish!

Try not to stay up very late doing divination when you need to get up early the next morn-ing. Nighttime may be a great time for looking into the future and tapping into your psychic energy, but even witches need sleep. And remember: You can do your magick at any time.

Webweaving

We know that you know the days of the week. Just keep in mind that they are named after the seven heavenly bodies of the ancient world—the Sun, Moon, Mercury, Venus, Mars, Jupiter, and Saturn.

Sunday (Sun ☉) Magick

The energy of Sunday, which is named for the Sun, is male. Sunday is the best day of the week to work with issues involving fathers and other authority figures. Sundays are great for working on questions of leadership, money, prosperity, and power. They are also good days to focus on your health, vitality, energy, and happiness.

Monday (Moon ☽) Magick

The energy of Monday is associated with the Moon and is female. This is a great day to work with Moon energy so you might want to do divination. This is also a good time to focus on issues involving mothers, nurturing, fertility, and growth. Monday is also a good time to work for clarity, beauty, or help with women's issues.

Tuesday (Mars ♂) Magick

Tuesdays are full of the male energy of Mars. This energy is one of courage, success, and lust. This is a good time to give attention to issues dealing with violence, competition, conflict, or survival. Tuesdays are also good for questions of money, endurance, and leadership.

Book of Shadows

The name **Tuesday** comes from the Germanic god Tiu. Tiu, like the Roman god Mars and the planet Mars, is associated with war. **Wednesday** comes from the Old English name "Woden's Day." This name was a direct translation of the Latin term *mercurii dies*, "day of (the god and planet) Mercury." When they translated the name, they also translated the god into one to which local people could relate. **Thursday** comes from the Old English and Old Norse for "Thor's day," a translation of the Latin name that meant "Jupiter's day." **Friday** comes from the Old English name *frigedaeg*, which is derived from the name of the Norse Goddess Frigg, who, like both the planet and the goddess Venus, is associated with love.

Wednesday (Mercury ☿) Magick

Wednesday is named for Mercury, a planet with male energy. This is a great day for working with communications, thought, self-expression, wisdom, and the arts. The energy of Mercury will also aid magick having to do with issues of addiction and psychology. Wednesdays are also good days to do divination.

Thursday (Jupiter ♃) Magick

The male energy of Jupiter prevails on *Thursdays*. This energy is conducive to work with growth and expansion, business, prosperity, abundance, success, and health. Thursdays are also great times to focus your magick on the big issues in your life.

Friday (Venus ♀) Magick

Friday is associated with Venus and has female energy. Fridays are great days for workings having to do with love, beauty, and romance. The Venus energy of Fridays will also aid magick involving healing, protection, loyalty, fidelity, trustworthiness, and women's issues.

Saturday (Saturn ♄) Magick

The Saturn energy of Saturday is female. This is a good day to work with divination and psychic abilities. Saturn energies will aid magick concerning the elderly, illness, death, and end of life issues. Saturday is also a good day to do binding spells and to deal with constrictions, limitations, or infidelity in your life.

Magick by the Season

You can also work with the energies of each season—the freshness of spring, heat of summer, preparations of autumn, and the turning inward associated with winter as we move through the cycle of the year. The change in energy as we progress through the seasons is probably familiar to you. Who hasn't noticed the fresh, new quality to spring or the hunkering down we experience in winter?

If you want to get even more specific about the energies that are in the air during different times of the year, you can take the signs of the zodiac into account as well. (To pinpoint the exact moment when we switch from one sign of the zodiac to another, consult an almanac or a witch's calendar.) One of the neat things about working with the signs is that you can buy (or mix) essential oils that represent the energy of each sign. For instance, if you have decided to work with the calm, dependable energy of Taurus during the month of Taurus, you might want to do some candle magick and anoint your candle with Taurus oil. And don't forget—the Moon will be moving through all of the signs of the zodiac during the month as well.

Spring: Bring Forth New Life

Just as trees unfurl new buds in the spring, you'll want to start on new projects, too. Spring is a great time to do magick dealing with issues concerning new projects and new beginnings. You might want to try using powders to do air magick at this time of year to take advantage of gusting spring winds. This is also a great time to do divination to see what is going to happen in the new season. The energies of spring will help you bring love toward you and will enhance any new project. If you're thinking of selling your house, this is a good time to make plans to do so.

So Mote It Be

Spring, of course, is a time of fertility and planting. If you are growing a magick garden, now is the time to prepare the soil and get ready for planting. Because it is the planting season, this is also a great time for Earth magick. You can double your magickal effect by putting your magickal energy into some seeds and planting them. The magickal energy with which you have infused the seeds will help them to grow, and when they burst forth with life, your magickal intent will manifest as well.

The Energies of Aries ♈: March 21–April 20

Start that new project now! The Aries energy in the air will help you do it. So, if there's a task or area of your life you've been meaning to work on for a long time, this is the time to go for it. This is also a good time to work magick around issues of leadership, assertiveness, aggression, and enthusiasm. Use that fiery Aries energy to get your magickal plans off to a blazing start!

The Energies of Taurus ♉: April 20–May 21

The energies out there under Taurus are still conducive to new beginnings. But the feeling is more stable and grounded. This is a great time to work magick concerning issues of prosperity, comfort, peace, harmony, and dependability, and you might want to take a look at your love life. You could also work magick on some volatile issues—if you have a lot of conflict at work, for instance—and the energy of the month would help to lend stability and steadiness to your task.

The Energies of Gemini ♊: May 21–June 22

This month the energy in the air has an amusing, witty quality. You might want to tap into that and bring some more humor into your life. Gemini energy is also concerned with knowledge, communication, flexibility, motion, and travel. This would be a great time to work magick to learn something new, facilitate communication, travel, and to change—especially your mind.

Summer: Strong and Sure

The energies of the summer are strong and sure just like the Sun in the sky. These energies can enhance magick dealing with beauty, healing, health, and nurturing. This is a great time to do workings concerning a project that you've had to restart. You'll also find that the energies are right to nurture a love affair that you have already begun. The energies of summer can bring strength and endurance. If you are selling a house, this is a great time to show it to perspective buyers.

The Energies of Cancer ♋: June 22–July 23

You can use the nurturing energies of Cancer to work magick having to do with your home, warmth, family, and family relations. This is also a good time to look at issues involving feelings, sensitivity, and giving of the self. You might want to work magick to allow you to give of yourself more freely, or you could do magick for someone else (with that person's permission, of course).

Alternatively, you could work magick to make others want to give of themselves and nurture. Activity in this vein could help bring your family together or build a strong team or support network.

The Energies of Leo ♌: July 23–August 22

The month of Leo is all about courage, showmanship, creativity, fertility, and willpower. You might want to do magick to enhance your leadership skills or to become the leader of a group. Leo energy will also help you with issues involving generosity, ambition, pride, physical appearance, and being in the spotlight. Yes, Leo, it is time for your close-up!

The Energies of Virgo ♍: August 22–September 22

The vibe while we are in the month of Virgo is one of service, organization, and self-improvement. This would be a good time to work magick to help you analyze and solve a problem that has been eating at you for a long time. This is also a good time to focus your magickal work on global problems and their solutions. Virgo energy will also aid you with issue concerning mental energy, health, employment, responsibility, and details, details, details.

Webweaving

You may know that the sign of Virgo is associated with virgins. But did you know that a virgin isn't just someone who is sexually inexperienced? A virgin is someone who respects and honors the sacred patterns of life, and realizes that we must be whole unto ourselves in pursuit of the divine.

Autumn: Accumulating and Taking Stock

In autumn, squirrels gather up food for the winter. They need to accumulate food and assess if they have enough to ensure their survival. For humans, this is a good time for similar activities—workings regarding possessions, money, prosperity, durability, survival, and employment. This is a great time to focus on what you have and ways that you can enhance what is already there. The energies of autumn are also associated with issues of spirituality, relationships, and family. If you have troubles in any of these areas, healing magick during the autumn could be particularly effective. Autumn is also a time to take care of any remaining tasks left over from projects you have already started. You should get ready for closure. For example, if you are selling a house, this is the time to figure out what you really need and strike a deal.

The Energies of Libra ♎: September 22–October 23

Libra energy is concerned with balance, harmony, and justice. This is also a good time to work magick with energies of charm, compassion, and idealism. You might want to use your workings to establish cordial relations with someone from who you have been estranged. This is also a great month for magick that has to do with mental energy, idealism, spirituality, love relationships, and issues of friendship and popularity.

The Energies of Scorpio ♏: October 23–November 22

This month you can use the intense energy of Scorpio to effect change in the areas of your life involving sexuality, desire, and power. This is another good time to work on issues involving leadership. You also could look at the profound questions—life, death, birth, sex, and transformation. Scorpio energy is also conducive to psychic awareness.

The Energies of Sagittarius ♐: November 22–December 22

The energies of Sagittarius are those of enthusiasm, exploration, freedom, independence, and fun. This is a great time to work magick to free yourself of the things that bind you—addictions, bad habits, objects that you don't need. You could also look at questions involving truth, honesty, optimism, philosophy, legal matters, and publishing. But maybe you'll want to tap into the fun vibe and do some magick to have a really good time.

Winter: Nurturing Within

Winter is a time when we naturally turn within. It's cold out there, so what better time to stay inside and reflect? This is a great time for meditation, divination, and working with past lives. You could also deal with banishing and issues having to do with survival and death. This is a great time to do some Nature magick to help the animals that live near you. Send your magick out so that they find the food they need to survive. You could also do some magick for your own prosperity so that you can be sure you have enough to share with others in need. Or you could work on sharing your energy and enthusiasm by volunteering for a community project. Many witches give a lot of their time to community service. The magick there is that others will see you involved and will want to pitch in and help make change, too.

So Mote It Be

You can try this in winter because it's a good time for meditation or at any at other time of the year: Get a deck of Tarot cards and check the astrological correspondences of each card of the Major Arcana. (If this means nothing to you, don't worry. We'll tell you about Tarot cards in Chapter 26, "Dreams and Visions.") Find the cards that correspond to the current sign of the zodiac. Shuffle them and pick one. Study the image on the card. Meditate on it, and see what it can teach you about the issues in your life or about any situation that comes up for you during the month.

The Energies of Capricorn ♑: December 22–January 21

The energies that abound this month are ones of ambition, achievement, and self-control. This is a great time to tap into that Capricorn vibe and reach your career goal. The energy of Capricorn is also concerned with efficiency, politics, structure, organization, responsibility, and helping others. You could do some magick now to allow yourself to take on responsibility of a community service project, or you could do some magick that would help others to shoulder some weight.

The Energies of Aquarius ♒: January 21–February 19

The energy of Aquarius is inventive, creative, and original. This is a great time to do something different, maybe even something revolutionary. Aquarius energies will also help you to bring something to light so that it is obvious. You might want to use this renegade energy to make a statement or take a stand on an issue. This is also a great month for humanitarian projects. So, maybe you'll use the psychic abilities this month fosters to come up with a revolutionary solution to the problems of homelessness and hunger in your community.

The Energies of Pisces ♓: February 19–March 21

Because Pisces energy is compassionate this is a good time for healing work of any kind. This is also a great time to work magick to develop spirituality in yourself or others. You might want to work with issues concerning emotions, faith, dreams, clairvoyance, and telepathy. The month of Pisces is also a great time to get in touch with your higher power.

Banish!

Avoid allowing feelings of being overwhelmed to stop you from doing your magick. Yes, we have thrown a lot of information at you. Remember you can do magick at any time. Consider the energies that are out there waiting to help you when you plan, but know that you don't always have to do everything at the best possible time. Sometimes we do things when we can, and sometimes we act when we have to.

Real Magick Takes Time

The type of magick that witches practice never yields immediate results on the material plane. Sorry, but that is the truth. What can happen quickly is the magickal change inside you—the feeling that you get when you practice ritual and know that your magick will happen. Often you can come away from your magickal workings with sense of empowerment and a "spiritual high." And, well, we do think that is magick!

Real change—and that is what real magick effects—takes time. And magick will take its time. The goal you are working toward will manifest when it is supposed to happen. Sure, on rare occasions you will put your magick out there, and the next day the phone will ring and that ace job that you have been after will be yours. But know that you have gotten it quickly because it was the time for the job to be yours. Usually you put your magick out there and then you wait a week or two, or a month, or more.

The Least You Need to Know

➤ You can do the magick you need to do any time of the day, day of the week, and month of the year.

➤ If you want to do your magick under optimum conditions, you should consider which natural energies are in force and pick your time based on how well they correspond to your magickal purpose.

➤ Magickal timing involves concepts that you already understand and use to judge the energies around you. For example, spring and the morning are times of new beginning, and because of this they are good times to start new things.

➤ Magick takes time. You will not snap your fingers or twitch your nose and effect real change. On the other hand, when you start to practice magick you may feel the internal transformation almost immediately!

Part 6

Witches' Brew: Notions, Potions, and Powders

It's time for you to start bubbling and boiling. You'll learn even more about magick in this part, and we'll talk about how you can write your own spells. But you're not totally on your own. We've provided a bunch of spells for you, and we'll tell you how to look into the future, your dreams, and take a glimpse into the beyond.

Candle
magick

weather
magick

This Magick ROCKS!

Sex Magick

Chapter 22

More Ways to Work Magick

In This Chapter

➤ Magick that's done and undone

➤ Light the candle or incense

➤ Magick of glamour and the kitchen

➤ What about the weather?

➤ Yes, more—clay, powder, paper, and flowers

Yes, there are even more ways to work magick. In this chapter, we'll give you some specific spells and incantations that you can use. We'll also give you some more general ideas for how you can use still other materials in your magick. Remember it is your magick and your creativity is a part of it.

Magick is like a recipe; it's a pinch of this and a pinch of that, plus your own personal intent. Magick works because you direct energy to make the desired result happen. As you know, you should always try the mundane solutions available to you before you turn to magick. If all of the everyday means of solving your problem fail, then you can use magick. But remember, even if you do magick, you must still continue to act on the mundane plane. You'll need to stick to your diet if you want to lose weight, and you'll need to send out those resumes if you want a new job.

Poppets

Poppet magick—magick involving a specially empowered doll—is great to use for binding spells, healing, or to lose weight. Some witches shy away from poppet magick because it reminds them too much of the stereotyped notion of *voodoo* dolls. Others avoid poppet magick because they don't want to do the work that it entails. But poppet magick is good, strong magick. And it lets you express your creativity to a high degree. Remember to keep any poppet you have made in a safe place. The doll you make represents the person for whom you have done the magick. So, you wouldn't want anything unplanned to happen to that doll.

Let's say you want to do poppet magick to heal a sick child. First, ask the child's parents if you have their permission to do magick for their child. If so, make the poppet while inside your magick circle, and put your healing intent and any herbs or other magickal ingredients that you want to use into it. Sew the poppet up while putting your intent into it and give it to the child in question. If the child is in the hospital, this could be a soothing reminder of your love and good wishes as the spell begins to work its magick.

You could also use poppet magick to stop someone from gossiping. Remember that you are binding the person's behavior and not the actual person or the person's free will. When doing a binding poppet, you should incorporate a small object that belonged to the person in question. Keep your intent in mind as you sew, then literally bind the poppet's mouth with cloth or string. Put the poppet away in a safe place where no one will disturb it, and the gossip will stop.

Book of Shadows

You've probably heard of **voodoo,** or voudou. Many of us carry a negative impression of this Afro-Caribbean religion, but we shouldn't. Healing is at the heart of voodoo, which is often described as a mixture of African ancestor reverence, Native American Earth religion, and European Catholicism. And voodoo, like Wicca, gives all women a central and powerful role.

What You Need for Poppet Magick

To do poppet magick you'll need some supplies:

➤ Fabric in a color that corresponds to your magickal intent (For a list of colors and their magickal associations, see Chapter 17, "Enhancing Your Magick Power." Or use white, which substitutes for all colors.)

➤ A needle and thread

➤ Stuffing (You can use scraps of cloth, cotton, wool, or fiberfill.)

Then you should add some of these:

➤ Herbs, flowers, fruits, or vegetables that correspond to your magickal intent

➤ Essential oils that correspond to your magickal intent

➤ Crystals or stones that correspond to your magickal intent (see Chapter 18, "Magick Powers of Nature")

➤ A piece of cloth, hair, or fingernail clippings that belong to the person for whom you are doing the poppet, or a photograph of that person

➤ Amulets or talismans

➤ Magickal messages or symbols (You can write these on paper or fabric and sew them into your poppet, or you can attach them to the outside.)

If you want to incorporate the elements into your magick, you could attach, sprinkle, or stuff your poppet with the following:

➤ Sand to represent the element of Earth

➤ Feathers to represent the element of Air

➤ Incense to represent the elements of Air and Fire

➤ A magickal potion to represent the element of Water

➤ Salt water to represent the elements of Water and Earth

➤ Holy water to represent Water and Spirit

After you are finished making the poppet, cleanse and consecrate it by passing it through each of the elements. The smoke of your incense represents Fire and Air and a sprinkling of salt water represents Earth and Water.

Webweaving

People also make poppets from wax. In England in 1609, Frances, Lady Essex, used a poppet to make her husband impotent so she could get her marriage annulled and marry Sir Robert Carr. She got to marry Carr, but in 1613 they were both imprisoned because of her magickal workings. Luckily, they were pardoned later.

Stopping the Magick

The biggest advantage to poppet magick is that the spell is easy to undo, so it can be used for magick that is of temporary duration. If you want to stop the spell, simply take the poppet apart. If you have done a weight-loss poppet for yourself, once you have reached your goal, you would dismantle the poppet so you would not continue to shed pounds.

When you undo a poppet, you can use this little chant:

With this spell I've begun,
I now wish the magick to be undone.

Be aware that the poppet represents a person and should be treated gently. You never, never want to burn a poppet. If you want to work with the element of Fire, you can try candle magick instead. In addition, you should make sure that the place you store your poppet is safe. The kids shouldn't play with it, and neither should the dog get his teeth into it. Store the poppet away until the magick manifests. Once the magick has come to pass, take the poppet apart and bury the pieces.

Candle Magick and Incense Magick

You can use candle magick and incense magick for just about any magickal purpose. You need to charge your candle or incense with your magickal intent before you light it. Then, when you do light it, you're sending out your magick. See the magick rising toward the Gods. You can help send the magick upward by using a feather as a fan.

What You Need for Candle Magick

Candles come in lots of shapes, sizes, and colors. You can buy a candle in the form of a cat, angel, devil, skull, cross, or human figure. You can also get candles that have seven knobs, candles that burn for seven days, bicolored candles, multicolored candles, floating candles, and ones that are one color on the inside and another color outside.

Here's what you'll need to assemble for your candle magick:

➤ A candle in a color that corresponds to your magickal intent

➤ A small pointed crystal or your bolline (magick knife used for cutting physical objects)

➤ An essential oil that corresponds to your magickal intent

➤ Herbs that correspond to your magickal intent

➤ A mortar and pestle

➤ A candle holder

To do a candle spell to bring yourself money, use your crystal or bolline to carve your desire on the candle. You need to be specific about what you write on the candle. Remember be careful what you wish for because you just might get it. It's nice to use a crystal because the crystal itself will also pull in energy and infuse the candle with added energy.

Then dress the candle with a magickal oil that represents your intent. When doing candle magick to bring something to them, many witches use this candle dressing method. Hold the candle so that one end faces you. Start applying oil to the candle from the middle and move your hand toward you. Then turn the candle around and coat the other half by moving your hand toward you. If you were doing magick to take something away, you would coat the candle with oil by moving your hand away from you. If you make your own magickal oils, you can empower the oil with herbs that also represent the intent of your spell.

You can also load a candle with magickal herbs. To do this, hollow out a hole in the bottom of your candle. Mix your herbs with some essential oil and fill the hole with the herb and oil mixture. Concentrate on your magickal intent while you work. Seal the hole up with wax, and your loaded candle is ready to use! When the candle burns down to your herb mixture, the herbs will ignite and blast your magick out to its destination. Be extra sure that you use this candle in an area where you won't start a fire because the herbs can flare up quite a bit. It's usually a good idea to place your loaded candle in a deep candle cup or in the bathtub to finish burning.

A Candle Magick Spell

Here's an example of a weight-loss spell using candle magick. You should do this on a waning Moon (see Chapter 13, "Esbats: Moon Magick"). You'll need a black candle on which you will write how much weight you want to lose. Be reasonable—don't put down so much that you may do harm to yourself.

As you empower the candle with your intent, chant the following:

> As this candle melts away,
> So do the pounds that hold me sway.
> As each day passes I will be
> Closer to a thinner me.
> This is my will, so mote it be!

Keep chanting and feel the energy in you build and build until you feel like you might pop. Grab the candle. See the magick happening and drive all that energy into the candle. Light the candle and know that your magick has come to pass. Let the candle burn all the way down. Remember, if you absolutely must put out the candle, never blow it out, because you will blow all the magick away. Always pinch it or stuff it out so you can relight it later.

So Mote It Be

When you mix herbs and essential oils together, it's easiest to add the oil to the herbs, not the herbs to the oil. As you stir the herbs, drip oil on to them a little at a time and mix them together with your mortar and pestle. If you try to add the herbs to the oil, they will just float.

Another Candle Magick Spell

After you have built your cone of power, put the energy into your candle, and lit it, you can use this all-purpose incantation to send your magick on its way:

> Loud is my message as the raven's cry,
> Send out this magick, send it high.
> Make it work, make it last,
> Tell the God's of this spell I've cast.
> Have it happen without complexity,
> This is my will so mote it be.

What You Need for Incense Magick

Incense magick is easy because you probably already have all the supplies you need. If you want, you can make your own incense from sawdust, herbs, and essential oils. Otherwise, you will just need the following:

Webweaving

Many witches make their own incense. Some believe that the smell of homemade incense is more pleasant. If you make it yourself, you'll know that it contains only natural ingredients. Another advantage is that you can mix in your magickal intent when you make it. Scott Cunningham's *The Complete Book of Incense, Oils, and Brews* (Llewellyn, 1989) contains some great recipes.

➤ Incense in stick, cone, or powder form that corresponds with your magickal intent

➤ Charcoal (to burn if you are using powdered incense)

➤ A censer or cauldron

➤ A lighter

An Incense Magick Spell

For this spell, which you can you can use for any purpose, you will need a feather in addition to your incense. Empower the incense with the following chant:

> Charge this incense strong and fast,
> To send out the magick I shall cast.
> Burn so quickly and burn so bright,
> This magick incense I will light.

Let the energy build and build. Then light the incense. With the feather, fan your incense to carry your magickal intent up into the air. You can visualize different birds carrying your message up to the Gods. Imagine that they are passing it from bird to bird, rising higher all the while.

String and Cord Magick

To do string or cord magick, all you really need is a length of string or cord. Make sure your cord is long enough to easily tie nine knots. Use a string or cord in the color that corresponds to your magickal intent. This type of magick is great for either bringing items to you or removing or sending items away from you. String and cord magick is another type of magick that is easy to undo. You could even use it for weather magick to prevent rain for a short period of time, like the day you are holding a rummage sale to support your local animal shelter. (Read more about weather magick a little later in the chapter.)

A Spell for String and Cord Magick

Put the energy of your magickal intent into the string or cord. Envision your magick happening, and while you do this, tie nine knots in the cord as you say your spell. With each couplet, tie another knot. Tie the first knot on one end of the string. Then tie the second knot at the other end. The third knot goes in the middle, and the fourth knot goes between the first and the third knots. Refer to the following chart to see where each knot goes.

Banish!

Resist the temptation to mess with the weather. Yes, it is something that you could do, but be absolutely sure you have really thought it through and that you are doing it for the good of all. Weather affects each and every one of us not just today, but in the future as well. If it doesn't rain today, it's possible that a farmer's crops may wither and that could raise the price of wheat, which could raise the price of bread, which could mean that many people will go hungry.

String or cord magick.

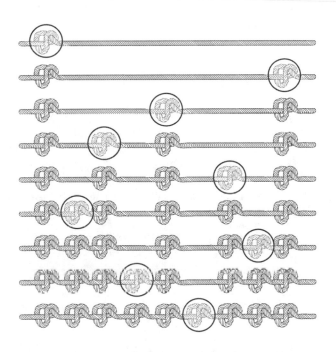

Here is a spell to say as you tie the knots:

By knot of one this string I tie,
Let the magick begin, don't let it die.
By knot of two it will come true,
Whether I make it for me or you.

> By knot of three it comes to be,
> The magick will happen as you will see.
> By knot of four my message will soar,
> Up to the gods whom we adore.
> By knot of five the magick's alive,
> It will happen, it will survive.
> By knot of six it will be fixed,
> The power increasing as the clock ticks.
> By not of seven this spell I'll leaven,
> As the message is carried up to the heavens.
> By knot of eight it will not wait,
> The magick will happen it won't be late.
> By knot of nine my magick will shine,
> It is my will placed in this rhyme.

When you're finished, place the tied-up string in a safe place. If you want this magick to be permanent, you can bury the cord in the Earth or you can burn it. But we think it is better to hang on to it. If you keep your knotted cord, you can undo the magick whenever you like.

Undoing String and Cord Magick

It was a beautiful day, and your rummage sale was a success; or perhaps you have been dieting and reached your ideal weight. Now it is time to undo the magick. Remove the knotted cord or string from its place of safekeeping. Locate the last knot that you tied when you did your spell. Untie it. Then untie the next to last knot that you tied. Untie all the knots in the opposite order that you tied them. Refer to the preceding knot-tying chart to help you keep track. When all the knots are undone, your magick will no longer be in effect.

You can chant the following over and over as you untie the knots:

> With each knot that I untie,
> Release the magick, let it fly.
> And it harm none, set it free,
> This is my will, so mote it be.

Mirror Magick

Mirror magick or glamour magick is a great way to help you (or someone else) deal with a difficult physical issue or the way you perceive yourself. A magick mirror allows you to see your own true inner beauty. You might want to make a magick mirror for someone who has been physically scarred in an accident or mentally abused about their appearance. This is also good for a child who is being teased at school about his or her birth defects. The mirror will allow a person to look beyond the surface and see that, despite any damage he or she may have sustained, that person is still beautiful. To use a magick mirror, look past the physical and emotional scars on the surface, and concentrate on seeing them melt away. Pull to the forefront all the wonderful things about yourself. When you focus on these aspects of yourself, you will enhance them. The more you use your magick mirror the more your inner beauty will shine forth. Your inner beauty will start to affect your outward appearance and you will become more and more beautiful all over.

A Mirror Magick Spell

You'll need the following ingredients (found in any herbal, health food, or metaphysical store, or grow your own) for mirror magick:

➤ A mirror of any size or shape

➤ ¹/₂ teaspoon of rose water

➤ ¹/₂ teaspoon of chamomile

➤ ¹/₂ teaspoon of rosemary

➤ ¹/₂ teaspoon of lemon grass

Mix the rose water and the herbs together. Make the mixture magickal by empowering it with your intent. Coat the mirror with the magickal herb mixture. As you coat the mirror with the magickal potion, chant the following while empowering the mirror with your spell:

> Magick mirror before my eyes,
> See my needs and hear my cries.
> Ring out the beauty that lies within,
> Start the spell let the magick begin.
> Though this glass my reflection I see,
> My intent, my will, so mote it be!

Webweaving

Many magickal craft recipes call for ingredients of equal parts. You'll find this is true for powders, essential oils, and incense. So, if you just see a list of herbs with no measurements given, you can assume that you will use equal measures of each one.

Your mirror will be ready to use. And you will start to see yourself in a whole new light. After you have empowered your mirror with magick, use it to bring out the beauty within. You should use it only for magick and should no longer use it for mundane tasks like checking your lipstick or fishing stray eyelashes out of your eye.

Storing Your Magick Mirror

Because you cannot use a magick mirror for mundane purposes, you must make sure that you put it away when you are not using it. Make a special storage bag for your mirror. (A little velvet bag in your favorite color will remind you of how special your magick mirror is and of how special you are.) Then store it in your magickal tool chest or cabinet.

Kitchen Magick

Kitchen magick is any magick that you can practice using ingredients or supplies that you would find in an ordinary kitchen. You can do kitchen magick by selecting culinary herbs based on their magickal properties and empowering them before you add them to your recipe. You can empower other ingredients as well. Or you can concentrate on putting your magickal intent into the food as you are cooking it. Remember that many ordinary fruits and vegetables have magickal correspondences as well. (See Chapter 17.)

Banish!

Okay, we've said it before, and we'll probably say it again. Please do not eat any herbs unless you are absolutely sure that they are edible. Many magickal herbs can be toxic!

Try this all-purpose culinary spell and see if it agrees with you!

Choose the food that you most associate with your magickal intent. Charge the food with your magickal intent by saying this chant:

> With this food I empower,
> The energy of this wondrous hour.
> As I ingest this magick meal,
> The power of this spell I seal.

Envision your magick coming to pass, and *bon appétit!*

Weather Magick

You can use weather magick to protect your home, family, and community from an oncoming storm. You probably won't be able to stop the storm altogether, but you should be able to keep it from doing serious damage. Be super careful when working with the weather. Remember, weather is something that affects everyone.

To lessen the impact of a storm, stand outside facing the direction from which the storm is coming. Hold your hands high in the air. Focus on your intent. Yell out this chant, sending your energy toward the storm:

> North, South, West, and East,
> Subdue this mighty weather beast.
> Calm its fury and make it pass,
> Protect my home with this spell I cast.

Notions, Potions, Powders, and More

As you have probably noticed, witches use a huge variety of materials when working spells. Besides all the things we have discussed so far, you can also work with clay, potions, powders, various kinds of paper, and even flowers.

Notions of Clay

You can make your own magickal notions—talismans and amulets with clay. If you were doing magick to bring yourself money, you could make a coin out of clay. To make the magick stronger, knead some money-drawing herbs or essential oils into the clay. Then, form the clay into a small, round flat coin and inscribe it with magickal symbols. Or write on it with a magickal alphabet. Clay comes in many colors and is easy to work with. There is even clay that you can bake; when it's done your object becomes permanent in shape.

You can also make small figures from clay, such as talismans in the shape of animals, which will give you the good qualities of each animal. For example, a fox-shaped talisman would help to bring you the quick and cunning energy of the fox. A talisman in the form of an otter would bring you a playful energy that could help you to have more fun. Historically, people have worn cat figures to bring them skill in divination. The cat shape also draws luck, protection, and a feeling of independence.

Potion Magick

Potions are probably among the first things that many people think of when they hear the word "witch." When you hear the word "potion," do you imagine a dark night, a bubbling cauldron of noxious brew, and three crones bent into the steam? Well, that sounds like a scene from *Macbeth* to us! But real witches do mix real potions. They usually make them in their kitchens, and the ingredients are rarely so exotic as to include eye of newt. Potions are infusions of magickal herbs that you can use to drink as a tea or to anoint an object, such as the mirror in the mirror magick spell discussed earlier in this chapter. Remember, never make a potion out of a poisonous plant if it is to be used for consumption.

Most potions are made by adding boiling water to magickally charged herbs and letting the herbs infuse for about 10 minutes, or by putting them into cold water and letting them sit in the sun all day to infuse naturally. If you heat your potion, it's best to cover the herbs while they are infusing so that none of the vapor escapes. Another way to make a potion is to place a jar of water and herbs in the light of the full Moon and let it set over night. Then, empower the solution and place it in a dark closet, until the next full Moon when it will be ready. Until then, remember to shake your potion gently once or twice every other day while it's brewing.

When the potion is ready, strain out the herbs and your potion is all set to do its work. You could use a potion made from banishing herbs to clean your house of a negative influence. You could add a love potion to your bath. You could also rub it on your skin or spritz it on a poppet. You can also make love potions using a wine base instead of water.

Powder Magick

After you have gained some experience with spells and working with herbs, you might want to try powder magick. To work powder magick, you mix up a powder and charge it with your magickal intent. Then you can blow the powder, and with it your magick, into the air. Or you can bury the powder, sprinkle it on the ground or around a room, place it inside a poppet, or mix it into clay for a talisman.

Magickal powders are made from finely ground herbs, a binder—such as benzoin, mastic, or *orrisroot*—and colored talc. You can also add glitter or powdered silver or gold.

Book of Shadows

Orrisroot is the root of a species of iris. It smells good and is used in the manufacture of perfumes and cosmetics.

Webweaving

Silver RavenWolf's book *To Light a Sacred Flame* (Llewellyn, 1999) has an excellent section on magickal powders. She even gives recipes for how to make several of her favorite powders.

Paper Magick

You can work paper magick without much in the way of special supplies. Build a cone of power and put the energy into a piece of paper by writing your magickal intent on it. Use magickal symbols or a magickal alphabet if you like. Then light the paper on fire and watch it burn. As it burns, concentrate on your intent and see your magick rise up and go to work. You could use colored paper in a shade that corresponds with your magick. You can also use fancy paper such as rag or parchment, but keep in mind that both of these burn quite slowly.

If you want to send your magick out quickly, buy some flash paper at your local metaphysical store. Flash paper has been specially treated to burn up in a flash. You light it and, poof, it is gone. Flash paper is great for magick that you want to send out with an extra kick, and is a great way to work with the element of Fire.

Flower Magick

We talked about herbs and botanicals in Chapter 18. But did you know that many common garden flowers have magickal properties? You can use them the same way you would use herbs. But please don't eat them. Many flowers are poisonous and others can be very irritating to the skin and the digestive tract.

If someone brings you flowers, save and dry them. Flowers that have been given as gifts have lots of great energy in them that you can use in your magick.

Flower	Magickal Properties
Blue Bell	Constancy, strength, luck, truth
Buttercup	Prosperity, happiness
Camellia	Gratitude, prosperity
Daffodil	Love, luck
Foxglove	Protection (poisonous plant!)
Geranium	Fertility, health, protection, love
Honeysuckle	Money, psychic and mental powers
Hyacinth	Love, protection, happiness
Lavender	Happiness, healing, peace, sleep, purification
Lilac	Protection, beauty, love
Lily	Protection, purity, breaking love spells
Lily of the Valley	Happiness, mental powers (poisonous plant!)
Marigold	Protection, dreams, psychic powers, business
Mullein	Courage, love, divination, protection
Periwinkle	Love, lust, money, protection
Primrose	Love, protection
Rhododendron	Peace, strength (poisonous plant!)
Snapdragon	Protection, friendship
Sunflower	Wishes, wisdom, health, fertility
Tulip	Love, happiness, dreams
Yarrow	Courage, protection, love, psychic powers
Zinnia	Love, lust, strength

To use flowers in your magick, dry the petals and grind them with your mortar and pestle. You can mix them with herbs or essential oils if you like. Or you can add flowers to a vial of oil to enhance its magickal properties. Flower petals also make a nice addition to dream pillows, the water of your ritual bath, or potpourri.

The Least You Need to Know

➤ Poppet magick is great for all kinds of spells. One of its biggest advantages is that the magick is easy to undo. The same is true of cord and string magick. Just make sure you keep your poppet or knotted cord or string in a safe place.

➤ You can send out your magick using candles or incense. In terms of supplies, candle and incense magick can be simple. Or you can add elements such as herbs and essential oils to fine-tune your magickal intent.

➤ A magick mirror will help you (or someone else) to see the beauty within. The more you see that beauty, the more it will shine, and the more beautiful you will become.

➤ You can practice kitchen magick and charge your ordinary recipes with a specific magickal intent. But please ingest only herbs that you know for certain are safe for culinary use!

➤ With weather magick you can influence the weather, but you probably should use this only to protect your home, family, or community in unusual circumstances. This magick is not for every day.

➤ You can make your own talismans and amulets. You can also make magickal potions from herbs and water or wine. Powders are another great way to use magickal herbs. You can even use ordinary paper or flowers in your magick.

Chapter 23

Spellcraft

In This Chapter

➤ How to write a spell

➤ Things you might want to use

➤ Casting that spell

➤ Spells that affect others

➤ This spell is broken!

You've seen some examples of spells in the last chapter and in other places throughout this book. You can use the spells we've presented or you can create your own. In this chapter we'll focus on exactly what you need to do to write your own spells.

Spells are like recipes. You use a pinch of this and a pinch of that, a drop of this and a drop of that. Add the right phase of the Moon, the right planetary correspondences, and most important of all, your magickal intent, and *voilà*—your magickal recipe is complete!

Using Spellcraft

Putting spells together is one of the central arts of witchcraft. Writing spells gives you a great opportunity to use your knowledge and creativity at the same time. Crafting a spell can take time and thought, although sometimes you'll see what you want to do all in one flash. The more familiar you are with all of the magickal substances—herbs, oils, and stones, to name a few—the easier it will be for you to tailor a spell to your specific intent and circumstances.

Remember, you resort to crafting a spell to attain your goal only after you have exhausted all the mundane ways available to you. If you haven't really tried to get what

Book of Shadows

A **spell** is a magickal recipe used to affect change. The Modern English word "spell" comes from an Old English word that meant "story" or "fable."

you want through ordinary nonmagickal channels, then you probably won't be able to focus your energy sufficiently, and it is unlikely that your magick will work.

What Is a Spell?

In order to make your goal manifest, you must visualize it first, then focus on it and direct your energy toward it. A *spell* is a recipe that you put together to help yourself visualize your magickal goal. Spells can have a number of different components, including ritualistic behavior, visualization, concentration, meditation, chanting, and physical objects. All these parts work together to help you make change happen.

Double, Bubble, Toil and Trouble

Many people are born with the ability to come up with rhymes and create jingles and verse. Those people (and Denise is one of them) are very lucky. Others have to work at it. But know that your spells don't have to rhyme or have meter, although it is catchy and fun when they rhyme, and the meter gives you a beat to stay with when you build a cone of power.

Macbeth watches as the three witches chant their rhyming spell in perfect iambic pentameter.

One way to develop your ability to make verse is to practice by talking to yourself. When you're driving or walking somewhere pick out the first object that you see, name it, then find other words that rhyme with the name by going through the alphabet. For example, say you pick out a tree. First ask yourself if you can think of a word that starts with an "a" that rhymes with "tree." Can't come up with one? No problem. Move on. Can you think of a word that starts with "b" and rhymes with tree? How about Brie? Then you would get Cree. And so on. Keep practicing. You will get quicker and quicker.

When rhyming word pairs start coming to you with speed, try making little two-line poems in the same way. You might come up with a couplet like this: "I see a cat in a tree. Let's hope this cat can see me." Practice creating two lines at a time until you feel comfortable. Then you can add two more lines. Once you get the hang of four lines, try rhyming every other line. So your first line will rhyme with the third line and the second line will rhyme with the last line.

Another technique that will help you to write spells in verse is to meditate and ask Spirit to give you the passion to put together a spell in verse. When you work on creating a spell, visualize what it is you want from the spell. Imagine what it will feel like to obtain your goal. Put that passion into writing your spell. Eventually you will be able to rattle off spells for any purpose. Write them down and you'll have a whole Book of Shadows ready for any magickal situation.

Remember, though, if you don't want to write spells with rhyme and meter you don't have to. You can just talk to the elements the way you would talk to a friend and speak to deity with awe and respect. When you build a cone of power, you can repeat one word—money or prosperity, for example—over and over again. Or you could chant the name of the particular element you are drawing on. What matters most is not clever rhymes and rhythms, but the passion and energy that you put into your words.

So Mote It Be

Make a commitment to practice rhyming for a week, and see if you don't make some progress. Make it a habit every time you get into the car or walk out of the house. Think of it this way: Rhyming all the way to work has got to be more fun than gnashing your teeth and worrying about traffic. At the end of the week, get out your notebook and write five rhyming couplets. See, you have learned something!

What Are Spells Used For?

Spells are used to bring about change. They do this by helping you to direct energy. The change could be for you or for someone else. Change could mean that you want to obtain an object or it could mean that you want to alter a situation for the better.

What Are You Trying to Accomplish with Your Spell?

By now, you know that you use magick only for the good of all. You should not cast a spell that will harm anyone. The outcome that you want to achieve with a spell must be crystal clear to you. If your goal isn't clear, you won't be able to use magick to reach it.

You can try to change many different things using spells. One of the first things you'll want to work on is yourself. After working on yourself, you will probably discover that many of the other circumstances that you had thought to change have corrected themselves as you have grown and become a better person.

You should make sure that you have pursued all the mundane means available to you before you turn to magick. You must also make sure that you are addressing your needs and not just a passing whim. You should never use spells for frivolous matters. You have to know the difference between your needs—food, clothing, shelter, love, acceptance, and spirituality—and your wants. You'll be better off if you address your needs first.

You may feel that you need a Lexus, but what you really could use is transportation and that could take the form of a bicycle, an old Datsun, or a convenient system of public buses. If you do address your needs first, some of your wants may very well disappear. If you have transportation and love, you may no longer desire a fancy car that will impress others.

Banish!

Don't rush ahead and do a spell to correct a situation that is bothering you. Before you act magickally, make sure you have exhausted all the mundane means available to rectify the problem. You also must think out all the possible outcomes to your spell.

Reexamining Your Intent

Before you go ahead and write a spell you'll want to reexamine your intent. Ask yourself questions. Look at what you want and see if your getting it is going to harm anyone or anything. If getting what you want will harm someone, stop and rethink your goal. You should also double-check that the outcome of your spell will not impinge on anyone's free will. In addition, you need to ask yourself how achieving your goal is going to affect you. Imagine how you will feel after your goal has been reached. Think through both the short-term and the long-term repercussions. If you are comfortable with all your answers and are willing to accept the karmic consequences, go ahead with your spell. Remember that you alone are responsible for your actions and for any side effects your spell might cause.

Writing Your Own Spells

Writing you own spells can be fun and empowering. Spell writing is a way to give voice to your passion and desires. It can also be a great creative outlet and that is healing in and of itself.

Be Creative: Your Spell Worksheet

After you have determined your intent and examined all the possible repercussions of doing magick to achieve your goal, you need to decide what kind of spell you want to do. Do you want to call on the powers of ...

➤ Fire?

➤ Water?

➤ Earth?

➤ Air?

➤ Or a combination of elements?

The element or elements you call will help to determine what you actually do in casting your spell. If you want to work with Fire, you might want to do a candle magick spell. You might decide you want to work with Fire because you want to draw fiery things—love, lust, or passion—to you. If you would rather work with Air, powders may be your thing. You might work Air magick because your goal involves thought and communication. If you were doing a spell that concerned communication with a lover, you could work with both Fire and Air at the same time by using incense in your magick.

Gather all your tools together. If you have decided to make a poppet or do cord magick, refer to the list of materials in Chapter 22, "More Ways to Work Magick." When writing any spell consider whether you want to use some of the following:

➤ Candles

➤ Clay

➤ Crystals or stones

➤ Essential oils

➤ Fairy dust

➤ Food

➤ Feathers

➤ Herbs, botanicals, or flowers

➤ Incense

➤ Paper or flash paper (a special quick-burning paper)

➤ Powders

➤ Seeds

➤ Soil or sand

If you are putting together a love spell, look at all the materials available to you that are associated with drawing love. You could buy an essential-oil mixture that is designed to bring love, take it home, and consecrate it. Or you could mix your own. When mixing your own, think about all the different aspects of love. Which ones do you want to emphasize? You could throw a heavy dose of lust and passion into the mix or you could design your blend for affection and stability. You could do this by adding herbs that represent these aspects of love to the essential-oil mixture. You could even add stone chips that represent your need or desire. Then shake it all up, empower the oil for your purpose, and your oil is ready to use in your spell.

Unless you are facing an emergency situation, figure out the best time to cast your spell. You could wait for a certain phase of the Moon or for a particular planetary alignment. Also consider whether or not you will do your magick within ritual or just on its own. And don't forget about color correspondences. You can use the color of your candle, stones or powders to fine-tune your magickal intent in many ways.

So Mote It Be

Get out your notebook and work on writing a spell. You might want to write one to aid your spell-writing abilities. Look over the lists of magickal herbs, stones, and essential oils throughout this book. Be creative. Use objects and materials that you are drawn to. When you are finished writing, review Chapter 20, "Magick's Astrological Correspondences," and Chapter 21, "Magickal Timing," and determine the best time to do your spell. Select a date and a time, make sure that you have all your materials beforehand, and cast that spell. Afterward, be sure to write down all the important information on a Magickal Record sheet.

Rhyming and Words of Power

It's nice to have a magick chant that you can say when casting your spell. So, even if you don't think you can do it, you should give rhyming a chance. As you write, think about what it is you want to accomplish. (Even if you aren't using rhyme, you should write out what you want to say as part of the spell.) You might want to call an element as part of your spell. A chant that draws on the element of Fire for love and passion might sound like this:

> Love is my heart's desire.
> I pull in the Element of Fire.
> The love I need put in my heart.
> Make it grow, give it spark.
> Don't make me wait. Send it fast.
> Bring to me love that lasts.

After writing a chant like this one you might decide to reconsider. Maybe you want to add some emotional Water energy to your spell:

> Fire's passion is in my heart.
> Hear these words, give it spark.
> Waters rise, and waters flow.
> Bring love to me, and make it grow.
> Instill my heart with love to be.
> This is my will, so mote it be.

Which elements you work with is your choice. Know that once you have decided on your words and invested them with your energy and passion, they become your words of power. Even if you think you can't write. Even if you think your rhymes sound silly. Your words represent your will and desire, because they come from your heart. When you repeat them over and over again, your energy will intensify, you will see your magick happen in your mind's eye, and your words will direct your power to manifest a change.

Remember to Keep Your Magickal Record

The reality is that when you first start doing magick you probably won't see much in the way of results. It's the rare person who can feel the full impact of his or her passion, who can focus and direct the energy with sufficient skill to reach a magickal goal the first time, but it does happen. There are so many factors involved in casting a spell that you need to keep records. Write down everything that you do when you work your spells. Your first six tries, for instance, might come to nothing, but one day, maybe on your seventh attempt, your magick will happen. When you discover that your magick has come to pass, you'll want to be able to look back at all the various factors and see what was different about the day the spell worked. If you don't have records, you could very well forget the important factor that made all the difference. You need to know what works for you.

A Step-by-Step Guide to Spellcasting

Your spell is written. You've gathered your tools. Now you are ready to cast your spell and send out your magick. You can work your spell inside ritual or you can do magick by itself.

Webweaving

In some traditions, instead of serving cakes and wine in ritual they serve cakes and ale. The expression cakes and ale has long meant "the good things in life." Yummy. We think so, too.

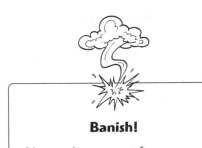

Banish!

Never take payment for your magick. Your magickal skills should not be turned into a business. Taking money may line your pocket with silver, but it will leave you spiritually bankrupt. And being a witch is primarily about your spirit. You also want to keep in mind that charging people for magickal workings is illegal and can get you into real mundane trouble, too.

If you plan on doing ritual, prepare your space. Get out all your tools, take your ritual bath, and dress in your ritual outfit. Cleanse and consecrate your space, pull up your magick circle, and start your ritual. Usually magick is done in ritual after you have called the God and Goddess and before you partake of cakes and wine.

If you are not going to do ritual, cleanse and consecrate your sacred space, pull up your magick circle, summon the element you need for your spell (or the Elemental of that element) or call deity, then do your magick.

If you have written a chant as part of your spell you'll use it to help you build your cone of power. It's a good idea to have all the steps of your spell written out. Bring that paper into the circle with you so you can refer to it while you are working. If you can memorize your magickal spell, that's even better.

Doing Magick for Someone Else

You already know that you should do magick for another person only if that person has asked for your help. If you do magick for someone without that person's permission, you are impinging on that person's free will and you will have to pay karmic consequences. That said, make sure the magick you have been asked to do is worth doing. You need to know if the person is sincere and if the magick is really for that person or if he or she really intends it for someone else. You also need to be certain that the person has done all he or she can do on the mundane level to achieve his or her goal.

When doing magick for someone else keep in mind that it is never okay to accept money for your magickal work. People will want to pay you, but you cannot take their money. First of all, moneymaking is not what magick is for. If you do accept money for your magick, your magick will start to lose its spiritual value. Taking money for your magick can also create greed within you. You also need to know that charging someone for magickal work is illegal.

The people you have helped will be very uncomfortable with the feeling that they owe you. What you can do is have them donate the money they would have given to you to the charity of your choice. If you like, they can write a check to the charity and send it to you. You in turn can send it along to the organization. Everyone benefits from this situation: You get to support a cause you believe in, they feel relieved to have made some payment, and the charity gets the money.

How to Break a Spell

Some spells were just made to be broken! In Chapter 22, we gave you spells for working poppet magick and cord magick. Spells using both of these types of magick are designed to be easy to undo. To undo a poppet spell, just take the poppet apart. For a cord magick spell, all you need to do is untie the knots in the reverse order that you tied them. If you like, you can say a little rhyme like the one in Chapter 22 while you do your undoing work.

You can also write a spell that undoes itself. Here's an example of a spell for enhancing karma that will break itself:

> Listen to this spell I weave, take heed in what is told,
> For your hatred and unkind deeds will return to thee threefold.
> By the rise of the next full Moon a Witch will sit and weep,
> For all the sorrow ye have sewn, thee will begin to reap.
> It's not too late to change your ways and break this painful spell,
> Replace the hatred in your heart so only love may dwell.
> So mote it be.

Once the person in question has stopped acting and feeling hateful, the spell will break itself. This is also an example of a spell that will influence someone else's behavior. Notice that the spell itself does not mete out any punishment. It just serves as a reminder to the individual that there will be karmic payback for his or her negative actions.

Another way to undo magick is to send the spell back to the person who cast it. For a spell that does just that, see the section "Breaking Another Witch's Spell" in the next chapter. If you want to break your own spell, you can try casting a new spell that will call the old spell back. When doing this, however, there are no guarantees. Your spell-breaking spell may not work, which is yet another reason to be absolutely sure of what you want and why you want it to begin with, before you decide to do magick to achieve it.

One way to try to recall a spell that you have cast is to take a cord and a pair of scissors, consecrate them, and empower them with your intent. Cut the entire cord into little pieces. Hold all the pieces in one of your hands and don't let them drop. As you cut up the cord, say the following chant:

> Recall the magick of this spell,
> The intent that I sent out,
> From me to there and back again,
> This time I have no doubt.
> Break the spell and set it free,
> This now is my command:
> The energy cometh back to me,
> Return it to my hand.

When you finish, take all the pieces and bury them in the Earth to ground the energy that you sent out.

The Pros and Cons of Binding Spells

There are many arguments in favor or *binding* spells. One of the chief advantages of binding spells is that the magick can be easy to undo. All you have to do is unbind or take apart the magickal object you used in your spell. And of course the purpose of binding spells—to bind up and stop a negative behavior—is positive. Getting rid of an unwanted behavior of your own or someone else's can certainly improve the lives of everyone. Certainly many people would benefit if your coworker, the one everyone calls "the gossip queen," was finally able to quit getting into everyone's business and spreading it throughout the office.

Book of Shadows

To bind means to tie or wrap with cord or to restrain. So, a **binding** spell ties up or restrains a person's negative behavior, but not the person him- or herself.

However, you also must consider the down side of binding spells. Even though you are binding the person's behavior and not the actual person, a binding spell can be seen as impinging on the free will of the individual because the person in question in some way enjoys the negative behavior. If you curtail someone's free will, you will bring yourself karmic payback. You need to assess if the behavior is truly causing more harm than pleasure. If you are dealing with a diabetic who can't stay away from sugar, binding the behavior could very well save that person's life. In such a case, you probably would not get hit with any negative karma. On the other hand, it wouldn't make sense to do a binding spell to keep Katherine away from chocolate because her indulgence isn't really doing anyone any harm. (Also she has never really tried mundane means to curb her intake of sweets.)

If a nasty neighbor were spreading vicious lies about another neighbor, you'd need to weigh the pros and cons before you take action. First determine that the liar is acting out of complete malice. Sure, that person is getting some gratification from his or her action, but what is it doing to the person being talked about? In a case like this, you could decide to bind the lying neighbor's behavior, even though you would be encroaching on his or her free will. It is possible that you might receive a small karmic nip in return, but it is unlikely that the karmic payback would be harmful or heavy.

The Least You Need to Know

➤ A spell is a magickal recipe with a number of components, including ritual, chanting, meditation, visualization, and magickal objects.

➤ Many witches like to write their spells in verse. Rhyme and meter are nice in a spell but, if you prefer, you don't have to use them.

➤ You should never accept money for doing magick. Taking money for using your magickal skills will strip the spirituality from your practice. It is also illegal, so don't do it.

➤ Poppet and cord magick spells are easy to undo. You just have to take the poppet apart or untie the cord. You can even write spells that undo themselves. It is possible to call a spell back, but it doesn't always work.

➤ You have to really weigh the pros and cons when doing binding spells. When you stop someone's negative behavior you could be messing with his or her free will and may incur some karmic payback.

Easy Spells

Because witches are a creative bunch, there's no end to the number of spells, chants, talismans, amulets, and potions that you will encounter. You'll want to start creating your own, too. Or maybe you have already begun. In this chapter, we'll give you some more spells and a couple of invocations. Use them if you like. Or use them as models to help you craft your own.

If you do plan to use the spells that follow, read through all the directions a few times before you begin your magick. And, when you are finished, don't forget to keep your magickal records.

More on Notions and Potions

We talked a little about making talismans, amulets, and potions in Chapter 22, "More Ways to Work Magick." Here are two spells you can use—one to empower an amulet or talisman and one for a potion.

Crystal Talisman or Amulet

You can empower a crystal to either draw something you want toward you—money, love, or luck, for instance—or keep negative energies away from you. To do this, choose a crystal to match your intent (see Chapter 18, "Magick Powers of Nature"). Cleanse the crystal of negative energy and then charge the crystal with your intent by chanting the following:

> This crystal I hold with intentions clear,
> To contain the magick within its sphere.
> Make it last and hold it long.
> Enhance the magick make it strong.

Envision your magick coming to pass while you chant. When you are finished, you can either carry the crystal with you or give it to someone else.

Webweaving

In the late 1500s, a Dr. John Fian tried to make a talisman to draw a particular young woman to him. He asked one of the woman's relatives, a young boy, to collect some of her pubic hair. The boy told his mother what the doctor wanted, and she decided to trick him. She sent the doctor some hairs from a cow instead. Fian did his magick, using what he thought were the hairs from the object of his desire. Lo and behold, the cow appeared at his door, and followed him everywhere he went!

Empowering a Potion

When making a potion, say this chant while envisioning your magick coming to pass:

> Bubble, bubble, toil, and trouble,
> Strengthen this potion on the double.
> Empower this magick, send it fast,
> And it harm none, make it last.

Blessings and Invocations

Witches have probably come up with more than a million different ways to bestow good energy on an object or to call in positive entities when doing magick. Here's an example of a blessing. And here are two more invocations that you can use in ritual.

Book Blessing

You can say this blessing over your Book of Shadows:

> In the realm of magick this book shall reside.
> No one but the chosen shall see what's inside.
> If breath be to Air as passion to Fire,
> Let harm come to none, this is my desire.
> If life be to Earth as Water to emotions,
> This book be filled with magical potions.
> May the Gods protect it, keep it from harm,
> And upon it bestow power, magick, and charm.
> No one without wisdom shall peer at its pages,
> Or the knowledge inside handed down through the ages.
> This book be it mine, it harbors no fears.
> The knowledge obtained through blood, sweat, and tears,
> My magick's my passion, the spirit's my guide.
> The love for the Goddess I hold deep inside.
> The book may she bless it with spiritual light.
> And let only her children read of its rite.
> For those of the Wicca truly can see,
> That this is my will, so mote it be.

So Mote It Be

Get some good-quality paper, such as parchment. Using your magickal pen and ink, write out this book blessing in your best hand. You can use a magickal alphabet if that feels special to you. Or type the blessing into your computer and fancy it up with a magick-looking font. Don't forget that you can use different colors, make borders, and add graphics. When you are finished, add the blessing to the front of your Book of Shadows.

Two Invocations

Use this quarter call at the beginning of ritual, or let it inspire you to write one of your own:

Winds from the North, that blow with cold,
Encompass this magick circle bold,
Sweeping away the old for the new,
Bring life to the Earth that is due,
Element of Earth come join us this night.

Winds from the east strong and fast,
Encompass this magick circle cast,
Communication swift and clear,
We summon you to guard us here.
Element of Air come join us this night.

Winds from the south, bring warmth to last,
Encompass this magick circle cast,
Burning with flames of hearts desire,
Fill us with longing and passions fire,
Element of Fire come join us this night.

Winds from the west born of ancient past,
Encompass this magick circle cast,
Emotional waters that ebb and flow,
Help spiritual oneness to flourish and grow,
Element of Water come join us this night.

If you have important magick to do, you might want to stir the Watchtowers using the Watchtower call. Remember to do so gently:

I gently stir the East's Watchtower,
Whose message is clear and filled with power.
Guard this circle with strength untold,
Protect us from harm with courage of bold.

I gently stir the West's Watchtower,
To direct the Water of emotional power.
Guard this circle with strength untold,
Protect us from harm with courage of bold.

I gently stir the North's Watchtower,
Encompass us with nurturing power,
Guard this circle with strength untold,
Protect us from harm with courage of bold.

I gently stir the South's Watchtower,
Stretching across us with flames of power,
Guard this circle with strength untold,
Protect us from harm with courage of bold.

Spells to Draw the Positive

We all want good things in our lives. These spells can help you draw what you want toward you. Remember that magick takes its own time, so don't expect results overnight.

Healing Necklace

You will need three lengths of blue cord or string, approximately two feet long. Sit in your magick circle and braid the strands together. As you braid, chant the following while putting your intent into the cord or string:

> Infuse these cords, send healing power,
> Have it grow with every hour.

Repeat the chant until you have finished braiding. Then say …

> This is my will, so mote it be!

If you like, you can add a bead made from a healing stone. Wear the necklace, or send it to the person you are doing it for.

Webweaving

There are many stones with healing properties. Healing stones include agate, amber, amethyst, beryl, bloodstone, calcite, flint, jade, and topaz, among others.

Love Candle

Remember that you must not direct a love spell toward a specific individual. You cannot make someone fall in love with you. To do so would impinge on that person's free will and would cause karmic repercussions for you. A love spell is meant to bring the right individual, no matter who that may be, to you. You will need a pink candle, a selection of herbs and essential oils that draw love and relationships, and a rose quartz crystal (see Chapter 18). Hollow out a hole in the bottom of the candle, about an inch deep. Save the shavings of wax. Grind the oils and herbs together with your mortar and pestle. While you do this, charge the herbs by chanting the following:

> True love, come unto me,
> Over mountain, land, and sea.
> Into these herbs of passions fire,
> Send to me my heart's desire.

Load the magickally charged herbs into the hole in the candle. Melt the wax shavings and seal the hole. Inscribe your magickal intent on the candle with the crystal and anoint the candle with blessing oil. Light the candle and send out the energy. Make sure you burn the candle in a deep candle cup because when the flame reaches the herbs they usually ignite and send the energy out quickly.

305

Fertility Poppets

Okay, folks, this spell involves sex between two consenting adults for the purpose of procreation. If you use this spell, it is very likely you will conceive a child. We just thought we would warn you.

You will need your spouse, partner, or mate, some stuffing, red cloth for your adult poppet, and green cloth for the baby poppet. You can use blue fabric for a boy baby or pink for a girl if you would like to attempt to influence the gender of the child you will conceive. You will also need some magickal herbs.

Sew a baby poppet out of the green cloth. Stuff it and add herbs. You might want to use carob for protection and health, carnation for strength, and clover for success. You can also add crystals such as bloodstone, which will also bring strength.

Fashion a mommy poppet from the red cloth. Stuff the mommy poppet and add herbs. You might want to use chickweed and hawthorn for fertility and hyacinth for love, protection of the fetus, and happiness during the pregnancy. You can also add crystals such as rose quartz for love and moss agate or salt for fertility. Don't sew her up all the way, but leave a space on the side of the stomach so you can insert the baby poppet at the right moment.

When the poppets are finished, set up for ritual by taking your bath. (You might want to do this together with your partner.) After you bathe, cleanse your space, be it the bedroom or another room of the house. It is your choice what room you would like to do this ritual in. Be creative. Before you begin your ritual, be sure to place the poppets in a location where you can send the energy from your love making to them. For example, if you make love in the bedroom you, place the poppet under the bed.

Banish!

Resist the temptation to do a fertility poppet spell without your partner's knowledge or consent. Because such a spell is likely to result in conception, this magick will affect both of you in a serious way. Consider all the repercussions seriously before you act. Then consider them all again.

Envision a circle of white light around the bed or area where you plan to make love. Turn on some soft music, light a few candles (be sure they will not be knocked over), and maybe light some incense. To begin your magick, start to make love. As you do this, envision the energy you are creating moving through you and down into the poppet under the bed. Imagine the energy as a red or blue light and envision the pregnancy happening. When you are finished making love, place the baby poppet inside the mommy poppet. Then sew up the adult poppet and placed it in a safe place until the spell has come to pass. After the child is born, the baby poppet can be used in a protection spell for the child.

Money and Prosperity

This money-drawing spell is fun to do. You can use play money or plain paper on which you draw any symbols that represent money to you. Cut the play money or paper into small strips. Mix in herbs and incense that correlate with money. Burn the mixture in your cauldron. The entire time the mixture is burning, chant the following:

> As this money is consumed with fire,
> Make it grow as I desire.

Once the paper is completely burnt, allow the ashes to cool, and mix them with green talc. Take the mixture outdoors, close your eyes, and blow it into the wind while chanting the following:

> As I blow this powder free,
> Money, money come to me.

If you try this spell, make sure to record what you have done in your Book of Shadows.

Or try the following spell for prosperity. You will need some tomato seeds and a place to plant them. Envision the seeds as seeds of prosperity and empower them with the intent that as the plant grows so shall your prosperity. As you empower the seeds, say the following chant:

> With these seeds I shall empower,
> The magick of this planting hour.
> As this plant grows it brings to me,
> The magick of prosperity.

Plant the seeds on the waxing Moon. After you have harvested the tomatoes, you can combine this spell with food magick. Envision your magick coming to pass as you eat the tomatoes.

Webweaving

Alfalfa sprouts and peas are two easily grown vegetables that will help bring you money. Oats and clover will, too, but, unless you are a lamb, you probably don't want to eat them!

Luck

We all could use a little good luck now and then. To enhance yours, try this spell.

You will need a white stone, an Apache's tear, or another stone that correlates with luck. You also will need some lucky oil—cinnamon, cypress, or lotus oil, or some combination of the three. Make sure your essential oils are mixed with a base such as almond or grapeseed oil. Anoint the stone with the oil and charge it with this chant:

> Into this stone before my eyes,
> Bless thee, and charge thee my power to rise.
> Enhance this stone with luck for me,
> This is my will so mote it be!

Keep the stone with you. Or give it to a friend who needs a lucky break.

Spells to Keep Away the Negative

When you cleanse and consecrate your tools and your sacred space you purge them of negative energies. You can also use spells to keep negative energies at bay. If you feel threatened, you can do a protection spell. If negative behavior, either yours or someone else's, is making your life hell, you could try a binding spell. And if your problems stem from another witch's spell? We even have a way to deal with that.

Protection Spells

Here are two protection spells that will protect you against anything from which you want protection. One of them uses essential oils and the other one employs dragon magick.

You will need: ⅛ cup of jojoba oil or almond oil; 5 drops of black pepper oil; 4 drops of pettigrain oil; and 1 drop of clove oil. Mix them together to make a magickal protection oil. Charge the oil by visualizing the energy leaving your body and infusing the oil. While you do this chant the following:

> I stand here in your guardian light,
> Empower this oil with your might.
> Protection from harm is what I ask,
> Please accept this as your task.

Banish!

Protection spells are great, and we hope that if you do one, it does help you feel more secure. But please avoid being careless. Casting a protection spell does not make you invincible. You still have to look both ways crossing the street, wear your seat belt, lock your doors, and exercise reasonable caution.

Once your oil is charged with energy, anoint yourself with it. With a small amount of oil, draw a pentagram on your forehead. (Make sure you don't let the oil drip into your eyes.) Now, feel protected!

For the dragon magick protection spell, you will need one white or purple candle to represent yourself and one candle for the Earth Dragon. Cast your magick circle. Stir the Dragon of the Element of the North (Earth). Light the Earth Dragon candle and chant these words:

> Earth Dragon strong and true,
> Send to me your magick new.
> Egg of protection we shall see,
> This is my will so mote it be.

As you chant, envision energy moving from the Dragon candle to the candle that represents you. See the energy around your personal candle as a green light in the shape of an egg. When you feel this has been accomplished, light your candle from the dragon candle. See your magick happening and know that you are protected. Snuff out your candle and put it in a safe space. Any time you need additional protection, light this magickally charged candle. Remember to snuff it out (don't blow it out) and store it in a safe place.

Binding Spells

Keep in mind when doing a binding spell that you bind a person's negative behavior and not the person. Binding a person would impinge on his or her free will. And that's a no-no, remember? (We talked about binding spells in Chapter 23, "Spellcraft.")

To do a cord-binding spell, you'll need a piece of black cord or ribbon, some paper, and a pen. (If you like, you can use this chant with some objects of your own devising. Be creative!) Write a brief description of the negative behavior on the paper. Roll it up tight. Wrap the paper with the cord or ribbon. As you do this, visualize the behavior being bound and chant the following:

> With this cord I now will bind,
> Stop this behavior and change your mind.
> This negative behavior that you display,
> Will now forever go away.

Or try this chant instead:

> It will stop now this unwanted behavior,
> Replace the bad with a positive favor.
> Let magick begin without wait,
> And harm it none this be their fate.

After you have bound up the paper, go outside and bury it deep in the Earth. If you need to undo this spell, simply dig up the paper and remove the cord. One of the advantages of binding spells is that you can undo them by unbinding the object that you tie up in ritual.

Breaking Another Witch's Spell

If another witch has put a hex on you, here's how to undo it.

You will need a length of silver cord and your bolline (magick knife used for cutting) or a pair of scissors. Tie one knot in each end of the cord. As you do this, visualize one knot representing you and the other the person who cast the hex. Cut the cord in the center, chant the following, and see the spell breaking:

> From you to me this spell I break,
> This was not right for you to make.
> Its path I will abruptly end,
> And back to you the spell I send.

Spells for Elemental and Fairy Magick

In Elemental magick, you work with the elements. You'll pick which element you will work with based on your magickal intent. As you may recall …

➤ Air is associated with thought and communication.

➤ Fire is associated with passion, courage, and change.

➤ Water is associated with psychic energy, emotion, and intuition.

➤ Earth is associated with growth, nurturing, and abundance.

When you use fairy magick, you summon the fairies and ask them to help you.

Air Magick

To make a powder, choose herbs that match your intent. Grind them with the magickal oil of your intent. Then stir in talc of a color that matches your intent. Empower the mixture by focusing on your intent and saying this chant:

> With this intent the magick I dare,
> To send out to the element of Air.
> The magick I cast this spell I'll see,
> This is my will so mote it be.

Or use this one:

> With this intent I call to Air,
> To cast my spell to the winds so fair,
> And bring my heart's desire to me.
> This is my will, so mote it be.

Go outdoors, put your back to the wind, close your eyes, see the magick happen, and blow the powder into the wind. Always remember that visualization is key with all spells. Visualize the magick happening as you feel the wind at your back and blow the powder into the air.

Fire Magick

You will need a pen, a piece of paper, and a cauldron or other nonflammable container. If you want the spell to happen quickly, use flash paper. If you want to see it happen over a period of time, use regular paper. Make your sacred space, cast your circle, and write your intent on the paper. As you write your intent, visualize the magick happening and chant the following:

> Element of Fire burning bright,
> I call you here with me tonight.
> Fulfill this desire sent to thee,
> Work this magick just for me.

Water Magick

You will need a stone and something to write with. Charge the stone with your intent and write the intent on the stone, if you like. If you have access to a pond, river, lake, or stream, cast the stone into the body of water. Know that the water will carry your intent and bring forth your magick. Chant the following as you visualize your magick happening:

> With my intent into this stone,
> Which in the water I have thrown.
> Water grant this spell to me,
> So that the results I soon may see.

If you do not have access to a body of water, you can use a bathtub or shower. As you sit in the bath water or stand in the running shower, allow the water to flow and carry your intent away from you as it goes into the drain. Visualize your intent and chant:

> Water running in the night,
> Underneath the Moon so bright.
> Grant to me this spell I weave,
> So soon my wish I will achieve.

Earth Magick

You will need a bowl of rich topsoil. Charge the soil with your intent and then cast the soil into a freshly planted garden. As you visualize your intent, chant …

> Into this soil through my hand,
> My intent I do command,
> Make it last, make it strong,
> From Earth to me where it belongs.

Fairy Magick

Be sure you really want to work with fairies. As we mentioned in Chapter 15, "Summon, Stir, or Call," fairies can work wonderful magick for you, but they are also very mischievous and difficult to get rid of once they have infested the house. If you've

Webweaving

It is said that when fairies are present, candle flames in the room will start to dance. So, even if you don't feel anything, watch the flames and see if they flicker.

Book of Shadows

Fairy dust is a super-fine glitter, similar to embossing powder. You can buy it in small vials at most metaphysical shops. Some people keep the vials closed and wear them as magickal jewelry.

decided you're ready to work with fairies, you will need—in addition to knowing your magickal intent—your magick tools and some *fairy dust*.

On a waxing Moon, sit in your magickal circle with your tools and fairy dust. Relax and visualize walking through the portal of the magickal Realm of Fairy. Walk through this wondrous place and drink in the magick. You may see the little critters peeking at you from their hiding places, flying overhead, or you may just hear a tiny giggle. Get the feel of what it is like to be around fairies. When you're ready, come back through the portal and open your eyes in your magick circle. Now you can begin by chanting this verse:

> Come little fairies, come to me,
> Make yourself known so I can see.
> Gifts I'll bring and respect I'll show,
> Fly all around me to and fro.
> Help me with my magickal quest,
> Make it strong then you can rest.
> Elemental gifts are my desire,
> Water, Air, Earth and Fire.
> Swift is the magick, make it so,
> Send high above and down below.
> Do not dawdle, do not tarry,
> Your job is my magick rite to carry.
> Come little fairies by dark and by light,
> Illuminate the magick have it take flight.
> Weave the intent of my magickal spell,
> Talk to the gods and make it work well.
> Come little fairies, come to me,
> This is my will, so mote it be!

When you are finished, blow the fairy dust around the circle. Then sit very still and quietly and wait for them to appear. You may not see them at first, but you may feel their presence as an itch or a tickle in your hair. After they have arrived, do your intended magickal work. When you have finished, leave some sweet milk out for them, some silver coin, or shiny objects.

The Least You Need to Know

➤ You can use spells to empower talismans, amulets, and potions with your magickal intent. Use one from a book, or write your own.

➤ Saying a blessing over an object gives that object positive energy and makes it special. Invocations can also draw good things—entities that help you with your magick.

➤ You can write spells (or use ones from books) that draw good things to you, such as love, fertility, prosperity, or luck.

➤ Protection spells protect you from negativity and harm. You can also use spells to help stop negative behavior—your own or someone else's.

➤ You can use fairy magick by summoning the fairies to help you, but be sure that you really want their help before you do so.

➤ You can work with each element—Fire, Water, Earth, or Air—separately. When you work magick with the elements, you also use their physical manifestations in your spells.

Divination

People have used a variety of divination techniques for centuries. In ancient Babylon, priests examined the liver of sheep to try to predict future events. Other popular ancient means of divination included examination of the behavior of drops of oil in a basin of water. We'll discuss several means of divination in this chapter. And we promise that none of them involve sheep.

The divination techniques we will discuss involve methods that are popular among Wiccans today. These techniques—runes, tarot cards, and pendulums, for example—have been used for centuries by people of many religions and cultures. Others, such as dousing, which is used to find water or oil, are employed by modern companies to this day. As a witch, it is important to be comfortable and familiar with at least one form of divination. Divination will help you with day-to-day decision making by allowing you access to divine guidance.

Tuning In with Your Psychic Mind

Learning to tune in to your psychic mind can be as easy as listening. Try to stay open to the messages that your subconscious mind sends you. The subconscious can pick up information that the conscious mind cannot. Some people believe that these messages come from spirit guides or from other entities. You can strengthen your psychic awareness with a few simple exercises.

Webweaving

The Psychic Pathway by Sonia Choquette (Crown, 1994) contains lots of suggestions for how you can become more psychic. She also addresses many of the fears that most of us harbor about receiving psychic information. *The Complete Idiot's Guide to Being Psychic,* by Lynn A. Robinson and LaVonne Carlson-Finnerty (Alpha Books, 1999) is another excellent resource for enhancing your psychic ability.

Book of Shadows

An **archetype** represents a character or a set of human characteristics that are common to all people throughout all cultures. The word can also mean "original model." In this respect, the characters of myth are the original models on which we base our understanding of the world and upon which writers build new stories.

Play a guessing game with yourself whenever the phone rings. Before you pick up, and without looking at the caller-I.D. box, guess who is on the line. Record the times you are right in your notebook. You'll be surprised to see how often you are correct.

When you get a letter in the mail, hold it up to your third eye (middle of your forehead), relax, and see if you can figure out what the letter is about. You can also try reading energy off objects. Pick up an object that you know other people have handled. Relax and let your breathing become even and regular. See if you get any sense of what kind of person has held the object before you. Maybe the person was angry and frustrated. Or maybe the person was carefree and full of laughter.

Another thing you should do is start paying attention when you get the sense that something is wrong. If you feel something is wrong, then it probably is. Haven't you ever gotten the feeling right before you've left the house that something wasn't right and later, once you're on the highway, you end up in a traffic jam in the rain with a flat tire? And you think, "I knew it! I shouldn't have left the house to begin with."

The more you listen to your psychic and intuitive messages, the stronger they become. All of us have the ability to use psychic information. Unfortunately, many of us have been taught from childhood to disregard our psychic awareness. Some of us have even been taught that our psychic abilities are evil. (They are not!) As a result, most adults have repressed these abilities. If you work with your psychic awareness, you can develop it, and it will grow into a wonderful tool to help you in your continued growth on the spiritual path.

Carl Jung, Archetypes, and the Shadow Self

Psychiatrist Carl Gustav Jung (1875–1961) studied many means of divination and concluded that divination systems allow us to tap into the collective unconscious, the subconscious awareness of all humans as a group. The knowledge of the collective unconscious is organized in symbols (remember that symbols, not words, speak to the unconscious) called *archetypes*. Archetypes are like characters from myths. Jung and many people after him (the mythologist Joseph Campbell, for instance) noticed that the characters in myths across all cultures had certain similarities. The Great Mother is an example of an archetype; so, too, is the Wise Old Man. Characters that fit these archetypes appear in many of our most popular stories and films—from *Cinderella* to *The Wizard of Oz* to *Star Wars*. The Shadow Self is the archetype that represents the dark, weak, ugly, or unacceptable side of each of us.

Using the Tarot

Tarot cards are a great divination tool that people have used for centuries. A few museums have decks (or partial decks) that date back to the fifteenth century.

A tarot deck consists of 78 cards—22 Major Arcana cards and 56 Minor Arcana cards. The cards of the Minor Arcana are much like regular playing cards in that they have suits and numbers or faces. The cards of the Major Arcana have pictures on them that represent the significant issues or phases in an individual's spiritual development.

> **Book of Shadows**
>
> A **tarot spread** is the pattern in which you lay out the cards when doing a reading. There are many different spreads that you can use.

Tarot's High Priestess is the key to intuition.

You can use the tarot in many different ways. One of the most common ways that people use it is to lay the cards out in a *tarot spread*. Spreads can involve lots of cards, or only a few. Usually you shuffle the deck and, as you do so, think of the question you would like to have answered. Then you, or the tarot card reader, lay the cards out in a spread. You can use a simple three-card spread, with three cards laid next to each other on the table, for a quick answer to a question. Or you can use a seven-card spread for a more in-depth answer. Some of the more complicated spreads involve more than 20 cards.

Webweaving

The Minor Arcana cards of the tarot deck are similar to cards in a regular deck—but they're not exactly the same. A regular deck of cards contains three court, or face, cards—King, Queen, and Jack—in each of the four suits. But the Minor Arcana in a tarot contains four court cards—King, Queen, Knight, and Page—in each of the four suits. Also, while both a tarot deck and a regular deck have four suits, the suits are different. Instead of the clubs, spades, hearts, and diamonds of the regular deck, the tarot deck has wands, swords, cups, and pentacles.

The Major Arcana: Archetypes for the Life Path

The images of the Major Arcana can be seen as representations of all the human archetypes. In addition, the cards of Major Arcana map out our path through life as we grow and develop. New souls start their journeys as Fools and mature in this life only to be reborn a bit further along the path. Because the cards allow us to see our archetypes, they can help us to receive psychic information.

Major Arcana Card Image and Number	Represents ...
The Fool (0)	Beginnings, innocence, an open mind
The Magickian (1)	Creativity, manifestation, skill
The High Priestess (2)	Intuition, psychic abilities
The Empress (3)	Abundance, fertility, nurturing, wisdom
The Emperor (4)	Authority, leadership, logic, planning
The Hierophant (5)	Traditions, conformity, conventional wisdom
The Lovers (6)	Romance, temptation, inspiration, choice
The Chariot (7)	Stamina, success, victory after struggle, health
Strength (8)	Compassion, unconditional love, calmness

Major Arcana Card Image and Number	Represents ...
The Hermit (9)	Truth, wisdom, silence, the inner voice
The Wheel of Fortune (10)	Luck, fate, fortune
Justice (11)	Fairness, pros and cons, judgment, balance
The Hanged Man (12)	Prophecy, self-sacrifice, hanging by a thread, release
Death (13)	Regeneration, rebirth, transformation, renewal
Temperance (14)	Patience, adaptation, discipline, cooperation
The Devil (15)	Materialism, temptation, addictions, obsessions
The Tower (16)	The unexpected, surprises, sudden change
The Star (17)	Hope, faith, wishes, prospects
The Moon (18)	Imagination, psychic development, intuition, unforeseen events, revelation of the truth
The Sun (19)	Contentment, peace, partnership, pleasure
Judgement (20)	Awakening, clarity, change in consciousness
The World (21)	Attainment, triumph, liberation, theend of karma

Cups, Wands, Swords, Pentacles

The suits of the 56 cards in the Minor Arcana represent the four elements. They also correspond to the suits of regular playing cards.

Major Arcana Suit	Corresponding Element	Regular Card Deck Suit
Cups	Water	Hearts
Wands	Fire	Clubs
Swords	Air	Spades
Pentacles	Earth	Diamonds

Using the Tarot in Wicca

Every witch needs a form of divination. Tarot is an excellent one because you can use it in many different ways—from a predictor of the future to a decision-making aid to a tool of spiritual growth.

Many witches use the tarot to help them predict what will happen in the future. One way to do this is to ask the cards, "What will happen if I remain on the same course?" Then lay the cards out in the spread of your choosing.

The tarot can also be used to help you make decisions. Say, for instance, you have a new boss and you don't know how to deal with her. Separate out the 22 cards of the Major Arcana, and set the Minor Arcana cards aside. Ask the Major Arcana cards how you should behave. Then pick three Major Arcana cards.

Let's say you drew The Fool, The High Priestess, and The Hermit. The Fool tells you that you may want to look at having a new boss as a new learning experience, that you need to approach the situation with innocence and an open mind. In your first meetings with this new boss, you should make sure that you don't come off as a know-it-all. And you'll want to make sure that you listen and learn from this new person in your life. The High Priestess tells you to take your intuition with you and listen to it. Allow your intuition to guide you to say the right thing and demonstrate your competence at your job. The Hermit also suggests that staying within yourself, listening and not talking a lot, is the best plan. If you were to bring a new member into your coven, you might want to use the cards in the same manner to determine how best to get to know the new member.

Webweaving

The Complete Idiot's Guide to Tarot and Fortune-Telling, by Arlene Tognetti and Lisa Lenard (Alpha Books, 1999) tells you everything you've ever wanted to know about the tarot, and probably more! It's a great, informative book. Denise even assigns it to her students.

So Mote It Be

Visit your local metaphysical shop and check out the tarot decks. Don't be in a hurry to buy, though. You should make sure that you have found the right deck for you. There are a lot of different decks, and some can be quite expensive with prices as high as $40. Look at as many cards as you can. Some stores will let you handle samples of the actual cards themselves. In other shops, you'll be able to look at the cards only as reproduced in a catalogue. Try to get an idea of the feel of each deck, and see which one speaks to you the strongest.

To use the tarot as a tool of spiritual growth, again you must separate out and use the 22 cards of the Major Arcana. Each card represents a step on the path toward spiritual enlightenment. You can choose a card at random and meditate on it. Examine the image on the card carefully and see what you can learn from it. You can also read all about the meaning of the card, but it is nice to really look at it first and see what the card means to you. If you prefer, you can start with The Fool card because we all start off as fools. Work with that card for a while, then when you feel you have learned the lesson of The Fool, move on to The Magician. You may get to a point where you feel that your growth has stopped. That is only natural. You can always repeat steps that you have gone through before. Few of us actually make it to the enlightenment of The World in this lifetime.

Another way that you can use the tarot as a witch is to develop spells around certain cards. For instance, you could build a spell around The Empress and use her wisdom and sense of control. Or you could pull on The Hermit if you want to develop your more reflective and inward nature.

Numerology: Going by the Numbers

We introduced numerology in Chapter 8, "Dedicate Yourself to the Craft," when we talked about using your Life Path and Destiny Numbers to help you determine your magickal name. You can also use numerology, the metaphysical science of numbers, to know yourself better and to look into your future.

Resonating with the Energy of Numbers

Scientists tell us that everything in the universe has its own energy or vibration. When using numerology, you take into account the energy vibrations of the numbers and names in your life. Numerologists believe that the names we carry are not arbitrary, but are meaningful expressions of who we are. They say the same thing about birth dates. So, are you ready to take a look at some of the significant numbers in your life?

Meaning of the Numbers 1 Through 9

Did you calculate your Life Path and Destiny Numbers in Chapter 8? Find those numbers if you did. If you didn't, you might want to refer to that chapter again and do it now.

The numbers 1 through 9 each have their own meaning. They are also associated with colors, stones, and the signs of the zodiac.

Number	Key Words	Color(s)	Stone(s)	Sign(s)
1	Beginning Individual Independent Leadership Courage Initiation	Red, garnet	Ruby	Aries

continues

continued

Number	Key Words	Color(s)	Stone(s)	Sign(s)
2	Gentle Sensitive Harmonious Balanced Cooperative Loving	Orange, gold, peach	Moonstone, gold	Libra
3	Self-expression Creative Enthusiastic Imaginative Optimistic Childlike	Yellow	Topaz	Leo
4	Solid Stable Traditional Practical Cautious Hard working	Green	Jade, emerald	Taurus
5	Freedom-loving Risk-taking Change Quick-thinking Communication Youthful	Turquoise	Aquamarine, turquoise	Gemini
6	Nurturing Family Balance Duty Love Service to others	Royal blue, indigo	Pearl, sapphire	Cancer, Libra
7	Solitary Mystical Philosophical Private Perfectionist Inventor	Violet, purple	Amethyst, alexandrite	Pisces, Virgo, Scorpio
8	Power Money Vision Achievement Strength Organization	Pink, rose	Diamond, rose quartz	Capricorn

Number	Key Words	Color(s)	Stone(s)	Sign(s)
9	Completion Perfection Compassion Forgiveness Dramatic Spiritual Idealism	White	Opal	Scorpio, Pisces

Banish!

Don't use what you have learned about yourself from numerology as an excuse to become passive in your life. Just because your Life Path or Destiny Number come out to a 2, meaning harmonious, balanced, gentle, among other things, doesn't mean you can't be a leader and a go-getter. By the same token, if you have 1s or 8s in your chart, showing independence and achievement, you don't want to become complacent—numerology may say that you are a leader and will have power, but you can't just wait for it to happen. You still have to act to fulfill your destiny.

Using Numerology in Wicca

As a witch, you can use numerology to look into your future or the future of others. Numerology can help you face the challenges of your life path by identifying some of the issues that you will encounter on the way. Numerology also can help you decide how to deal with new people in your life. If you study the numbers in your life, you may find which times are best for you to venture out and which times you'd be better served by sticking to familiar turf. You can also draw on the energy and symbolism of a particular number in magick.

Other Kinds of Divination

There are many other kinds of divination. If the ones we've just described don't appeal to you, check out some of the others. It's important that, as a witch, you have a system of divination that you like.

Palmistry

Palmistry is the art of reading the hands. The palmist looks not just at the line in your hands, but at the overall shape and size of the hand, and the length of the fingers relative to the palm. Believe it or not our hands are continuously changing. You can learn a lot about a person—physically, mentally, and emotionally—from studying their hands. A person's hand will also tell you about that person's past, present, and future.

Four of your fingers carry the names of Roman gods: The index finger is named for Jupiter, the middle finger for Saturn, the fourth finger for Apollo, and the little finger for Mercury. And what about the thumb? Well, the thumb is really important, but it's still just the thumb.

Dowsing and Pendulum Magick

Dowsing is an art that was practiced by the ancient Scythians, Persians, Greeks, and Romans. Usually it is used to look for things that are hidden in the ground—water, oil, or minerals. A dowsing rod is a Y-shaped stick, which is held by the two short branches. The tail of the Y is then used to point toward the ground. The stick rises up or drops down sharply to indicate the presence of the desired substance. Today dowsing is used by oil companies and by farmers in search of water. People who specialize in locating water underground through dowsing are called dowsers, but in Wicca, we call them water witches. You can also use a dowsing rod to answer yes or no questions.

Pendulums are very popular among witches because they are so easy to use. You can use anything as a pendulum—a fishing weight, a piece of jewelry, a spool of thread, or a crystal hung from a string. (Crystals are especially nice to use because they pull in energy.)

To use a pendulum for divination, you ask the pendulum a question and watch its movement to determine its answer. Before you ask the pendulum a question, you need to decide the meanings of movement in each of the directions. Many people make a card with the pendulum's answers on it that look like the following figure.

Hold the string of the pendulum in one hand and let your pendulum hang down. Wait for it to become still. Then ask your question. Or swing the pendulum in a circle while asking your question. Eventually, the pendulum's movements will change to indicate your answer. You can also hold your pendulum over a group of crystals to help you decide which one to buy. It will swing and point to the crystal that is for you. Many witches carry pendulums with them so they can have a quick consultation any time. A pendulum can even help you pick out fruit in the grocery store (provided you don't mind the stares of the other customers).

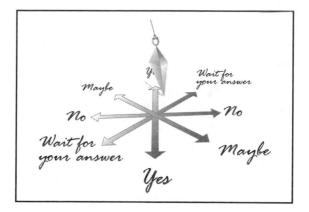

Channeling and Ouija Boards

You've probably heard about channeling—contacting spirits and having them talk through you. Channeling is not an easy thing to do. You have to build up your psychic ability first. Many people are frightened by the idea of dealing so closely with spirits. But if you are scared, you probably won't be open enough to channel.

Another way to "talk" with spirits is through a *Ouija* board. Many people are frightened of Ouija boards and believe that they can be harmed or haunted by them. Really there is absolutely nothing to be afraid of. The board itself is not the thing that does the communicating with the other side. The person using the board is the one making the contact with spirits. Many people first start to channel by using an Ouija board.

If you do encounter an obnoxious spirit when using a Ouija board, you can just tell it to go away. If it won't stop bugging you, put your board away. Don't worry, the spirit will not come after you. Before you start your session, you might want to envision a white light surrounding you and the board to safeguard yourself against bratty spirits. When you do so, ask that only positive spirits communicate with you.

It's best to work in a group of three when using a Ouija board. That way, two people can hold the planchette on the board and the third person can write down the answers as they are spelled out. Sometimes the messages that you receive will be abbreviated. For instance, you might get "I C U" for "I see you." Other times the planchette starts moving and picking out letters so fast that you'll have a hard time keeping track unless you assign someone to record each letter.

Book of Shadows

The name **Ouija** (pronounced *WEE-gee* or *WEE-jeh*) comes from the French word *oui*, meaning "yes," and the German word *ja*, which also means "yes." So these boards that bear the alphabet, which have been trademarked by Parker Brothers, are really "yes-yes" boards.

Tea Leaves

The reading of tea leaves dates back to seventeenth-century Europe. To read your leaves, you'll need some loose tea, a teacup, a saucer, and a question. Brew a cup of tea and drink it until there is just a little bit of liquid and the leaves left at the bottom of your cup. Swirl the tea and the leaves around and turn the cup upside down on the saucer. Think about your question. Let the remaining liquid drain away from the leaves for a few minutes then turn the cup right side up.

Your tea leaves will be stuck to the inside of the cup. Spend some time looking at them until images begin to emerge. Some of the images may be on the sides of the cup and some may be on the bottom. The closer an image is to the cup's rim the sooner the event that it symbolizes will come to pass. You can interpret the images in your leaves based on what the symbols mean to you or you can buy a book about tealeaf reading that explains the meanings of the various leaf formations.

Webweaving

Psychiatrist Carl Jung spent a lot of time studying the *I Ching*. It's a fascinating system that has been used by Chinese emperors and just regular people for centuries. In fact, in the second century B.C.E. the knowledge of the *I Ching* (which is pronounced *ee-CHING* in English) was a prerequisite for government service.

I Ching

The *I Ching* is an ancient Chinese book that details 64 different life situations. It is both a system of divination and a guide on your path through life. *I Ching* means the Book of Life Changes. Each of the 64 situations is represented by a hexagram made up of six lines. To use the *I Ching,* you can cast three coins six times, once for each line of the hexagram. You then write down the pattern of heads and tails that you generate and match the pattern that you have thrown to one in the book.

Runes

There are several different types of runes. Basically runes are old alphabets that were used by the ancient Anglo-Saxons, Germans, and Scandinavians. Each letter in the runic alphabet also has symbolic and magickal significance. According to legend, the god Odin hung upside down from a tree for nine days. After this ordeal he gained understanding of the magickal meaning of runes and became the only true rune master. Only he completely understands the significance of each rune. Many witches see The Hanged Man in the tarot deck as Odin, hanging upside down reading the runes.

Each rune is usually written or inscribed on its own piece of wood or small clay tablet. You can think of them as magickal Scrabble tiles. You can use runes in some of the same ways you use tarot cards. You can meditate on one rune and its meaning. You can draw three runes from a bag to help you decide how to deal with a situation in your life. You can also pull on the energy of a rune when doing your magick.

Scrying

Scrying involves looking into a reflective surface to see images that may tell you about the future. Scrying can be done a number of ways. For example, you can look into water, a crystal ball, a piece of obsidian, or a candle flame.

When scrying with water, fill a black pan—one of those old cast-iron frying pans would be ideal—with water. You can also put water in your cauldron. Some witches add a drop or two of ink to the water to make it darker. Light a candle and pull up a white protective light all around you, much in the same way that you pull up a magick circle. Stare into the water. After some time, you may start to see images or a swirling mist. You might even hear things. You can also use a scrying glass (a special piece of black glass in the shape of a hand mirror) or a piece of obsidian in the same way.

When looking into a crystal ball you should let your conscious mind get lost in the crystal ball's clearness so that your unconscious mind can connect with your super conscious mind and allow you to communicate with spirits. Some witches like to use candle flames for scrying. Others, and Denise agrees, think that staring into the flame is too hard on the eyes. However you decide to do it, try it a few times and see what you can see.

The Least You Need to Know

➤ Everyone has the ability to receive psychic information. Most of us have repressed this ability, but if you work on it, it will work for you.

➤ Psychiatrist Carl Jung believed that divination systems allow us to tap into the collective unconscious and its system of archetypes—mythic characters and images that help us to make sense of the world around us.

➤ You can use tarot cards to look into your future or to help you with a decision or a problem. You can also meditate on the images of the Major Arcana to aid your spiritual growth or pull on their energies in your magick.

➤ Numerology will tell you all about the energy of the numbers in your life. You can tap into this information to help you grow and learn. The energy of numbers can also be used in magick.

➤ Every witch needs a system of divination—whether it's the tarot, the *I Ching*, a pendulum, a crystal ball, or a combination of several methods. Find at least one that works for you.

Chapter 26

Dreams and Visions

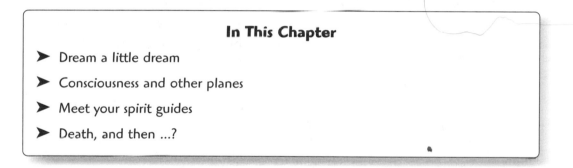

In This Chapter

➤ Dream a little dream

➤ Consciousness and other planes

➤ Meet your spirit guides

➤ Death, and then ...?

We all dream. In fact, we all dream every night. Some cultures have seen dreams as visions of events that occurred in the past or will come to pass in the future. In the present day, some individuals see dreams as a means to work out personal problems and conflicts. Some people think of dreams as their nightly entertainment. Other people use their dreams to help themselves grow emotionally and spiritually. And still other people don't pay any attention to their dreams at all.

Do you remember your dreams?

Dreamtime: Pillow Magick

People have been fascinated by dreams for thousands of years. The Bible is full of stories of people having prophetic dreams and visions. The Indian Upanishads (Hindu treatises), which date from 1000 B.C.E., record the interpretation of dreams, and so does the ancient Babylonian Talmud (200 B.C.E.–200 C.E.).

In the present day, some people foresee the future in their dreams or receive visions of places they have never been. Others receive messages from deceased relatives. While you sleep you can even work magick—pillow magick!—which we'll tell you about a little later. At the very least, dreams are a testament to the human powers of creativity.

And by studying your dreams you can learn more about yourself—your hopes, fears, needs, and desires.

Freud's Royal Road

Remember Sigmund Freud, the great pioneer of psychoanalysis? Well, it was actually Freud who coined the term "the unconscious." Back then, it was a pretty radical idea—the thought that we all have hidden thoughts, feelings, and desires that are too intense and primitive to be shown in society or even acknowledged to ourselves. Freud believed that in dreams we reach a compromise with our unconscious wishes and are able to express them in a way that does not offend our sense of propriety. Because he saw dreams as a way into the unconscious, Freud referred to them as the "royal road to the unconscious." So, let's take a walk down the royal road and see what is on your mind—your unconscious mind, that is.

Dream Symbols: Your Personal Archetypes

Dream dictionaries and interpretive guides have been around since at least the year 200 C.E. But today, there is no general consensus for how to interpret dreams. Some people believe that the symbols in dreams are universal; others argue that the symbols are culturally bound. For example, if you are an urban American and dream of a cow, some people believe the cow has a different meaning to you and your culture than it does to, say, a country dweller in India. Another way to look at dream symbolism is to assume that it has meaning for you in personal terms only. Maybe as a child you always slept with your stuffed cow Moo-Moo. Or maybe you were once chased by a cow and badly frightened.

Webweaving

Mary Summer Rain's *Guide to Dream Symbols* (Hampton Roads Publishing, 1997) is a super-useful book. In its 608 pages it contains 10,000 dream symbols!

One way to help yourself understand your dreams is to ask yourself how you feel when you first wake up. Are you angry, sad, elated, or grumpy? Does your feeling stem from your dream? A happy dream about a cow may have a very different meaning from one that made you feel enraged when you woke up.

If you can't figure out what images or themes from your most recent dream mean, consider these general guidelines:

➤ Animals or one special animal could be your spirit animal or one of your spirit guides. Or it could be someone else's spirit animal come to deliver a message to you.

➤ Death can refer to changes in your life and the concept of rebirth. Much like in the tarot, this could mean that you are going through some major life transitions. Dreaming of the death of a loved one, especially if that person has been ill, could also foretell their impending demise. Some people have seen their relatives visit them in dreams to say goodbye.

➤ Falling dreams usually occur when you feel anxious, insecure, or vulnerable.

➤ Famous people in your dream could indicate a desire on your part to hide from the reality of your present situation.

➤ Flying in a dream can be about ambition or a desire to escape and attain freedom.

➤ Glued to one spot in a dream? It could be that your unconscious desires are paralyzing you and preventing you from acting.

➤ Healing in a dream can be about physical or emotional issues. Such a dream might give you insight into your eating and health habits or could alert you to a health problem that is waiting to happen.

➤ Water imagery in dreams can represent deep feelings, intuition, and the unconscious.

Colors in your dreams can also have significance. Here are some of the colors you may encounter while your eyes are closed:

➤ Brown—comfort, nurturing, laziness

➤ Black—calm, peace, fear

➤ Blue—calm, sadness

➤ Gray—wisdom, calm, ambivalence

➤ Green—envy, abundance

➤ Orange—power, assertiveness, energy

➤ Purple—passion, spirituality

➤ Red—passion, lust, anger

➤ Yellow—cowardice, distrust, clarity

➤ White—purity, hope, emptiness

Check out some books on dream symbolism if this topic appeals to you. If someone else's strategy for interpreting dreams works for you, by all means use it. But trust your intuition. We're talking about *your* dreams and *your* symbols after all.

Divination Through Dreams

Some witches have dreams that tell them about events that have yet to happen. Such divinatory dreams can be quite simple. For example, you dream that you are walking through a strange house where you have never been before. Three days later you visit a friend who has just bought a new house. You walk in the door and have a sense of *déjà vu*. Then you realize that you are in the house you had dreamed about a few nights earlier.

So Mote It Be

Try making yourself a dream pillow in order to have prophetic dreams. If you want to find answers to some of the questions that you have about your love life, select pink or red cloth for your pillow. Stuff the pillow with some fiberfill, and then add herbs such as chamomile or hops. Remember that you can mix the herbs in any way you choose. If you want a passionate love (and some lust), you should add more lusty herbs, such as cinnamon. If you want gentle love or stability, look for herbs with those qualities, such as lavender and chamomile. Throw in some mugwort for prophecy, and then meditate with the pillow before going to sleep.

You can try to induce dreams of divination by using pillow magick. Stuff a small pillow or bag with herbs. If you want to see the future love of your life in your dream, use herbs that represent that kind of love. You can grind the herbs with an essential oil, too. (See Chapter 18, "Magick Powers of Nature," for lists of herbs and essential oils and their magickal properties.) Pin the small pillow to the pillow that you sleep on. Before you get into bed, meditate on what it is you want do. And sweet dreams!

Another way to see visions of things to come that involve you and another person is to obtain a small belonging from that person. Prepare a dream pillow with herbs to facilitate your divination. Hold the person's object in your hand while you meditate on what will happen between you. Keep the object in your hand and go to sleep. When you wake up, look for messages in your dream that could shed light on your relationship.

Visitation in Dreams

You can have visitors while you are dreaming. You can also go visiting yourself. Did you ever wake up and feel certain that someone else was just there? Many people report that their deceased loved ones visit them in dreams. They come to give advice, to check up on you, or to let you know that they are okay.

You can try to go visiting in dreams yourself. Sometimes you can even do it without trying. Before you go to bed, meditate on flying and going to see the person you want to visit. Usually you will dream that you are getting up out of your body. You rise above the bed where your body still rests and fly off to Paris or wherever it is that you want to go. You can check on your brother in Los Angeles or your sister in Montana. Is her house really such a mess?

If an animal comes to you in a dream, it also could be a visitation. Maybe one of your friends has sent his or her spirit animal to deliver a message (see Chapter 15, "Summon, Stir, or Call," for more on spirit animals). You can send messages to people this way too. Sometimes this can be a great way to tell someone something that he or she might not want to hear. Often people take dream warnings more seriously than warnings that they receive in person.

If you want to understand your spirit animal better, you can travel with it and see what it sees in your dreams. Before you go to bed, meditate on your spirit animal and be prepared for a night as a different species.

Keeping a Dream Journal

How can you keep a dream journal if you don't remember your dreams? Try this: Before you go to bed, sit down and meditate; tell yourself that you will remember your dreams. When you first wake up, don't jump out of bed and start doing things right away. All that rapid activity will knock the memory of your dream out of your head. The first thing you should do when you wake up is start writing in your dream journal, even if what you put down is just fragments. Often one fragment will lead to another, which leads to another, and pretty soon you've remembered most of your dream.

Make sure to keep your dream journal and a pen that you like next to your bed. Use a pen that writes quickly. You don't want anything to slow you down and cause you to forget an interesting detail. If you wake from a dream in the middle of the night and want to remember it, write it down then, even if it is 3 A.M. If you wait till it is time to get up, you will have forgotten it.

Also make sure that you write the date at the top of each dream journal entry. The date will be important when you go back and look through the records of your dreams. Without the dates you'll find it harder to see the patterns in your dreams and to identify any recurring dreams. Having the date on each dream will also help you to see the relationship between the actual events in your life and the occurrences in your dreams. It just might

Banish!

Dreams can carry important information that will help you in your waking life. But avoid becoming obsessed with your dreams. One woman we know was concentrating so hard on remembering her dreams that she couldn't sleep at all!

Webweaving

Here are two more books about dreams that you might enjoy: *Dreaming the Divine: Techniques for Sacred Sleep,* by Scott Cunningham (Llewellyn Publishers, 1999) and *The Complete Idiot's Guide to Interpreting Your Dreams,* by Marci Pliskin and Shari L. Just, Ph.D. (Alpha Books, 1999).

be significant that the night after you had that big meeting with your boss you dreamed of falling down the stairs over and over again.

Altered States of Consciousness

In many cultures all over the world, people achieve altered states of consciousness to gain spiritual insights. Dreaming, meditation, and trance are all natural states of altered consciousness. We don't have to learn how to sleep in order to dream, but meditation and trance work take practice and concentration. Trances can be induced in a number of ways. Some people can enter a light trance state by listening to a sustained and regular pattern of drumming. Others can learn to hypnotize themselves and enter a light trance in this manner.

There are other ways to achieve an altered consciousness. In Native American traditions, people consume peyote, a powerful hallucinogen, to attain this altered consciousness and to see visions. In some traditions, fasting and physical exertion are used to bypass the conscious mind and achieve an altered state.

Vision Questing, Astral Travel, and Bilocation

Some witches practice the techniques of vision questing and many do not. In vision questing an altered state of consciousness is achieved in order to see visions of spiritual significance. This is a *shamanic practice* that is shared by many of the Native American tribes. Fasting, sweat lodges, and peyote are often used to aid or induce the vision quest. Vision questing can be extremely physically rigorous and should not be attempted by anyone with respiratory or cardiac problems.

Book of Shadows

Shamanic practices are activities that shamans engage in. A shaman is a medicine man or priest from a nontechnological culture. Shamans use astral projection a lot. They also use fasting, sleep deprivation, and drugs to help themselves attain altered states of consciousness.

Astral travel is travel on the astral plane. The astral plane is thought by many to be another layer of reality that is separate from the one that we ordinarily experience in our waking lives. Some people consider the astral plane to be the realm of dreams. The astral body, which includes your aura, is thought to actually leave the physical body and visit other locations. So, some dreams can be thought of as astral travel. If you dream of flying, especially if you see yourself leave your body behind, you may have experienced astral projection in your dreams. Some people will dream of an event, say a wedding or a baseball game, only to discover that the very same event was occurring across town while they were sleeping. In a case like that, astral travel just might explain how that happened.

In astral projection, you decide that you want to travel on the astral plane. You can attempt this by practicing meditation. And it will take practice! You will be able to focus sufficiently only if you have a regular meditative practice. In your meditative state, you envision the astral body leaving the physical body, but the two bodies are connected by an umbilical cord of white light. Then the astral body can travel to distant locations or can visit the different layers of the astral plane. Before you attempt such travel, do your homework. You should read a lot about astral travel and projection before you try it so you know what to expect. You don't want to wander into a situation you're not prepared for and scare yourself.

Bilocation is another technique that allows for travel while leaving the physical body behind. To do this you enter a meditative state and envision a filmy image of yourself leaving your body behind. This double of you can go out into the world and allow you to see what is going on without you having to leave your house.

Banish!

Does the idea of astral projection creep you out? If you don't like the idea, avoid thinking about it! It is not something you have to do to be a witch. In fact, many witches don't practice astral projection at all. There's plenty for you to work with without you having to leave your body.

It is probably best to learn these techniques of out-of-body travel from another witch who has a lot of experience with this kind of work. Often mastering these techniques can take years of practice. And you have to really have the passion to want to do it. Many witches don't bother with these kinds of experiences. Some feel that out-of-body techniques are just a little bit creepy. Others who have tried them don't like the feeling of loss of control that goes with out-of-body travel.

Accessing Your Spirit Guides

Many people first see their spirit guides (see Chapter 15) in their dreams. If you have a dream in which you are following another person, that character may be one of your spirit guides. In a dream of this type, you will feel very strongly that the person you are following is trustworthy. If you are someone who has trouble trusting other people, your spirit guide might appear to you as a particularly attractive animal.

Psychologist Carl Jung thought that our spirit guides are part of us that we want to embody but can't. According to this theory, if you are really shy, the part of you that wants to be self-empowered might manifest itself as your brave and assertive spirit guide. Other people believe that spirit guides are spirits that have been sent to watch over us.

Once you have seen one of your spirit guides in a dream, you will find it easier to communicate with that being. Spirit guides usually send you subtle messages in dreams, or you can hear then as your small inner voice. Even if you have not seen your guides in a dream, you can arrange to meet them on a meditative journey.

Once you have met your spirit guides and understand what they look like, they start to send you messages in dreams. Or they will make small things go wrong on the physical plane to prevent you from doing something that you shouldn't do. Spirit guides that take the form of animals will use their animal instincts to keep you out of danger. You can also communicate with your spirit guides through a Ouija board. When you start listening to your guides, to your inner voice, you will find that life goes a lot smoother.

So Mote It Be

See what books your local metaphysical store has on spirit guides. Many books on the subject contain guided meditations to help you meet them. The easiest way for you to use a meditation from a book is to tape record yourself reading it out loud. It's much easier to listen to the tape than it is to read while trying to meditate. The other advantage to making your own meditation tape, as opposed to buying one, is that you will be more comfortable with the sound of your own voice (even if you do think you sound funny on tape) than you will be with the voice of a stranger.

Beyond This Life

What happens when you die? Where does the spirit go? And what does it do when it gets there? Questions such as these have been central to human consciousness since time immemorial. Wiccans have a number of answers to each of these questions. Hey, you knew there couldn't be just one answer per question.

Edgar Cayce: The Akashic Records

Edgar Cayce (1877–1945) was a noted psychic and healer. He believed that there is a place on the astral plane where there is a book called the *Akashic Records*. Everything that you want to know about everyone is in the Akashic Records—who they were, what they accomplished, when they were born, and when they will die. The Akashic Records also contain this information for people who have yet to be born.

Book of Shadows

The **Akashic Records** are an enormous collection of data that exists on the astral plane. Witches and psychics can access this information, which includes facts about the lives and accomplishments of every human who ever lived and who has yet to live.

Cayce himself visited the Akashic Records frequently. In them he discovered cures for many diseases that had yet to be invented in his time. His methods were considered rather unorthodox. He started an institute of healing in Virginia that bears his name. Cayce was also able to project himself across the country to check on what someone was doing. He was able to report on their activities with a high degree of accuracy.

Once you have learned to travel on the astral plane, a skill that can take years and years of training to master, you can visit the Akashic Records. If you like, you can even look yourself up.

Final Resting Place?

Are you afraid of graveyards? Witches usually are not afraid of cemeteries. Some even use gravesites to work magick. Of course there are two schools of thought on this issue. Some witches believe that there is no point in visiting graves or working with them because the person whose is buried there is not there. Their spirit has reincarnated so there is nothing left in the grave but an empty shell. Other witches believe that cemeteries have special energy because many people visit them to remember their dead. Also the ground of graveyard has been consecrated, so it is sacred space. You can take dirt from a gravesite and use it to help you communicate with the person who was buried there. But before you take dirt from a grave, you should ask permission from the spirit whose grave it is.

You can sprinkle dirt from your ancestor's (or from someone else's) grave around your magick circle in ritual to invite that person to ritual. Don't pick just any old dead person to invite. You should deal with someone whom you know a lot about, because when you invite these spirits to ritual, you invite them into your magick circle, and some unknown spirit could prove to be a nasty and unwelcome guest. If you know the spirits you are dealing with, you don't have to worry. They won't hurt you. And they may have a lot to tell you.

You might want to spend some timing visiting graveyards to make yourself more comfortable in that kind of environment. Read the old stones, because often their inscriptions will tell you a lot about the person buried there. If you find a stone you particularly like you can make a gravestone rubbing to take home. Before you do a rubbing make sure that rubbings are allowed; some cemeteries forbid them because of possible damage to very old stones. Try packing a picnic when you go to visit a graveyard. After a while you will feel comfortable and will start to see graveyards as simply the place where the body goes after death.

Webweaving

Wiccans believe that all animals have souls. The souls of animals are so pure that they have no lessons to learn in this life. They are just here to be here and enjoy life. Yup, that is exactly what the cat is doing when she is chasing string or stretching in that spot of sun by the window.

Book of Shadows

Summerland is where spirits go after death to rest and reflect in the company of the God and Goddess, and to decide how they are going to reincarnate. In Wicca there is no heaven or hell.

Summerland Beckons

Summerland is not heaven and it is not hell. Witches believe the summerland to be a place of reflection for the spirit. After death, spirits think about the lives they have just lived and plan where they will come back next. Ultimately each spirit, after it has learned all it needs to learn and taught what it needs to teach, is reunited with the All. In each lifetime, the spirit advances toward this ultimate goal.

When you enter the summerland, sometimes you sleep and reflect for a long time to recover from difficult life experiences. Other souls don't spend much time resting, because they are anxious to get back to Earth and continue their journey.

Reincarnation: Rebirth

After the soul has rested sufficiently, it decides when to reincarnate. Before it leaves the summerland each soul has already chosen who it will be and what lesson it will learn in its new lifetime. Once it has reincarnated it doesn't remember what its lesson is, but must find out by living through all the experiences of its new life.

If a soul doesn't wish to reincarnate right away, it may become a spirit guide. Or if it has learned all it needs to and does not need to reincarnate, it will reunite with the Goddess.

Some witches believe the idea set out by Edgar Cayce, that all spirits travel through time in groups or soul families. According to this theory, we know each other over several lifetimes. Maybe next time you will know your spouse, not as your partner, but as your boss, your child's teacher, or your next-door neighbor. Others believe that we will meet the same spirits again, but that each spirit moves on its own.

Wiccans believe that we each have a job to do in this lifetime. We have things to learn and things to teach. If a young man dies suddenly people often ask, "Why did he have to go?" The Wiccan answer would be because he obtained what he had to in this lifetime. He learned what he needed to learn and taught what he needed to teach. His job was done. Sometimes the death of a young person can help the people around him or her to grow. In that respect, the death was not senseless. There was a reason for it.

Even if the person is gone, the effects of that person's life continue in the lives of everyone who was touched by that person and by that person's actions. And the person's spirit moves on to summerland and then is reborn into a new life of spiritual lessons and teachings.

The Least You Need to Know

➤ People have believed in the power of their dreams for thousands of years. As a witch you can learn from your dreams the way everyone does and you can use them in magick.

➤ People have used altered states of consciousness for centuries to induce spiritual visions and out-of-body experiences. Some witches use these techniques, but many do not.

➤ If you dream that you are following a person or an animal you may be catching a glimpse of one of your spirit guides. You can meet your spirit guides through meditation.

➤ Wiccans believe that we die after we have accomplished what we were supposed to do in this life.

➤ After death, spirits go to the summerland to rest and choose their next incarnation.

➤ Souls reincarnate until they have perfected their knowledge. Once they have achieved that, they can be reabsorbed into the All.

Resources

Listed below are some excellent books and videos that will help you learn more about Wicca and witchcraft. There's a great wealth of published material on the topic, from the general to the very specific. This list is just a starting place. When you go looking for one of the titles listed here, browse the books in the area and see what else catches your eye.

Suggested Reading

Adler, Margot. *Drawing Down the Moon: Witches, Druids, Goddess-Worshippers, and Other Pagans in America Today.* New York: Arkana, 1997.

Beyerl, Paul. *A Compendium of Herbal Magick.* Custer, WA: Phoenix Publishing, 1998.

———. *The Master Book of Herbalism.* Custer, WA: Phoenix Publishing, 1984.

Briggs, Robin. *Witches and Neighbors: The Social and Cultural Context of European Witchcraft.* New York: Penguin, 1996.

Brown, Karen McCarthy. *Mama Lola: A Voudou Priestess in Brooklyn.* Berkeley, CA: University of California Press, 1991.

Buckland, Raymond. *Buckland's Complete Book of Witchcraft.* St. Paul, MN: Llewellyn, 1986.

Budapest, Zsuzsanna E. *Grandmother Moon: Lunar Magic in Our Lives: Spells, Rituals, Goddesses, Legends, and Emotions Under the Moon.* San Francisco: HarperSanFrancisco, 1991.

Bullfinch, Thomas. *The Age of Fable or Beauties of Mythology.* New York: Heritage Press, 1942.

Campbell, Joseph. *Hero with a Thousand Faces.* Princeton: Princeton University Press, 1990.

Choquette, Sonia. *The Psychic Pathway: A Workbook for Reawakening the Voice of Your Soul.* New York: Crown, 1994.

Cunningham, Scott. *Cunningham's Encyclopedia of Crystal, Gem and Metal Magic.* St. Paul, MN: Llewellyn, 1988.

———. *Cunningham's Encyclopedia of Magical Herbs.* St. Paul, MN: Llewellyn, 1985.

———. *Wicca: A Guide for the Solitary Practitioner.* St. Paul, MN: Llewellyn, 1988.

Curott, Phyllis. *Book of Shadows: A Modern Woman's Journey into the Wisdom of Witchcraft and the Magic of the Goddess.* New York: Broadway/Random House, 1998.

Eisler, Riane. *The Chalice and the Blade.* New York: Harper & Row, 1987.

Farrar, Janet, and Stewart Farrar. *The Witches' Goddess.* Custer, WA: Phoenix Publishing, 1987.

———. *The Witches' God.* Custer, WA: Phoenix Publishing, 1989.

Frazer, James G. *The Golden Bough: The Roots of Religion and Folklore.* New York: Avenel Books, 1981 (reprint of 1890 edition).

Gerwick-Brodeur, Madeline, and Lisa Lenard. *The Complete Idiot's Guide to Astrology.* New York: Alpha Books, 1997.

Gile, Robin, and Lisa Lenard. *The Complete Idiot's Guide to Palmistry.* New York: Alpha Books, 1999.

Graves, Robert. *The White Goddess.* New York: Noonday/FSG, 1948.

Grimassi, Raven. *The Wiccan Mysteries.* St. Paul, MN: Llewellyn, 1997.

Hamilton, Edith. *Mythology: Timeless Tales of Gods and Heroes.* Boston: Little Brown, 1969.

Hopman, Ellen Evert, and Laurence Bond. *People of the Earth: The New Pagans Speak Out.* Rochester, VT: Destiny Books, 1996.

Hutton, Ronald. *The Triumph of the Moon: A History of Modern Pagan Witchcraft.* New York: Oxford, 1999.

Jacobi, Jolande. *The Psychology of C.G. Jung.* New Haven, CT: Yale University Press, 1973.

K, Amber. *Covencraft: Witchcraft for Three or More.* St. Paul, MN: Llewellyn, 1998.

Lagerquist, Kay, and Lisa Lenard. *The Complete Idiot's Guide to Numerology.* New York: Alpha Books, 1999.

McCoy, Edain. *Entering the Summerland: Customs and Rituals of Transition into the Afterlife.* St. Paul, MN: Llewellyn, 1996.

Melody. *Love Is in the Earth: A Kaleidoscope of Crystals* (updated). Wheat Ridge, CO: Earth-Love Publishing House, 1995.

Pliskin, Marci, and Shari L. Just. *The Complete Idiot's Guide to Interpreting Your Dreams.* New York: Alpha Books, 1999.

RavenWolf, Silver. *To Light a Sacred Flame: Practical Witchcraft for the Millennium*. St. Paul, MN: Llewellyn, 1999.

———. *To Ride a Silver Broomstick: New Generation Witchcraft*. St. Paul, MN: Llewellyn, 1999.

Robbins, Rossell Hope. *The Encyclopedia of Witchcraft and Demonology*. New York, 1981 (reprint of 1959 edition).

Simms, Maria Kay. *The Witch's Circle: Rituals and Craft of the Cosmic Muse*. St. Paul, MN: Llewellyn, 1994.

Starhawk. *The Spiral Dance*. New York: Harper & Row, 1979.

Stone, Merlin. *When God Was a Woman*. New York: Harvest/HBJ, 1976.

Teish, Luisah. *Jambalaya: The Natural Woman's Book of Personal Charms and Practical Rituals*. New York: Harper & Row, 1985.

Tognetti, Arlene, and Lisa Lenard. *The Complete Idiot's Guide to Tarot and Fortune-Telling*. New York: Alpha Books, 1999.

Videos

Buckland, Raymond. *Witchcraft: Yesterday and Today*. 60 minutes; 1990.

Farrar, Janet and Stewart Farrar. *Discovering Witchcraft: A Journey Through the Elements*. 87 minutes; 1998.

———. *Discovering Witchcraft: The Mysteries*. 60 minutes; 1999.

Magickal Record

Type Of Ritual: _____

Date & Time: _____ Approximate Length: _____

Phase of the Moon: _____

Planetary Positions

Weather: _____

Sun in: _____ Moon in: _____ Location of Ritual: _____

Mars in: _____ Mercury in: _____ _____

Venus in: _____ Saturn in: _____ Purpose of Ritual: _____

Jupiter in: _____ Uranus in: _____ _____

Neptune in: _____ Blue Moon: Yes / No Physical Health: _____

Deities Invoked: _____

Ritual Tools Used: _____
_____

Chants/Music Used: _____

Oils/Herbs/Crystals Used: _____
_____

People taking part in Ritual:
_____
_____

Magick Performed/Spells etc:
_____

Format: _____
_____
_____
_____
_____

Date of Manifestation: _____ Results: _____
_____

Index

361